Christianity and Belonging in Shimla, North India

Bloomsbury Studies in Material Religion

Bloomsbury Studies in Material Religion is the first book series dedicated exclusively to studies in material religion. Within the field of lived religion, the series is concerned with the material things with which people do religion, and how these things – objects, buildings, landscapes – relate to people, their bodies, clothes, food, actions, thoughts and emotions. The series engages and advances theories in 'sensuous' and 'experiential' religion, as well as informing museum practices and influencing wider cultural understandings with relation to religious objects and performances. Books in the series are at the cutting edge of debates as well as developments in fields including religious studies, anthropology, museum studies, art history, and material culture studies.

Christianity and the Limits of Materiality, edited by
Minna Opas and Anna Haapalainen
Figurations and Sensations of the Unseen in Judaism, Christianity and Islam, edited by Birgit Meyer and Terje Stordalen
Food, Festival and Religion, Francesca Ciancimino Howell
Material Devotion in a South Indian Poetic World, Leah Elizabeth Comeau
Qur'anic Matters, Natalia K. Suit
The Religious Heritage Complex, edited by Cyril Isnart and Nathalie Cerezales
Museums of World Religions, Charles D. Orzech
Space, Place and Religious Landscapes, edited by Darrelyn Gunzburg and Bernadette Brady

Christianity and Belonging in Shimla, North India
Sacred Entanglements of a Himalayan Landscape

Jonathan Miles-Watson

BLOOMSBURY ACADEMIC
LONDON • NEW YORK • OXFORD • NEW DELHI • SYDNEY

BLOOMSBURY ACADEMIC
Bloomsbury Publishing Plc
50 Bedford Square, London, WC1B 3DP, UK
1385 Broadway, New York, NY 10018, USA
29 Earlsfort Terrace, Dublin 2, Ireland

BLOOMSBURY, BLOOMSBURY ACADEMIC and the Diana logo
are trademarks of Bloomsbury Publishing Plc

First published in Great Britain 2021
This paperback edition published in 2022

Copyright © Jonathan Miles-Watson, 2021

Jonathan Miles-Watson has asserted his right under the Copyright, Designs
and Patents Act, 1988, to be identified as Author of this work.

For legal purposes the Acknowledgements on p. x constitute an extension
of this copyright page.

Cover design: Maria Rajka
Cover image © Jitendra Singh / Getty Images

All rights reserved. No part of this publication may be reproduced or transmitted in any
form or by any means, electronic or mechanical, including photocopying, recording,
or any information storage or retrieval system, without prior permission in writing from
the publishers.

Bloomsbury Publishing Plc does not have any control over, or responsibility for, any
third-party websites referred to or in this book. All internet addresses given in this book
were correct at the time of going to press. The author and publisher regret any
inconvenience caused if addresses have changed or sites have ceased to exist,
but can accept no responsibility for any such changes.

A catalogue record for this book is available from the British Library.

A catalog record for this book is available from the Library of Congress.

Library of Congress Control Number: 2020945420

ISBN: HB: 978-1-3500-5017-4
PB: 978-1-3501-8529-6
ePDF: 978-1-3500-5018-1
eBook: 978-1-3500-5019-8

Series: Bloomsbury Studies in Material Religion

Typeset by RefineCatch Limited, Bungay, Suffolk

To find out more about our authors and books visit www.bloomsbury.com
and sign up for our newsletters

For Tara

Contents

List of Figures ... ix
Acknowledgements ... x

1   Sita's Red Dress: Introduction ... 1
    i)   The mystery of the Cathedral on the Ridge ... 1
    ii)   Sacred landscapes and material culture ... 3
    iii)   Postcolonial life in the Land of the Gods ... 6
    iv)   From academic ancestors to a discordant ethnography ... 10
    v)   Sita's tears: disrupting academic authority ... 13
    vi)   Substance of the book ... 18

2   Christ in the Land of the Gods: Context ... 23
    i)   Searching for Mount Meru: the sacred centre out there ... 26
    ii)   Saffron priests and Christian Sadhus ... 28
    iii)   From East to West: the Christian Maharishi ... 34

3   Recreating Mount Olympus: From Shymla to Simla ... 39
    i)   Dùthchas, rain and replication ... 40
    ii)   White robes and riding dresses: material religion in Simla ... 48
    iii)   Living in a ghost town: the materiality of spirits in Shimla ... 55

4   Churchscape, Landscape and Material Religion ... 59
    i)   Displaced sacred space and implicit mythology ... 60
    ii)   The centre of the spiral: a key myth ... 65
    iii)   The materiality of myth in the shimla hills ... 66

5   Worshipping with Ghosts: Implicit Mythology in the Shimla Hills ... 71
    i)   Worshipping beyond the boundaries of faith ... 72
    ii)   Engaging with the material trace of past worship ... 74
    iii)   Churchscapes, material religion and ghosts ... 78
    iv)   Ghosts, ancestors and myths of becoming ... 81
    v)   Beyond binaries: landscapes, myth and history ... 88

6	Materiality, Heterodoxy and Bonding at the Hidden Cathedral	91
	i) Cathedralscapes	92
	ii) In search of the Hidden Cathedral	95
	iii) Heterodoxy and harmony in the Cathedralscape	101
7	Ritual, Materiality and Skill	103
	i) Skilful worship	110
	ii) Weaving material religion	117
	iv) Becoming one with the landscape	123
8	Pipe Organs and Satsang	129
	i) Tensions, tears and ruptures in the landscape	130
	ii) Landscapes of group expansion and group maintenance	139
	iii) Hindu and Christian or Jesu Bhakti	142
9	The Salt in the Stew: Conclusion	145
	i) Prophetic anthropology and the wisdom of the hills	146
	ii) Christians and the Cathedralscape	147
	iii) Salt, sugar and dilithium crystals	151
	iv) Developments and future areas for exploration	153
Notes		159
References		163
Index		177

List of Figures

1.1	Christ Church Cathedral. Photo by author.	3
2.1	The high Himalayas of our imagination. Image by manbartlett is licensed for reproduction here under CC BY 2.0.	24
2.2	Categorising Singh and Stokes. Diagram by author.	36
3.1 A	Simla as Mount Meru. Diagram by author.	44
3.1 B	Simla as vertically central. Diagram by author.	44
3.2	Shimla monkey. Photo by author.	45
3.3	Historical photograph of the Mall. Reproduced with permission from Durham University Oriental Museum.	47
3.4	Historical postcard of Christ Church Cathedral. Reproduced with permission from Durham University Oriental Museum.	50
4.1	Painting of Shimla by Aruna Mahajan. Reproduced with the permission of the artist.	60
4.2	Rooting the ancestors in the walls. Photo by author.	68
4.3	Homans' memorial. Photo by author.	69
5.1	Heritage and identity sign. Photo by author.	79
5.2	Mapping myth's journey. Diagram by author.	87
6.1	Cathedral Village by John Serafin. Reproduced with the permission of the artist's estate.	94
6.2	Sacred nodes of Shimla. Diagram by author.	95
6.3	St Andrew's Kirk. Photo by author.	96
6.4	St Michael's Cathedral. Photo by author.	98
6.5	Entering St Michael's Cathedral. Photo by author.	100
8.1	Christmas worship at Christ Church Cathedral Shimla. Photo by author.	130
8.2	Christmas at Christ Church Cathedral. Photo by author.	134
8.3	Shimla crowd. Photo by author.	135
8.4	Mixed responses to ecstatic music. Photo by author.	136

Acknowledgements

This book is built on almost 15 years of research and I am extremely grateful for all the support that I have received over this period. Not least from my family, especially, Sukanya, who has been a constant support throughout. This book would never have been possible without the people of Shimla, whose kindness, passion and insight inspired the project and guided its development to this stage. I am particularly grateful to the warm and wonderful communities (congregation and clergy) that surrounded Christ Church Cathedral and St Michael's Cathedral, the members of Shimla Amateur Football Club, Pankaj (and the Himalayan Institute), Jaswant, the Wilson family, the Fernandes family, Francis Chug, Siddharth Pandey and Professor Madan Sharma. Special mention must be made of my family in the hills at Tawi, especially Mohini Auntie, without whom our time in Shimla simply would not have been the same; I will always remember playing Holi with our little community, including Kali, not long before she was taken by a leopard.

I am grateful to the ESF for providing €100,000 funding for the fieldwork elements of this research and the universities of Tallinn, Luther and Durham for being supportive places to develop further this research. Especial thanks are due to Professor Margaret Kenna who has my thanks for her early encouragement to carry out research in this area and Dr Amy Whitehead for her encouragement to move my findings towards publication in this manuscript. I am grateful to the anonymous reviewers for their supportive and helpful feedback and to Lalle and Lucy at Bloomsbury for their belief in this project and patience throughout the writing process.

1

Sita's Red Dress: Introduction

i) The mystery of the Cathedral on the Ridge

December 2006, I am making my way up a smooth, broad, path in the Indian Himalayas. My instinct is to move through the thin mountain air quicker than is wise, but my progress is slowed by loose clusters of wool-wrapped people from the plains. They leisurely drift up the path, moving as much side-to side as forward, while I pant past like a steam-train, momentarily losing the sound of my breath in the upsurge of their exclamations. I pause, my way barred by a group of Bengalis, who expansively gesture at local crafts, displayed in the windows of the mock Tudor riparian; and, at that moment, a different kind of chatter catches my attention, drawing my eyes up to the jagged roofline, where frantic monkeys have caught a crossed line with the tourists below. The humans simply ignore the frenzied communication of the assembled simians, effortlessly filtering them out of the landscape and (with the tension resolved) I turn to the road ahead. But I do not move forward, I stand rooted to the ground, for as my eyes refocus, I see clearly the sharp outline of Christ Church Cathedral, softened by a haze of gently falling snow.

From this vantage point the Cathedral only partially reveals itself through the mountain rock and deodar leaf that stands between us. Yet, the Cathedral still manages to somehow dominate the view, as though the hint of its future revelation is enough to overcome the limits of its present manifestation. Its tall, Gothic style, tower, painted a bright yellow, contrasts with both the grey of the sky and the muted vegetal colours that surround it: rock mountainside, tin roof, tree branch and tree leaf. As I draw closer, the verdant softness falls away and all that is left is the sharply sloping mountainside and soaring Gothic parapet, at once imposing and inviting – inviting perhaps because it seems to speak to the mystery of this place and its people; imposing perhaps because it speaks of a history of imposition that I would rather forget. There is then a dual allure here, a sort of salty-sweetness, of something at once strange and familiar. The Cathedral appears to be a place out of place, it whispers complex histories and in so doing threatens to reshape my comfortable understandings of the unfurling of life, the expression of faith and the nature of identity in these hills.

As I draw closer to the Cathedral I move through a corridor of buildings that have an increasingly substantial feel. They are grander now, although still largely Tudor in style, and house up-market, international, clothing brands, eateries and coffeehouses. Throughout my ascent the Cathedral is a constant reference point, revealing different aspects of itself in relation to the landscape around it, sometimes in dialogue with the cluster of Tudor buildings below, sometimes setting its relation to the blanket of the deodar trees that cover Hanuman's sacred hill behind, and sometimes speaking to the distant peaks of the high Himalayas, which form the horizon. My sense of the city at this moment is of a spiral, wound around a sacred, central axle, for it is the Cathedral that binds together the triadic elements of this landscape: colonial buildings below, postcolonial people around and pre-colonial high peaks above.

The silver peaks, which zigzag the horizon, speak to a time before history, what Eliade would call '*Illud Tempus*' (1963: 169), a contraction of then and now, human and Divine. These mythic summits contrast to the two, time-marked, landscapes of the foothills below, acting as a spatial representation of local chronology. Time and space begin to emerge at this point then as key concerns of both the landscape and this book. Within which, we will be led to explore the combination of the visible trace of history with the time obliterating powers of mythological landscapes, as well as the way that myth and history are held in balance by the flow of postcolonial life in these colonially scarred and timelessly sacred mountains.

These mountains are the converging ranges of the South Western Himalayas, which are found in Himachal Pradesh, they form the key setting for this book's exploration of sacred landscapes. However, rather unusually, this book is concerned not so much with life on (or travel to) the high peaks as the life of the Christian communities in the comparatively lowly (and often overlooked) state capital, Shimla. Although these Christian communities may seem like an unusual group to make the focus of a work of Himalayan anthropology, I will show that putting their account at the centre of this work is natural, transformative and (precisely because it is counterintuitive) necessary. The book draws on over 10 years of fieldwork in the region, blending ethnography, auto-ethnography and textual study, as it moves to explain the mystery that lies at the heart of Shimla's Christian communities; the pursuit of this mystery will lead us to challenge the established paradigms of postcolonial theory, South Asian studies, global Christianity and material culture.

ii) Sacred landscapes and material culture

Back on the trail the path spirals upwards, moving me around the Cathedral before eventually bringing us face-to-face. Seen from across the broad expanse of the ridge, the Cathedral seems a less imposing and more inviting site. Its bright yellow appearance gives it a festive feel that is further underscored by the crowds of people, popcorn sellers and pony rides that stand between me and it (depicted in Figure 1.1). Moving slowly through the crowds, I come before the four cornered Galilee and there I pause; like a penitent waiting for the removal of transgressions, only I do not know yet what my transgressions are. I am not yet aware that it is the very denial of the obvious role of the lives lived in and around this building that is my academic transgression; I only know that I want to be drawn deeper into the mystery of its being. This encounter formed the starting point for the relationships forged in and around this and other similar

Figure 1.1 Christ Church Cathedral.

buildings that have resulted in this book, which is both an exploration of the mystery that the Cathedral represents and an account of the blended material religion that I found in this postcolonial city. This is therefore a book about relationships with places as much as with people, what Plate (2015: 4) calls the material aspects of religious life.

Although a focus on materiality is a seemingly obvious outcome of research with a fieldwork component, it has been less central to ethnographic accounts than might at first be presumed (Conkey 2006: 356). That is not to suggest that there has been no attention to material artefacts in anthropology, to do so would be disingenuous, given the long history of development in this area. The work of Boas (1927) is heavily focused on artefacts, Malinowski (1922) famously discusses the circulation of objects and Lévi-Strauss (1975) masks, to name but a few. There is however a sense that, at least since the 1980s, there has been a growing movement towards the recognition of the centrality of material artefacts to our understanding of human-society. This book is therefore able to draw on the literature and momentum surrounding this 'material turn' (cf Hicks and Beaudry 2015, Miller 2009, Woodward 2007, et al) at the same time as looking beyond it to the nature of a life lived in relation to sacred materials.

The religious significance of materials has historically been overshadowed by approaches to religion that have focused on philosophical questions of existence (Plate 2015:4). A material turn in religion seeks to refocus attention on the everyday reality of engagement with materials, which is a fundamental process of human existence. The material religion movement of today is therefore clearly linked to the wider material culture movement but has gathered real momentum as an independent entity over the last ten years. At the time of writing there are two edited volumes (Morgan 2010, Plate 2015), a journal (*Material Religion*) and a conference[1] dedicated to the study, as well as, of course, this book series. This emerging and ever strengthening body of literature can be seen, for our purposes, to have two distinct approaches within it, which I will term 'object centric' and 'craft centric'.

An object centric approach focuses on material artefacts as completed objects that offer alternative insight into the underpinnings of a more vernacular religion (Bowman and Valk 2012) than the traditional attention to the philosophical/ theological formal religious thought of religious elites (Hume 2013, Kilde 2005, Roose 2012, et al). Although this body of work usefully highlights the importance of both the everyday and the physical elements of religion it does not sit well with the demands of my field site. The situation that I encountered requires serious attention be paid to the importance of human relations with the non-human elements of the material landscape, which forms a series of ongoing processes. Consequently, this book has less interest in the finished artefact as a gateway to the human mind (or minds) that lie behind it and instead focuses on the ecology of relationships (Bateson 2000) that that form at a node of sacred significance.

This more dynamic understanding of materiality jars with an object centric approach to material religion and suggests that Christ Church Cathedral requires a different tack be taken. In doing so the book distances itself from the several works of material religion that specifically address Christian Cathedrals of Western-Europe (Aravecchia 2001, Irvine 2011, Shackley 2002, Sheldrake 2001). That is not to say that these texts are irrelevant, indeed, it was no doubt partly because of the way that these works conditioned my initial response to the environment that Christ Church Cathedral first appeared to me as a mysterious and alluring building, prompting questions about both historical creation and contemporary relation (or recreation). This hook initiated the research project and forms a starting position, however time spent with the cathedral led in a rather different direction and demanded that questions centred around understandings of creation, creator and owner be replaced by questions of belonging and becoming, which naturally arise through a craft centric approach to material religion.

A craft centric approach forms a clearly emerging vein in the material religion literature (Grimes 2011, Meyer 2015b, Whitehead 2013). This approach engages material religion with theories of personhood that are typically drawn from the work of phenomenological thinkers, including Bateson (2000), Ingold (2015) and Merleau-Ponty (1962). These theories draw inspiration from ongoing mutual processes of becoming that drive much of the contemporary environmental art movement (Goldsworthy 2009). This is the vein of material religion that I will follow in this book, for it is through this approach that I am able to unlock the mystery of how Shimla's historical processes of sacred crafting are hidden in plain sight. I therefore adopt an Ingoldian (2007a) switch from artefacts to ongoing, multiple acts of becoming as way of gaining insight into the ways that postcolonial populations (through everyday acts of worship) overcome the traumas of history. Crucially, this involves a broadening of our understanding of the relationships under discussion: moving from a model of creator and created to a series of ongoing, mutually constitutive relations, which encompass a wide-range of people and materials – a movement from religious objects to sacred landscapes.

I find the idea of sacred landscapes a useful way to phrase the issues with which this book is concerned. In distinction to the closely (and perhaps more fashionable) term space, landscape has a sense of dynamism to it, and of interplay between human and non-human (Olwig 1996) that captures the relational aspect, which my fieldwork revealed as central to life in the Shimla hills. In its contemporary use, by geographers, such as Wylie (2007), and anthropologists, such as Ingold (2000, 2011), there is a common trend of understanding landscape as a 'polyrhythmic composition of processes' (Ingold 2000: 201). From this perspective landscape is not something that is perceived, nor is it the backdrop that human action unfolds upon, rather it is a mutual constitution of person and place through action (Ingold 2000: 198–201). As people flow and knot around certain places, landscapes are formed which bind together the human and the non-human, the animate and the inanimate, the past, the present and the future. This temporal blurring is facilitated by a duel process of narrativization (Basso 1996) and actions, which leave a trace that others will to some extent have to reckon with in the future (Ingold 2007b). From this perspective landscapes are never complete; they are in a constant state of becoming (Ingold 2000). Threads in the landscape are drawn together as they wind and knot around sites of significance, where they become entangled, each enmeshed in the being of the other (Ingold 2011).

The above understanding of landscape resonates strongly with my experience of life lived in and around Christ Church Cathedral, a sacred site enlivened by worship, but not limited to being a place of formal worship. It exists at the centre of a nexus of relations and actions that are constantly coming into effect as people wind around the place. Christ Church is a Cathedral that I experienced as both geographically and symbolically central to the life of people in this Himalayan city and a reflection on the processes by which it becomes and remains central is a core concern of this book. Through a demonstration of the operation of these processes I seek to stretch established material religion theory and demonstrate the need for a radically new understanding of postcolonial life in the region.

iii) Postcolonial life in the Land of the Gods

It is November 2006 and I am sat with Urmi and her two teenage children in their South Delhi apartment. We sip sweet tea and nibble namkeen (a fried snack), the roar of the city below is transmuted to a murmur, a background gurgle, by the time the gentle breeze brings it through the open fretwork windows. Cocooned in this comfortable setting, our talk turns to the thrill of the possibilities of fieldwork in the Himalayas. The tranquil atmosphere is however transformed when I casually suggest Shimla as somewhere that I would like to explore before moving on to the higher Himalayas in search of a 'real' field site. At hearing this Urmi looks distinctly unimpressed, her expression communicates her dismissal even before she replies:

> "We don't like Shimla, it's not as a hill station should be".
> Surprised by the way that a casual mention of Shimla has prompted such a visceral response I probe further,
> "How'd you mean?".
> "Well", she replies, "it's too built up, too popular,
> there're too many people, it's not like the Himalayas ... they put a lift there! A lift in a hill station!"

Although Urmi's words were meant to ward me off a visit to Shimla they had the opposite effect, opening instead a sense of intrigue, and for the first time I felt the allure of Shimla's mystery. I was left with a nagging question: why should Shimla illicit such a strong negative response from someone whose connection to it is so limited? I decided that a visit to Shimla would remain part of my plans. After all, I reasoned, it was a convenient stop on my way to higher climbs. I had, however, not reckoned on how powerful a snare this mystery could be, nor did I have any sense of the way that Shimla would come to dominate the next decade of my life.

I have encountered many similar reactions to a mention of Shimla, over the years that have passed since this conversation, often from people with a fleeting connection to the place and occasionally from people who have never visited. The objections raised to Shimla in these conversations are nearly always some form of rejection of its landscape. In particular, it is suggested that humans have somehow ruined the landscape through both their continuing presence and the trace of their historical presence. Landscape, in this discourse, is implicitly defined as something, given and natural, perhaps shaped by the gods, but only debased by humans. There is then a dichotomy of 'natural' and 'cultural' products, which is precisely the sort of binary that the idea of landscape as a process is supposed to dissolve (Ingold 2000: 197). Yet, it cannot be denied that these understandings both exist and inform a great deal of interaction with Shimla and indeed the wider Himalayan region.

This is perhaps not surprising; I encountered similar reactions when walking with people from India's metros in rural Himachal Pradesh (Miles-Watson & Miles-Watson 2011). There, as here, the reaction was born from a history of imagined engagement with these regions, which lends the Himalayas a high degree of importance for millions of people who have never been there. In both classical Hindu texts and popular imagination, the Himalayas are a place shaped by the actions of mythical figures in the time before time and they are of central importance as a mediating space between mythic and lived reality (Eck 2012: 3). The high Himalayan peaks are said to be full of *tirthas*, or sacred crossing points, where the Gods and humans meet in a more powerful way than the home shrine (Eck 2012: 7). The Himalayas play an important cosmological role for the millions of people that come under the broad rubric of Hinduism, despite the fact that many thousands of miles may lie between the mountains and the devotee. This cosmic understanding of the Himalayas however seems to have no place within it for urban cities like Shimla, which have the marks of historical processes, both colonial and post-colonial, so clearly inscribed on their landscape; such places jar with expectations and if they cannot be filtered out of the experience they are re-categorized as a place, out of place, a broken landscape.

No doubt such an understanding lay behind Urmi's dislike of the city; indeed, it is clear that the scale of development in Shimla is directly proportional to the strength of her reaction, for Shimla is perhaps the most dramatically developed of India's Himalayan cities. Shimla is the state capital of Himachal Pradesh, a small largely rural state in the central North West Indian Himalayas. It immediately jars with the image of this region as a place of timeless tradition, cut off from the flows of modern life, because of both the mass of people present and the fact that it draws economic migrants in from all-over the country. In total, around one hundred and seventy-five thousand people are considered as residents of the city, but over half of these are classed as a floating population (Chandramuli 2011: 47). Shimla's political networks extend well beyond the city's borders and it is the home of the state government and the state university, as well as a wide selection of service and retail industries. Shimla is then, in many ways, more a hypermodern city (Coleman and Crang 2002: 1) than a Shangri-La (Hilton 1933).

Shimla's sites of postmodern capitalism are places with an obvious history that stretches back beyond the living and captures something of the actions and desires of those who are now dead. One of the reasons that so many tourists flow from the plains into Shimla each summer is the perceptible presence of colonial history among these hypermodern spaces. Although the city was renamed Shimla in 1983, as part of a pan-national project, old Simla (as this city was once called) still proudly proclaims its past. Indeed, many local residents will still refer to what they see as the meaningful parts of the city by the old name of Simla. This recalls its time as the summer capital of British India and the seat of

European power in the subcontinent (discussed further in Chapter Two). It is internationally famous today primarily for that connection, but it is always more than that and while it resonates with a wider colonial process it is a unique place. Sadly, in the popular imagination and the countless historical novels that it has inspired, the unique nature of Simla is lost in the mist of nostalgia for an imagined empire, thick with Orientalist (Said 1979) assumptions.

The most recent manifestation of this popular nostalgic view of Simla is the British drama 'Indian Summers', which made the remarkable decision to use a costal location on an Indonesian island as the film site for a drama set in Simla, presumably because it assumes that all colonial towns in the Orient look the same (Miles-Watson 2015). The assumption 'Indian Summers' makes of a pan-oriental unity in the colonial experience that may connect to assumptions that many colonials recorded. However, Indian Summers neo-colonial disregard of altitude moves it away from the colonial understandings, where combinations of virgin-mountainside and colonial construction were the two key ingredients for the birth of places like Simla. This book operates to undermine these assumptions, it stands clearly against the neo-colonialism of the Indian-Summers' crowd and moves both with and against the old colonial viewpoint. For, I will demonstrate that they were indeed right to pay attention to the importance of being on top of a mountain, but were wrong to assume that the moulding of the mountains was a one-way process, for the mountains were working on them at the same time as they were working on the mountains. In this book we will therefore explore this assumption critically before moving to communicate something of the emplaced, richly varied reality, of both old-Simla and modern Shimla.

The modern city of Shimla is a place where the trace of the past is very present, yet the city is not a museum and its forward movement is equally as palpable. It can be presumed therefore that modern Shimla provokes strong reactions because it is at once too postcolonial for the Indian Summers' crowd and too colonial for the likes of Urmi. However, Urmi's rejection of Shimla seemed to have as much to do with postcolonial developments, such as the lift, as colonial developments, like the Cathedral. What is more, the rejection of Shimla, as a place out of place, can be found in some of the earliest colonial accounts of the city (Pubby 1988: 7). This sense of disquiet that some colonial officers had with the landscape of colonial Simla is discussed further in Chapter Two. These accounts suggest that the Simla landscape, even in the colonial period, has a sense of artificiality about it; not really a British landscape in the hills, but also not a native landscape, which is implicitly seen as being more in-harmony with the natural world. This view is echoed by a certain postcolonial discourse and this correlation suggests that it is not simply the turn from the colonial to the postcolonial that renders Shimla a place out of place, rather it is the way that its landscape manifests an imaginative fusion of European and non-European elements that is uncomfortable for those who wish to keep them separate.

The way that Shimla so obviously manifests the tensions of past action and present life, which lie behind most postcolonial cities is precisely what I was drawn to. Yet, in 2006 I was not yet able to fully appreciate this and certainly had no inkling that the city would capture my imagination in the way that it has. No doubt a large part of this had to do with the way that the Himalayas featured in my own imaginings and how I brought these with me to the field. For, the idea of the Himalayas resonates well beyond Hindu India and countless people, all over the world, are able to imagine a Himalayan landscape. This is because of the stories that they have heard told about such places, stories which on the whole have little place for Shimla; a city that does not fit neatly into the ideal of either a Shangri-La, or a wild, deserted landscape (Pinault 2001:110).

iv) From academic ancestors to a discordant ethnography

The anthropologist is not a traveller, they do not so much move through areas as dwell within them. What is more, they do so armed with a history of scholarship and interpretation that generates a different type of engagement and ethnography to popular discourse (Wheeler 1986). Academics, however, also live in wider social contexts and as such are also influenced by popular behaviours, beliefs and narratives. Of course, academic analysis seeks to move beyond popular discourse through both its method and its engagement with canonical literature. However, there is nothing objective about the (perhaps uniquely) subjective experience of fieldwork and the ethnographic record therefore is neither truly objective or all encompassing (Lévi-Strauss 1981). As is now well established, the ethnographic record creates its own narrative (Stoller 1994) and has the effect of guiding the way that we come to understand the material culture of any given place. This guiding effect acts as both a magnifying glass, allowing the academic to easily detect subtle elements of the landscape, and a filter, directing our gaze to such an extent that it filters out other aspects of life in any given region (Miles-Watson and Miles-Watson 2011). It is necessary, therefore, to now consider how this book is both influenced by pre-existing literature and seeks to pull away from this, directing attention to aspects of both the region and the religion that have previously been overlooked.

The Himalayas certainly has a strong and lively tradition of ethnography devoted to it, from the earliest colonial anthropological accounts (such as Hutton 1921 and Von Fürer-Haimendorf 1939), through the twentieth century (notably Beremen 1972, Madan 1965, and Sax 1991), and into the new millennium (including, Hausner 2008, Joshi 2012 and Wagner 2013). Many of these ethnographic texts echo the popular ideal of the Himalayas as a spiritual destination by focusing on pilgrimage (Hausner 2008, Sax 1991, Snellgrove 1961, et al). Others reinforce its popular connection with Shangri-La through a focus on villages (Madan 1965, Mathur 2014, Parry 1979, et al) and tribes (Bhasin 1988, Gooch 1998, Wagner 2013, et al).

Collectively they establish a trend for viewing the region as a timeless place of tribal peoples and religious ascetics loosely populated and dominated by the 'natural world', which is viewed as Divine; in this, the academic literature strikingly resonates with popular understanding. What is more, this trend cannot be dismissed as simple orientalism, for it can be detected in both Indian and Western publications; it is exemplified by two important collections: the Indian based *Anthropological Survey of India's* volume on Himachal Pradesh (Sharma and Sankhyan 1996) and the *Modern Anthropology of India* (Berger and Heidemann 2013), which is a product of the western academy.

The Anthropological Survey of India (hereafter referred to as ASI) is a government funded project (established in 1945 and still ongoing) that aims to document the communities of India. A key strand of this project (from 1985–1992), known as the People of India, proceeded on a state by state basis to analyse the 'communities of India, the impact on them of change ... and the links that bring them together' (Singh 2016). The findings of this were then published in an extensive series of volumes. Himachal Pradesh is represented here and has a weighty seven-hundred-and-fifteen-page volume devoted to it, but this volume focuses almost entirely on essentialist descriptions of different tribes and is written entirely in the ethnographic present. We are told, for example that 'the Badhai, or Barhai, *are* a community of woodcutters and carpenters ... *The* people *are* non-vegetarian ... Women *enjoy* almost an equal status ... [and] *the* community *demands* at least one son' (Sankhyan 1996: 40–44, my emphasis). The dual use here of both essentialisation and presentism, when combined with a focus on rural/tribal identities is a clear and explicit presentation of the way that the ethnographic record of the region reinforces popular understandings, at the same time as drawing attention to specific aspects of life in the hills that are then presented as representative of the whole.

The *Modern Anthropology of India* (2013) is a recent attempt, by largely western scholars, to provide a description of the peoples of India that is better engaged with 'on-going theoretical debates' (Berger and Heidemann 2013: xiii). In contrast to the ASI's desire to be comprehensive, *The Modern Anthropology of India* aims to draw out key texts, themes and ideas, acting as a gateway for further research. It condenses this material into a single volume, which (like the ASI project) proceeds to deal with the country by moving systematically from one region to the next. Such an approach implicitly reinforces the ASI's denial of mobility and transformation, despite the explicit desire to not do this. The *Modern Anthropology of India* captures well the marginalisation of the region of Himachal Pradesh by the western academy. Himachal Pradesh is discussed in a chapter that it has to share with its neighbour, Uttarakhand, which is notably called 'Uttarkhand and Himachal Pradesh' (Sax 2013); even as a combined chapter, the text only runs to nine pages in a book that averages eighteen pages per chapter (Sax 2013: 276–285). What is more, within the chapter, the discussion of Himachal Pradesh is limited to around one page (Sax 2013: 278) and Shimla, the state capital, fails to get a mention at all (ibid). To some extent, this regional blindness is only natural for a book that works primarily by mapping existing ethnography. However, this continuing marginalisation has the (perhaps unintended) unfortunate consequence of reinforcing the pattern of scholarship, drawing the attention of future ethnographers away from Himachal Pradesh, towards other seemingly more interesting regions. Yet, I cannot help but feel that this is something of a tragic oversight, given that Himachal is such a culturally rich and diverse state, with both a famous history and a key role to play in the future of the wider region.

The neglect of Himachal may well be simply a case of people following established patterns of scholarship, which lead them to (somewhat innocently) only see what they have been taught to see. However, it also needs to be considered that the double neglect of Shimla, a famous place with both a powerful historic role and contemporary political position, is as much a deliberate neglect as an overlooking. For, it seems to me that Shimla has been neglected not so much in spite of its historic and contemporary relevance as because of it. Shimla's existence as a modern urban, dynamic, multicultural zone jars with both popular and academic notions of the Himalayas, at the same time as its contemporary relation to colonial history disrupts academic narratives about the postcolonial period (Van De Veer 2014) and unsettles our established hermeneutical frameworks – Shimla is the elephant in the hills!

In its inability to confront the reality of contemporary Shimla, the academy reveals itself as something that has never fully been able to move beyond its colonial foundations. Indeed, there is nothing new in the discomfort that the academy shows in discussing Shimla and regions like it: colonial officers in India were so concerned about the threat of the Colonial impact on 'native' landscapes that they urged local rulers to establish reserves for Pahari culture (Kennedy 1996: 81); it is striking that after independence, these same reserves became the key focus of anthropologists (ibid.). The ethnographic material contained within this volume is then truly a first step in the reconfiguration of the academic field by drawing attention to Shimla's Christians and the uncomfortable questions that their lives provoke. In 2006, I was part of the problem, heavily enmeshed in the ways of seeing described above, I was intent on largely following the path set before me. Like all good researchers, I had spent time in the library and came to know the region through academic literature well before I travelled there.

When I finally came to the Himalayas I did so with a strong interpretive lens, which meant that I filtered out Shimla's urban communities, partly because of habit and partly because of a subconscious recognition of the uncomfortable questions that they posed for the academy's understanding of religion, identity and postcolonial practice in this region and beyond. However, the reality of spending time in Shimla allowed the place to work on me and the whisper of the mystery to enter into the peripheries of my consciousness, drawing me deeper into the lives of these people. Yet, on that first snowy day, I had no real sense of what I had stumbled into. Although Christ Church had led me to it, it took a further, quite dramatic, event for me to realise that I had already begun my research, taking my first steps on a journey into the lives of these quite remarkable sites of worship and the people, past and present, Christian and non-Christian, who both make them and are made by them.

v) Sita's tears: disrupting academic authority

Whenever I summon a vision of Christ Church Cathedral, it is always haunted by the image of a woman wearing a vivid red dress. She is sat on the ground outside the church, her head is down, her hair partially covering her face, and she is weeping. Although the image of her desperately crying in this glorious red dress is now so vividly present, my field notes show that this is something of a fiction, or at least a symbolic crystallisation of a historically observed situation. Two weeks after I had first come to Shimla, my future research was indeed shaped by Sita crying outside of Christ Church, but she was not sat on the ground, nor was she wearing a red dress. Instead, Sita was stood slightly apart from a crowd, dressed in jeans and a simple top, the colour of which I did not record and has long since faded from my memory. She did not sit in solitude, but rather stood in conversation with me, for I was present, shaping the event at the same time as I was shaped by it. Despite these discrepancies my vision expresses reality as much as it is obscures it, for while she was not sat, seated worship was part of her lament, and while she was not wearing a red dress, she was weeping over a red dress – a red dress that she was to wear at her wedding.

I had by this time been led by the allure of the Cathedral into the lives of Shimla's Christian communities, but I had not imagined that I had arrived at a place that was going to be the focus of my research efforts for the next ten years. To the contrary, my understanding of what research in the region entailed was so guided by the ethnographic record that I was unable to see that my research had already begun. I imagined instead that I was still in a position of waiting to undergo real research, which would be undertaken at a later date, high in the Indian Himalayas, with tribal, Hindu, communities. Research in a former colonial capital that was today an urban centre with educated, middle class, Christian pillars of the community was not the sort of research that people travelled half-way around the world to do. However, these communities actually were disruptive anarchic forces, not so much in terms of their resistance of the public centre as their ability to disrupt the academic and popular discourse, reshaping established paradigms. My own disruption began suddenly with Sita's tears and moved from there to a refocused position of harmony. That journey is recreated in this book, with the intent that it will similarly disrupt wider complacent assumptions, thickening the discourse and allowing for a refocusing on an equally important other.

Part of the reason for my initial oversight was the very identification of anthropology with Christianity. Today such a position is unlikely, but in 2006 it was commonplace. The explosion of interest in the anthropology of Christianity over the last decade is quite remarkable and has undeniably transformed the subdiscipline of the anthropology of religion. However, when I stood next to tearful Sita, fourteen years ago, the anthropology of Christianity in general was in a nascent state. Both the Cannell (*The Anthropology of Christianity*, 2006) and the Engelke and Tomlinson (*Case Studies in the Anthropology of Christianity*) volumes, which together announced the sub-discipline to the global stage, appeared later that year and the landmark Bialecki, Haynes and Robbins text (*The Anthropology of Christianity*, 2008) would not be published for a further two years.

My research with the Christian communities of Shimla has therefore unfolded and developed against the backdrop of a turn towards the study of Christianity within anthropology, which both benefited my work and complicated it, especially when my own experience has contradicted key assumptions of the anthropology of Christianity movement (detailed in chapters five and six). If, in 2006, the anthropology of Christianity was a marginal area, then the anthropology of South Asian Christians was doubly marginalised. Even today, South Asian Christians are clearly less central to the anthropology of Christianity debates than say African Christianities, and it is common for people to assume that work in India focuses on Hindus, while work in the Himalayas draws primarily on Buddhists. The situation has however improved since Rowena Robinson was able to complain that 'writing about Christianity in India suffered from enormous neglect' (Robinson 2003a: 12).

Over the last fifteen years the development of the anthropology of Christianity (Bialecki, Haynes and Robbins 2008, Cannell 2006, Engelke and Tomlinson 2006 et al) has combined with a more widespread interest in popular Indian Christianity (Raj and Dempsey 2002) to help generate a far richer ethnographic record of Indian's Christians (Jain 2009, Raj 2002, Schmaltz 2010 et al). Great progress has been made over the last fifteen years in broadening understanding of contemporary global Christianity in general and Christianity in India in particular, there are however still notable gaps in the ethnographic record. It is still the case, for example, that the majority of material written about Christians in India focuses on the South of India and avoids certain regions, such as Himachal Pradesh, altogether. When, in 2006, I first began working with Christian groups in Himachal Pradesh I understood the main contribution of my work to be that of adding an account of the Christians in this region to the ethnographic record, presenting a missing piece of the puzzle.

It soon became clear, however, that the study was pushing me beyond this humble goal, for the lived reality that I was entering into transformed the discourse, by moving beyond the ideal types, colonial politics and Indian power structures that are commonly used to understand Christian groups in this region (Robinson 2003b: 864). For, although the Christians that I was working with in Shimla have a connection with the colonial period that is attested to by many now classical studies of India's Christians (Fuller 1976, Mosse 1996, Robinson 1998 et al), the issues that I saw surrounding colonialism focused more on landscapes of worship than on caste. Shimla's contemporary Christians have been airbrushed out of the ethnographic record precisely because of their centrality to life in the contemporary city and the wider trends this points to.

This ethnography then has the power to unsettle established discussions and theories at the same time as it joins with them.

Historians, unsurprisingly, have had little trouble in placing Christian communities at the heart of colonial India and there have been several notable historical studies of Christianity in South Asia (Bayly 1989, Baumann 2008, Frykenberg 2010, Phan 2011, Robinson 2003a), which present survey histories that focus on the developmental scheme of Christianity from the earliest days, through the colonial period into the present. I have found one of the most useful aspects of such studies, for this research, to be that they succeed in highlighting the diverse roots of Christianity in the region. In particular, where they draw on the heritage of precolonial Christian missionaries, colonial Christian missionaries (Catholic Portuguese, French and Protestant, largely British and American), as well as postcolonial impulses, which are largely driven by American evangelism. The detail of these historical surveys has tended to focus on certain regions and communities, especially those in South India, including Mar Thomist and Portuguese Catholic, communities; there are several excellent histories of certain groups and regions in the South of the subcontinent. These texts pick out the important histories of, especially caste politics (Caplan 1987, Dempsey 2001, Mosse 2012), but also inculturation (Collins 2007) and gender (Kent 2004) in the historical development of minority communities' identity.

The, largely monoculture, south Indian, historical, studies that have dominated the academic discussion provide a useful comparator for my own engagement with the multicultural, contemporary, North Indian, Christian communities of Shimla. At certain points, this book sings in resonance with the picture that is formed of Christianity in India by the collective weight of the historical record, however at other times my experiences are strikingly discordant and it is precisely in these discordant moments that this ethnography opens understanding of the contemporary situation in this Himalayan region. This ethnography is therefore a necessary corrective to the paucity of modern scholarship, historical or otherwise, that addresses the churches in the North West Himalayas. By drawing previously overlooked, distinct, voices into the conversation I am able to present an alternative vision of Christian practice in India that is at points strikingly different to the established narrative yet equally as authentic. Through this I open understanding of the complexity of faith in the modern Indian nation. There are however very useful accounts of the life of Christians in the North West Himalayas that date from the colonial period, which largely explore the development of Christian mission in the region.

I have found, in particular, the *Parochial History of Shimla* (Wilkinson 1903) and *The Rural Church in the Punjab* (Lucas and Thakur Das 1938) to be two key primary source documents. These, along with other, harder to find, archival data, provide a backbone of archival material that supports the contemporary, ethnographic descriptions. Indeed, it is impossible to deal with such a rich historical environment (and movement) without engaging in some way with ethnographic history (cf Saika 2004). That said, this book is not intended to be another historical account, it is born from engagement with contemporary societies and it is to the contemporary situation that it primarily speaks.

When we turn to the present day, scholarly material discussing contemporary Christianity in the region is limited to one unpublished thesis, produced by a member of Shimla's Catholic community, as part of the requirements for a degree in Political Science at Himachal Pradesh University (Chug 2000). This work is not in any way ethnographic and is largely a presentation of statistical survey data. I have found the survey data to provide a useful quantitative balance to my own more qualitative research and use this to help understand how the specific instances that I am describing might fit into wider trends. This book is not an attempt to capture the entirety of Himachali Christianity, rather it is interested in communicating the important lessons that I have learnt during specific interaction with Christians and Hindus whose material religion entangles in and around the two active Cathedrals of Shimla. It looks to the past and the future but is clearly situated in a particular point of these communities ongoing development, by drawing on ten years of fieldwork in this region (between 2006–2016). This fieldwork was at times undertaken on my own and at times undertaken with my wife, but always with the generous support and guidance of those Himachali people that I had the privilege of spending time with. While many people (both human and non-human) shape this work I have to acknowledge that it never would have come about were it not for the revelation offered by Sita's tears.

I had met Sita a couple of weeks earlier, when she joined me and another congregant for coffee after a church meeting. She was then in her twenties, a local educational professional, who seemed confident, bright and articulate. Two weeks later, it was a rather different aspect of herself that she revealed and in so doing opened my eyes to the necessity of the research that is encapsulated in this book. We had travelled together to a large and unusual inculturated Christmas event that was taking place in the courtyard of Christ Church Cathedral (discussed in detail in Chapter Six). As the service unfurled behind us, Sita turned to me and began to tell me that she was facing a dilemma in her life because she was to be soon married in a red dress, but it was her desire (and as I understood it a family tradition) to get married in a white dress. It was clear that this seemingly minor detail of her life tapped into something of greater significance as she became ever more distraught, pleading with me for answers in what could only be a rhetorical fashion:

> "Why is it that we [and she used the plural] should always be the ones to compromise?"

And then again as the Christian Swami's song filled the air she asked with tears in her eyes:

> "Why is it that our traditions are not viewed as authentic?"

In that moment, moved by the vulnerability that this relative stranger had displayed, as the Christian sannyasin reached a new octave, the finely spun enchantment of the academy was broken by the force of the material experience. I felt Sita's comment personally; it was as though I had been doubly wounded by both her confession and her seeming assumption that I was somehow a source of aid, for I was not only without a solution, but part of the problem. I was one of the 'them', I had gone to Himachal precisely with the sort of understandings that were now impacting so severely on her life: understandings about the nature of religion and authenticity in the Himalayas, understandings about the nature of proper anthropological research, the issues of distancing, and the other, not to mention understandings about the nature of inculturated worship and local material culture – in short, the issues that this book explores.

My epiphany led me to the understanding that if I was to do research that had real integrity then I had to allow the alternative vision before me to be given validity. I had to take seriously the testimony and way of life of people like Sita. This book then is in many ways a seditious work, for it presents a tale of Christian stability and order in a region that the academy has variously described as Shangri-La (Buckley 2008), the Land of the Gods (Elmore 2016) and the Anarchist's Refuge (Shneirerman 2010); it presents a vison of the world that is gained from being attentive to the everyday lives of ordinary middle-class Indians, in a continent so often characterised by accounts of extraordinary ritual (Hausner 2008) and crippling poverty (Jeramiah 2013). Finally, this book talks of religious harmony and peace (both through and within time) against a trend to stress religious divisions and turmoil (Hinnells and King 2007).

vi) Substance of the book

This book presents a theoretically engaged ethnographic exploration of the material religion that surrounds nominally Christian sacred sites in Shimla, a Himalayan Hill Station. This crafted material religion is an active ongoing process, informed by a colonial past, but also shaped by both the postcolonial present and more distant geological/mythic times. Although the material religion centres on landscapes that are identifiable as Christian, it will be shown that Hindus, atheists and Sikhs all have a role to play in the mutually constitutive relations of animate and inanimate that lie at the centre of these nodes of sacred entanglement. After this initial discussion, we turn in the next chapter to the geographic location of Shimla, which both presents a problem of identity for its contemporary post-colonial population and an opportunity for the development of new understandings of the relation between the past and the present in postcolonial India.

In the second chapter (*Christ in the Land of the Gods*) I draw on archival, ethnographic and autoethnographic material to locate Shimla's communities in their geographic and historic context. This process of contextualisation begins with the seemingly natural and mythologically suggestive geography of the western Himalaya. It then moves to explore the way that Christianity came to be integrated into these landscapes through both the trace left by the material action of wandering Sadhus for Christ and the relating of toponymical mythology today. In particular we focus on two key figures Sadhu Sundar Singh and Samuel Evans Stokes, exploring how they came from opposite directions and met in the middle, before Stokes became a Hindu and Singh went to join the ancient Maharishi of Kailash. The chapter concludes by considering the value of viewing the lives and ministries of Stokes and Singh as part of a broader development of a certain kind of inculturated Christian material religion, which has strong roots in the Shimla district, even if its lack of purchase in the city is equally as marked.

The third chapter of the book (*Recreating Mount Olympus*) narrows the focus to the urban and historically rich geography of the state capital, confusingly also called Shimla. The chapter aims to introduce the nature of life in the modern hill station, however in order to achieve this the chapter has to take account of the important colonial history of this region, where reckoning with the past is an inescapable part of life in the present. We will focus especially on the striking contrast between the material religion of the hills (outlined in the previous chapter) and the material religion of the city. The disjunction between these urban and rural material religions will then be used as a spring-board into the complex (and yet central) issue of why the landscape of Shimla is unsettling and uncanny for some, yet so reassuring and enticing for others. This in turn leads us to consider the relationship of the Shimla Hills to other sacred mountains, especially when viewed through three important theoretical lenses: homeland, weather world and replication.

The first of these concepts is perhaps the most rooted of the three and this is captured by the idea of *dùthchas*, a sense of home that is rooted in relations (built up over successive generations) with human and non-human aspects of the landscape. The second area of focus moves us to consider how local weather relates to more global issues of climate. By exploring the importance of weather worlds for material religion we therefore move to a more mediated position. The final theoretical concept, that of replication, allows for a focus on the connection between local and global practices, especially when replication is viewed as a device for bridging separately conceived points in space and time. When placed together, these thematic areas of focus help us to approach both the locatedness of material religion in Shimla and the importance of its connection to other places and eras.

Chapter Four (*Churchscape, Landscape and Material Religion*) sharpens the focus again as it explores Christ Church Cathedral as a geographical and spiritual centre of contemporary Shimla. We consider the depiction of Christ Church Cathedral in local art work and the importance of the narratives that surround it for the contemporary population. This leads us to consider the way that past residents are memorialised in the contemporary space and the role of these memorials as a connecting thread through the traumas of history. In order to move towards a deeper understanding of this material we develop here the concept of mythology as a source of truth and explore why it is problematic (from the perspective of material religion) to set history apart from mythology. Crucially, the chapter introduces the specific concept of implicit mythology and its capacity to enrich explorations of material religion. In doing so this chapter develops the core arguments and understandings of this book, which are used in the subsequent chapter to unlock the mystery of the Cathedral on the Ridge.

In Chapter Five (*Worshipping with Ghosts*) we return to the understanding of materiality as implicit mythology, as developed in the previous chapter, this time employing the theoretical construct to interpret experiences with the ghosts of Christ Church Cathedral. These experiences, the book argues, are central to the processes that allow for the postcolonial Christian community to negotiate the material religion of the very visible colonial past. The chapter draws together ethnographic information and theory to both illuminate the site and rework established theoretical understandings. By the end of this chapter a core understanding of the mystery of Shimla's landscapes will be in place. The chapter builds upon the firm foundation of understanding that earlier chapters in this book have established before moving to present the book's central revelation, which will be returned to again in every subsequent chapter. Each time that we return to this central revelation it is complicated and thickened in relation to further data, loosely following the spiralling method that Lévi-Strauss outlines at the start of his mythologiques project in the overture of the *Raw and the Cooked* (1990: 35). At the heart of both this chapter and the book lies Christ Church Cathedral and the revelation of its transformative powers that is revealed by engagement with Lévi-Strauss' canonical formula ($fx_{(a)} : fy_{(b)} \cong fx_{(b)} : f^{a-1}_{(y)}$). The results of applying this formula to the implicit mythology of Christ Church, which are presented in this chapter, are employed in subsequent chapters as a cypher that enables the decryption of the various mysteries of the Shimla Hills.

Chapter Six (*Materiality, Heterodoxy and Bonding at The Hidden Cathedral*) shifts the focus to the broader churchscapes of the city and in particular, St Michael's Cathedral. Although less visibly central, it plays an important role as a more variegated space of contemporary Christian Material culture than Christ Church, demonstrating alternative ways of nuancing the received elements of material religion and society in the region. The site is particularly strong in a bonding form of religious capital and we use this as a way to explore the value of group identities, before turning to explore (in Chapter Eight) the tensions and issues that surround tightly entangled identities. The chapter then moves from considering people as generators of capital towards an understanding of people as part of a wider process of landscape capital. The chapter deals critically with established notions of landscape and spatial capital and then moves to posit a more complex understanding of a particular type of landscape capital, which I term Cathedralscape capital. The chapter is notable for its lack of centring on Christ Church Cathedral and this allows us to present an important complimentary way of weaving the material threads of postcolonial futures and colonial histories in this region to that already explored in this book. Through this exploration we are naturally led to open the idea of skill, as a core concept for understanding the weave of material religion in this landscape and beyond.

In Chapter Seven (*Ritual, Materiality and Skill*) we develop the core concept of religion as skill, or (to be more precise) as a process of enskilment. The section makes important contribution to wider themes in the study of religion and in particular demonstrates that my conception of religion as a skill and Bergmann's Theological understanding of this are distinct evolutionary forms that draw from a common point of origin. Through engagement with participant observation we are led to emphasise skill as a process, rather than a value and this allows us to make the shift from skill, to enskilment. We will also, in this chapter, begin to explore the importance of this concept for understanding the field site and suggest possibilities of its importance for reconfiguring wider understandings of religion. In order to do this, we return to St Michael's Cathedral (introduced in Chapter Six) and in particular the way that the landscape processes that surround it operate. The chapter ends with a methodological consideration of the role of the researcher within the landscape and the need to reveal this both as an ethical issue and as a way of generating insight into the processes of enskilment that I am terming 'Prophetic Anthropology'.

Chapter Eight (*Pipe Organs and Satsang*) brings the ideas and accounts of the previous four chapters dramatically together, as we move to consider the material culture of one core, calendrical, ritual, which is centred on Christ Church Cathedral, but engages members of St Michael's Cathedral's congregation. Crucially, we also move out of the restricted consideration of the Cathedralscape from a Christian perspective moving into the wider realm of the Cathedralscape's role in the city's Hindu cosmology. The chapter refocuses the pluralism debate in South Asia, moving away from notions of the intermingling of substances and towards the idea of the entwining of lines, in an attempt to demonstrate that Hindu communities can be profitably explored as an integral part of Christian worship in contemporary India. Through this consideration we are led into a more general theoretical discussion of the important, but often overlooked, area of mixed-faith identities and the importance of these for challenging assumptions about the nature of contemporary religious identity.

In the final chapter (*The Salt in the Stew*) we return to the central mystery of Shimla that the book began with and now offer an answer to the mysteries of the cohesiveness of material religion in this historically ruptured region. We explore new developments in the landscape, especially around the development of technology and nationalism and put forward new theories for the operations of religion and research more broadly. In doing so we will be led to calls for a reconfiguration of not only our understanding of this region, but also the wider fields of postcolonial theory, South Asian studies, global Christianity and material culture. In particular we will return to the central idea of the book, the call for a prophetic anthropology, which is a consequence of a shift from viewing material religion as a category to a process of enskilment. This in turn demonstrates the value of a focus on landscape for the crucial tasks of rehabilitating mixed-faith identities and destroying unhelpful (often harmful) communal divisions.

2

Christ in the Land of the Gods: Context

Shimla is located in Himachal Pradesh (literally the Snowy Region), a small Indian State at the western end of the, formidable, Himalayan mountain range. Himachal's geography and mythology connects it to this wider chain of mountains, which stretches over one thousand five hundred miles and (at its highest points) reaches beyond the clouds to over eight thousand eight hundred metres into the sky (Colebrooke 1827: 35–373). Although the Himalayas are easily identifiable as a unit on a map, or a satellite image, they are on the ground a remarkably varied region that is nonetheless united in the popular imagination by the powerful symbolism of the mountains. If the reader closes their eyes and imagines the Himalayas it is certain that a strong image will be quickly conjured, possibly of snow-capped mountains (depicted in Figure 2.1). This is of course in keeping with much of the Himalayas, but there is more to this region than simply snowy peaks and generally the people who move across this landscape spend most of their time in one of the highly diverse and considerably less snowy valleys than on these unifying peaks. Indeed, Shimla, the focus of this book, is rarely blanketed in snow, even though snow is often visible from it and never far from either the imagination, or conversation of its people. Snow then is not something that this book can afford to dismiss entirely, but it is important to mention that (in my experience) the more time people have been able to give to engagement with Himachal Pradesh the less central snow is to their conceptions of it.

If we return again to the reader's vision of the Himalayas, although it may already be shifting now, I would venture that it initially had (and still retains) an emotional resonance of some sort, it is not simply an image that the reader conjures, but an image with emotional force. What is more, I believe that this will be the case with the vast majority of this book's readers, regardless of if they have ever set foot on these mountains. I suggest this because I know that the stories that are woven around these mountains are both widely circulated and have a certain phenomenological pull, which has seen the lives of a large percentage of this planet's population drawn into some sort of correspondence

Figure 2.1 The high Himalayas of our imagination.

with them. These mountain stories speak to deeply held cultural assumptions about the word and trans-cultural phenomenological encounters within the world. As such, they become more than just stories and live within us as 'values' and 'beliefs (Davies 2011: 105, 362). They generate ideas that carry an emotional charge, which when bound up with our sense of identity becomes a belief (ibid). It is therefore possible to say that the Himalayas are a part of widespread and disparate belief systems, which range from the orientalist Shangri-La (Buckley 2008) to the Puranic Mount Meru (Eck 2012: 122–125).

At one end of the continuum of belief systems sits the Edenesque myths of the Himalayas, which we are here organizing under the category of 'Shangri-La'. The name Shangri-La draws from Hilton's classic 1930s novel 'Lost Horizon', which has seen innumerable reprints and adaptations for film, radio and stage (Mather 2017: 233). It tells of a British diplomat who, following a plane crash, happens upon a magical valley, high in the Himalayas where people live long and harmonious lives within a spiritually rich, benevolent, bounteous and truly beautiful environment (Hilton 1933). The story may connect with local ideas of Shamballa (discussed below), but what is important for our purpose is that it connects with a wider Western mythology of a lost Eden in the hills that both predates the book and stretches beyond the zenith of the book's popularity (Mullen 2016: 2). Western populations of the last few centuries have found something deeply alluring in the notion of the Shangri-La myth type, regardless of the exact naming of the location, and this attraction continues to exert a strong influence, even as the name Shangri-La recedes from folk memory (Bishop 2000: 10). The seductiveness of this myth type derives from a European impulse to posit an uncorrupted and unchanging landscape. A landscape where humans act in 'harmony' with other elements, which has the capacity to act as a sort of counterbalance to the fractured known landscapes of home. In this binary model the West is associated with a dynamic existence outside of a subjugated natural realm and this is satisfyingly opposed to a Shangri-La in the East, where the marked feature is a harmonious existence within nature that harkens back to the dawn of humanity.

At the opposite end of the continuum of myths about the Himalayas stands a conception, here termed 'Mount Meru', which is deeply rooted in the literature and traditions of the subcontinent. However, it is important to note that this understanding is richest in material that is found not in the Himalayas themselves but on the great plains bellow. From here the Himalayas were conceptualised as a sacred and set aside place, associated with healing and encounters with Divinity, as well as being a place to be journeyed to at set times and (mostly) returned from, after a relatively short period; although it was once geographically central and remains cosmically central, it is experienced largely as geographically peripheral. This concept will be discussed in detail in the next section, what is important for our purposes here is to note that this understanding differs from the Shangri-La conception in a highly revealing way. From the perspective of the Indian plains dweller their subcontinent is both horizontally bounded by the Himalayas and vertically joined to the heavens, through the geography of the mountains. Thus, while the Shangri-La myth type places the Himalayas in opposition to the known world, the Mount Meru myth type makes the mountains a mediator between the earth and the heavens.

At one end of the continuum of myths of the Himalayan mountains we therefore have a vision that draws from an oppositional model, while at the opposite end we find a vision based on a model of mediation. Despite these differences, the two concepts are crucially united in a conception of the Himalayas as at once cosmologically central and experientially peripheral. Both the oppositional and mediatory conceptions of the Himalayas are brought together by the sense of the region as an Eliadeian *sacred centre out there* (cf Eliade 1959, Eck 1987, Turner 1973). In this understanding, which finds full form in unifying Theosophical discourse (McKay 2015 410–426), the Himalayas are a geographical marker for the symbolically central cosmic pole, or axis mundi, which not only unites, but also provides a centre to an expanded, more than human, cosmology. In order to therefore understand the complex network of emotionally charged resonances that surround this region we must now therefore explore further the Eliadean idea of the Cosmic Mountain, beginning with its roots in Hindu understandings of the Himalayan region.

i) Searching for Mount Meru: the sacred centre out there

For most contemporary Hindus, there is a canonical, scriptural, importance placed on the Himalayas, which is evident in the earliest texts and increases gradually through the millennia, into the modern era (McKay 2015). For our purpose, it is convenient to follow the trend of splitting the Hindu textual traditions into three, admittedly hazy, categories (Lorenzen 1999: 636). The first of these is the Vedas, which represent the earliest texts and contain treaties that have tended to be ideologically distant to the everyday life of the majority of contemporary Hindus (Thapar 1989: 212). The second cycle of Hindu mythology is the world of the great epics, namely the Ramayana and the Mahabharata. These are well known both through study of their classical texts (which possibly date from as early as the sixth century BCE (Keith 1915) and from engagement with popular performances, which range from folk theatre to television and film productions (Gillespie 1995). The final category is a group of oral and recorded texts known as the Puranas, or old stories, this is a highly diverse group of material that encapsulates the main body of the contemporary Hindu mythical universe (Nagar 2006: 496). The Himalayas have a sacred significance in all three of these categories and yet it is certain that the breadth and depth of material exploring the importance of the Himalayas dramatically increases as we move closer to the present day.

The mountains emerge as a significant cosmological region and source of healing in the earliest of the Vedic scriptures, which are still studied by experts today and have enjoyed a revival of interest in recent years that is partly tied to a rise in nationalism (Nanda 2003: 37–94). The Himalayas also make their presence felt in the great Hindu epics and (particularly in later recitations of these exploits of Gods and heroes) they form an important part of the cosmological landscape. Through these, the mountains become places associated with a wider geography of mythical actions and actors that helps to give sense to the modern nation of India. However, it is in the Puranas, that we find the Himalayas beginning to take central stage, as a place where the Gods dwell still and paradise can be found. In particular, the Markandeya Purana, an early and widespread text, describes in detail a Cosmic mountain that both acts as an axis mundi that joins the worlds of man and the Gods and a centre around which the cosmos revolves (Dutt 1896: 103). The mountain becomes both a point of crossing, or *tirtha*, between the world of the Gods and the world of men and a source of power, or *pitha* (Eck 2012: 217–293).

In the Markandeya Purana, which is a non-sectarian text (Rangachar 1964: 154), the mountain is the abode of many celestial deities and has large flat top that allows for the housing of all the divinities. However, in popular tradition Mount Meru is most closely associated with the God Shiva, who is one of the Great Gods (Maha-deva) and the chief deity of the sectarian Saivite movement (Whitmore 2018: 74). Saivite renouncers are ideologically positioned in opposition to householders, having abandoned the life of owning possessions, having stability and working towards order, to instead seek out communion with the wild God Shiva, often in the mountains that are closely associated with him. The association of Shiva with these mountains is furthered by the human presence of these ascetics, as well as by Saivite temples and numerous local myths that associate various mountain peaks with the Divinity, his actions and/or his body parts (Hausner 2008: 68). The ascetic renouncers are known for meditating in high Himalayan caves for years at a time, as well as for wandering between the worlds of men and the sacred sites of Shiva, coordinating their movements with those of the sun and the moon to arrive at points of significance at significant times (Hausner 2008: 125). These meaningful wanderings are mirrored in the pilgrimage activities of millions of Hindus, who each year travel to the Himalayas as a way of entering the land of mythology and (in a way that harks back to the Vedas) in search of healing and good health. Many of these travellers journey to sites associated with Shiva and the cries of 'Jai Shankar' (Hail [Shiva] the Beneficent), resound around the pilgrimage trail. For these people this Western Himalayan region is then clearly a sacred centre out there. It operates as part of a wider system of cosmology that both places it at the periphery of everyday life and the centre of spiritual revelation.

We have seen therefore that there is a substantial, Indian, tradition, or complex of traditions, that consistently connect these mountains with conceptions of the Holy and (over time) develop increasingly rich narratives around the mountains, alongside patterns of specialised (perhaps ritual) action that brings people either into direct contact with the mountains, or by proxy (such as through associated shrines of replication). This rich tradition however neither positions the mountains as uninhabited, nor regularly inhabited by 'ordinary people'. To enter into the mountains then is to enter into, or at least draw near to, the realm of a particular element of the sacred. One that is associated with healing and health on the one hand and the abandonment of security and bodily desires on the other. These seemingly contradictory conceptions are held together by the complex fabric of meaningful action that surrounds the mountains and ensures that they have a strong emotional resonance for Hindus throughout the subcontinent and (especially today) beyond.

ii) Saffron priests and Christian Sadhus

The high peaks of Himachal Pradesh are intimately connected with Hindu cosmology, but they also had great appeal to several Christian holy men, who were drawn into the mountainous region of Himachal Pradesh by both its association with Divine revelation and the traditions of the Shaivite ascetics. Although the practice of Christian pilgrimage to the peaks of Himachal Pradesh may not have been as widespread as its Hindu counterpart, its historic practice is still highly significant for our understanding of the contemporary material religion of this region. Oral history has largely distilled the practice of the complex of Christian encounters with Himachal Pradesh into the common recitation of the lives of two remarkable Christian figures, Satyanada Stokes and Sadhu Sundar Singh, who both left a lasting imprint in these hills. As we will see, Stokes and Singh are drawn to the mountains from opposite starting positions. They meet briefly in a cave, on the mountainside, before their paths cross over each other and each is increasingly drawn into the space that the other once occupied.

Stokes and Singh present a neat example of the range of possibilities for both the operation and understanding of Christian holy men in the Himalayas, as well as a wonderful example of how human lives can extend their significance beyond death through the sparking of narratives that have a perduring, significant, symbolic resonance. Crucially, I will argue that the ongoing resonance of Stokes and Singh is not a disruptive (or rupturing) force, for it is integrated seamlessly into the wider structures of balance that govern the region. Although Stokes and Singh both have a good range of hagiographical literature devoted to them by interestingly often separate communities, I first became aware of them through the way that they naturally entered my life and discussions while living in Shimla. Perhaps somewhat predictably, I came to know of Sadhu Sundar Singh through conversations with Church congregations, aided by sweet tea. Rather more surprisingly, I was first introduced to Samuel Evans (Satyanada) Stokes, while playing football with Himachali Hindus.

During my time in Shimla I set up a small amateur football club that held regular practice sessions in a picturesque village, located around 20 miles east of the city centre. Flat, grassy, land in Shimla was at a premium and although Annandale, located at the foot of the city, hosted in 1881 the first football cup competition in India, the postcolonial period had seen access to it severely restricted (Kapadia 2001: 18). I thought on one occasion that I had scouted a suitable alternative, this time not below, but above the city's central mall, but this site also met with local objections and even prompted a local resident to compose a protest poem. So it was that we ended up training at some distance from the city and through this move I was gifted my own set of effervescent experiences in the Shimla Hills.[1] These began with the not insignificant journey to the training area, which involved an hour's motorbike ride along roads that wound around the mountainside, followed by a 30-minute trek, through dense forest, before finally arriving at a suitably flat plateau, a clearing in the forest that the mountains gazed down on like giants around a cauldron.

If I was a little apprehensive about doing football training so far from the city at first, once I had undertaken the journey, I never doubted that it was indeed a blessing. I recorded a great exhilaration (even effervescence) about these training sessions, which partly came from the communitas of joining with my fellow residents in a collective act of coordinated movement and partly came from joining with the environment of rural Himachal Pradesh (cf Turner 2012: 43–54, 143–165). Our little Shangri-La was a flat, soft, green shelf on a steep mountainside that was both mellowed by gently swaying deodars and reflected in the bright, white, rocky outcrops that ringed the mossy-green clearing. As we ran our studs joined the goats in turning the humic soil and our shouts joined the Himalayan Griffon in piercing the soft blanket of sound made by the whispering trees and chattering bulbul. Looking back now (and in the moment then) it is clear that I felt a loss of the boundedness of myself as I both spilled out into and was gathered up within the environment; this almost religious moment of communion (or communitas) seemed to affect us all and leave us with a lasting sense of contentment. The narrativization of this fieldwork, if we can call it that, which I have offered here is important for three reasons. First, it points to the way that my own life is entangled in the very weave that we are here trying to unpick. Second, it demonstrates the way that sacred experiences, religious narratives and seemingly secular action are naturally blended in the everyday unfolding of life in this region. Finally (and perhaps most importantly for our immediate purposes) it presents an important context in which the legacy of Stokes first entered meaningfully into my life. Looking back now, it is striking that this Christian missionary entered my world quite by chance while engaged in activities that could be seen as secular (playing sport) and in the company of people who would identify as Hindu.

I have made much above about the significance of sport and nature for sacred revelation, but in truth the revelation of the importance of Stokes' ministry did not come during the playing of sport, but rather arose from a discussion surrounding playing sport. I have many fond memories of sitting with Rohit, Prem and a few other members of the group relaxing in the gentle, afternoon sun (after we had finished playing/training) and allowing conversation to take us where it would. It was during one of our earliest engagements of this nature that Rohit turned to me and generously said "You are going to be the Samuel Evans Stokes of our age". Although I was not fully aware of it at the time, it was a significant compliment and one that I could never live up to, for despite us both coming from outside of India, choosing to live in Shimla and being married to Indians, he was able to achieve wide-reaching political and economic reform, whereas I changed little and often took steps to dampen my impact on the region (as will be further discussed in Chapter Nine). Despite these differences, as time went on, I found that it was not unusual for my presence to solicit a recounting of the Stokes mythology, which was commonly known by both Christian and non-Christian residents.[2] It was always recited with fondness and any comparison was, I am convinced, intended as great praise, even if it both presented an archetype of the incomer that I would never come close to embodying and cast into relief the comparative insignificance of my life and actions. In what follows I will detail aspects of Stoke's life that are drawn from a combination of archival sources, the published writings of his close family members and oral recitations as a way of helping to draw out the complexity of his engagement with the landscape of Himachal Pradesh and the life that I lived there.

The story of Stokes typically began by situating him in Kotgarh, which is a small village around 50 miles from Shimla and could variously involve presenting him as an economic reformer, a social rights activist, or a famous Christian Sadhu depending on the context of the oral recitation. Typically, I found that the Christian aspect of his work was highlighted by people within the church, whereas the local Hindu population preferred to focus on the good social and economic reforms that Stokes was involved in, at the expense of an account of his later engagement with Hinduism. All versions of the myth however share certain common features that are largely supported by the historical record. I will first present these as a way of contextualising the shaping of the landscape by historical Christian actors, before turning in a later section (Chapter Eight) to explore further the differences in these narratives, as well as the centrality of these contestations for understanding the contemporary population's meaning making systems.

Stokes ended his life in Shimla and spent much of it in Kotgarh, but his story begins in North America, where, in 1882, he was born to a family of Quaker engineers, based in Philadelphia (Clymer 1990:54). This was a practicing Quaker household and Stokes therefore entered the world within the frame of a tradition that valued community, quiet reflection, questioning of authority (both religious and secular), as well as Biblical revelation (West 1992). These predispositions remained with him throughout his life, albeit nuanced and emphasised in different ways at distinct times, but he can be readily as beginning life within a particular Western, Christian, tradition. A tradition which I argue remained with him even after his conversion to Hinduism. Stokes journey to that point of conversion and into the landscape of Himachal Pradesh began at the age of twenty-two, when he had a highly formative meeting with the Presbyterian missionary Marcus Carleton (Clymer 1990: 54). Carleton came from a remarkable (although largely today forgotten) family of American Presbyterian missionaries that collectively made a substantial contribution to the development of health care facilities in Northern India (Amherst 248). Carleton's father had established a hospital in Ambala and his sister (also a medical doctor) was highly active in India, running hospitals and leprosy dispensaries (Sharma 2008: 3).

Marcus Carleton was actively involved in a leprosy hospital in the Shimla region when he met Stokes and it seems that Carleton inspired stokes to abandon his studies and go directly to India, while still in his early twenties, to help with this relief work (Kashyap and Post 1961: 25). However, after his arrival in India Stokes himself became ill and his own struggles with Typhoid resulted in him relocating to Kotgarh, a small settlement, located around 50 miles North East of Shimla city (Clymer 1990:55). Stokes was eventually to settle in Kotgarh and he married there Agnes Benjamin, who was a local Christian of Rajput descent (Sharma 2008:17). It is commonly said that although Stokes came to Himachal Pradesh as a missionary, he was less focused on formal conversion than bringing people to God's love through good deeds, and many are quick to recount tales of how he both effectively worked with the sick and was an avid social reformer. For example, it is commonly said that his very earliest encounters with India led him to the realisation that the best way to help the people of the region was by increasing their means to engage profitably with the emerging market economy. Typically, Stokes' response to the realisation of the centrality of market forces for wellbeing is phrased around two linked areas: agriculture and law.

When Rohit first mentioned Stokes he also described how Stokes transformed the Shimla hills by introducing a radical new crop and he rather strangely saw a connection between this and my own humble, ultimately ephemeral attempts to introduce a footballing culture into the region. Of course the two actions are so tenuously linked that there is no real justification for the comparison, but what is interesting is that in searching for a frame of reference for a Westerner trying to develop something in the region it was Stokes, an outside and missionary, not a formal colonial officer that came to Rohit's mind. What is more, it was the tangible, agricultural innovation and legacy of this Christian missionary that brought him into our conversation. This is because Stokes introduced new methods for the development of apple trees farming in the region and introduced new species of apple, although not as is often claimed, the apple itself (Tucker 1982: 122). Stokes innovation in the region of apple farming was so successful and left such a lasting legacy that today Shimla is known throughout India as a place that cultivates scrumptious apples (Sharma 1997). The initiative that Stokes began has then dramatically changed the landscape in a very tangible way as orchards sprang up among the hills, villages became more prosperous and new transport infrastructure was introduced. It is also at this time that in a large part thanks to a small wooden church, known as St Mary's, made its way unassumingly into the Kotgarh valley, although this is seldom commented on.

The second area that Stokes sought to make improvement was through his social work and in particular his attention to improving the official legal and social status of ordinary, rural, Himachalis. To this end, he was famously involved in a fight to remove the *beggar and beth* system, which was a traditional form of compulsory unpaid service due to the landowners by the peasantry, which many British officials exploited for their own gain (Negi 2002: 17). Stokes saw that this system of indentured labour removed the independence and rights of the ordinary people and he believed it to be akin to a form of bondage (Sharma 2008: 125). He therefore believed that he was called upon to fight this violation of fundamental human rights in the same way that his ancestors had been called to fight the practice of slavery (ibid). Stokes organized a highly effective combination of peaceful non-cooperation, negotiation and publication that resulted in an official climb-down by the British government, who consequently effectively abolished the practice in the region (Sharma 2008: 131). Through these actions Stokes effectively aimed to improve the cultural capital of Everyday Pahari folk at the same time as improving their economic capital. He was highly successfully in both endeavours and the advancement of these two areas has combined to leave a lasting legacy, transforming the socio-economic landscape of the region.

Stokes' work as a social reformer and political dissident were clearly the most important aspects of his contribution to Himachal for my Hindu friends. From this perspective what is important with regards to his Christian missionary roots is that this (and the associated fears of conversion) were not an issue for the acceptance of the indirect benefits that emerged from his social engaged religious practice. The tangible societal benefits of his ministry, despite his missionary orientation brought him the praise of key figures in the Indian independence movement. Mahatma Gandhi, for example, praised Stokes as the ideal immigrant and the chief reason that he did not want all people of western origin to quit India (Clymer 1995). At the same time, Stokes' movement into the sphere of Indian life moved him outside of the acceptable sphere of action for a colonial at that time and brought him the ire of the British government, leading to his eventual arrest and detention (Sharma 2008: 147). At this point, I would argue, Stokes moves outside of the bridging, liminal, status that he had previously held and becomes more firmly associated with the emerging world of the Indian citizen than that of the Western colonial. It is as if we reach a point where the stretching of the Western category towards that of the East reaches a snapping point, catapulting him firmly into the Eastern category, as Gandhi comments, from this position 'his white skin [can no longer] protect ... him' (Singh 2013: 1) A similar, trajectory of movement to the centre and then crossing to the other side can be discerned in Stoke's religious categorization, if not formation. The overtly religious aspects of Stokes' life tend to be downplayed in contemporary recitations of his life, yet religion was clearly an integral part of his life and it factors meaningfully into both the classifications that his contemporaries, put upon him and implicitly in the classificatory systems that are deployed to understand him today.

Stokes approached his Presbyterian missionary endeavour in a way that both drew on his Quaker roots and paved the way for his later engagement with Hinduism. An early correspondence with his mother demonstrates a strong desire to learn about religion in India, especially Hinduism as a way of creating a more equal dialogue (Singh 2013: 1). He soon came to believe that there was a lot that was worthwhile in Hinduism and that if the Christian message was to ever find root in India it would have to do so through the sort of dialogue with Indian society that the Late Roman Stoa had enjoyed in the west (Griffiths 1982). For Stokes this dialogue was not to be found at purely an intellectual level, but also through the material culture and the lived landscape of the religious traditions. Stokes therefore adopted local dress and practices of worship that were familiar to local Hindu Holy men, or Sadhus, who could be found in the

Himalayas (Emilsen 1998: 94–96). He spent time meditating and even came to exemplify the Khadi (wearing of locally spun, natural fibres) movement, even going so far as to call for the banning of all imported clothes (Clymer 1990: 64).

Stokes is remarkable within the region and a somewhat unusual missionary figure, but he is far from unique. He can be seen as somewhat following the footsteps of earlier missionaries, such as Robert De Nobili, a seventeenth century Christian Missionary in South India, who adopted (amongst other things) the material culture of Hindu worship in order to encourage high caste conversion to Christianity (Waghorne 2002: 17). In more recent years this practice has grown ever more popular (as we shall see in Chapter Eight), buoyed up in part by the legitimation of Vatican II. With many Christians, both before and after Stokes, taking the adaptation of Material culture even further (Emilsen 1998: 94–96). Sadhu Sundar Singh is one notable saffron sadhu for Christ who crossed paths with Stokes both literally and metaphorically before the two journeys lead them to progresses along their opposite, if intersecting, trajectories and it is useful to develop a complementary outline of his path here.

iii) From East to West: the Christian Maharishi

Sadhu Sundar Singh is rarely evoked in Shimla and has been far more central to discussions about Shimla that have taken place in Europe and America than those that I have enjoyed within Shimla itself. However, for many, Singh's saffron robes are the iconic image of material Christianity in this region, easily eclipsing Stokes' (little known, yet substantial) contribution to the Khadi movement. I believe that this is due to the way that Singh affected the landscape and the contrasting degree of fit between this impact and the dominant etic and emic narratives of Christian material religion in this region. The most notable discussion that I had in Shimla about Sundar Singh happened away from the town centre and arose, unprovoked, as an exasperated cry about the lack of evangelical impulse in the dominant church narrative of the time (as will be discussed in Chapter Eight). Outside of Shimla, Singh is well known and frequently mentioned, normally in relation to Christianity in this area, often as an exemplar, sometimes as a warning.

Singh is an iconic Christian figure in the region who is instantly striking for his association with the saffron robe and iconic turban (Dobe 2015: 166). This powerful use of material religion combined with his naturally oriental looks to create a widespread impression of him as a messiah like figure capable of leading a Christian renewal in its old and decadent heartlands (Cox 2002). The fact that Singh was not born to Christianity but came to it after a road to Damascus type experience further cements his image as a Paul of the modern era capable of both extending and reshaping the notion of what it is to be part of the Christian community (Dobe 2015: 153). It is common to begin the narrative of Singh's life with reference to the fact that he was born into the Sikh religion with an early interest in the study of South Asian religious thought, but a hostile reaction to the Christian Theology that he encountered in Punjabi missionary schools (Thompson 2005: 1–12). Then, at the age of sixteen, it is said that Jesus appeared to him in a vision and spoke to him in Urdu (Sharpe 1990: 176: 51). From that experience, it is claimed, he was led to become a wandering sadhu, following a traditional Indian practice at the same time as spreading the message of the Gospels (Thompson 2005: 45). He eventually left behind the plains and headed towards the Himalayas, where he believed people were closer to God (Streeter and Appasamy 1921: 14–15).

His Himalayan journey lead him to Shimla (then Simla) where he was formally baptised, not at Christ Church, but at what was then known as the 'native church' (Buck 1925: 123). This church was interestingly located on the lower bazaar, which was then (as it is largely now) a less obvious, more organic network of twisting shop lined streets that snake around the mountain between the upper Mall and the lower cart road. Interestingly, the lower bazaar was seen by many Europeans, during the colonial period, as an unwanted incursion of the India of the plains into their European enclave in the hills (Kennedy 1996: 193). As such, it is perhaps not surprising that Sadhu Sundar Singh's Christianity, which is associated more with the mystic allure of the Himalayan peaks of Himachal Pradesh than the ordered streets of Shimla, finds an association with the city in the area of it that spoke to so many of something other than the dream of a European town in the hills.

Singh later travelled with Stokes, the pair sharing together certain ideals of Christianity that drew from a shared belief in the inspirational value of the life of St Francis (Thompson 2005: 53–57), as well as a shared conviction that the most appropriate form of Christianity for India was one that engaged with wider patterns of religious practice in South Asia (Chug 2000: 65). Sundar Singh's influence was not limited to the Indian Himalayas and he was arguably more popular in Europe than in India. In 1921, during a tour of Europe, he is reported to have preached to a crowd of ten thousand at Neuchâtel (Cox 2002: 231). Through such high-profile events Sundar Singh became for many Europeans the archetypal image of both Indian Christianity in general and the Christianity of rural Punjab in particular. If Stokes therefore represents the European dream of Christianity being reinvigorated by contact with India, then Singh represents the equally European dream of India being transformed by contact with Christianity.

The two come from opposite directions and meet in the middle, with perhaps Stokes crossing Singh to end in a position commensurate with Singh's starting point (illustrated in Figure 2.2). For, partly drawn by love and partly pushed by fear, he ended his life abandoning Christianity and fully adopting a local form of political Hinduism.[3] In contrast to Stokes gradual drift to Hinduism through engagement with an inculturated from of Christianity, Singh moves quickly (and dramatically) to Christianity. Despite this seemingly rapid change of orientation of faith, Singh seemingly remains rooted in an eastern material religion, while happily employing religious concepts and understandings from the West, as well as broadening his sphere of political influence to the West. It is notable, however that both Stokes and Singh have their transformations nurtured in the liminal space that the Himalayas provides, and both can be understood within an established archetype of Himalayan Spirituality. It is, therefore, possible to view the lives and ministries of Stokes and Singh as part of a broader development of a certain kind of inculturated Christian material religion that has strong roots in the Shimla district. However, it is important to note (as depicted in Figure 2.2) that they circle (clockwise in the diagram) around Simla city without ever being as central to its material landscape as might be expected.

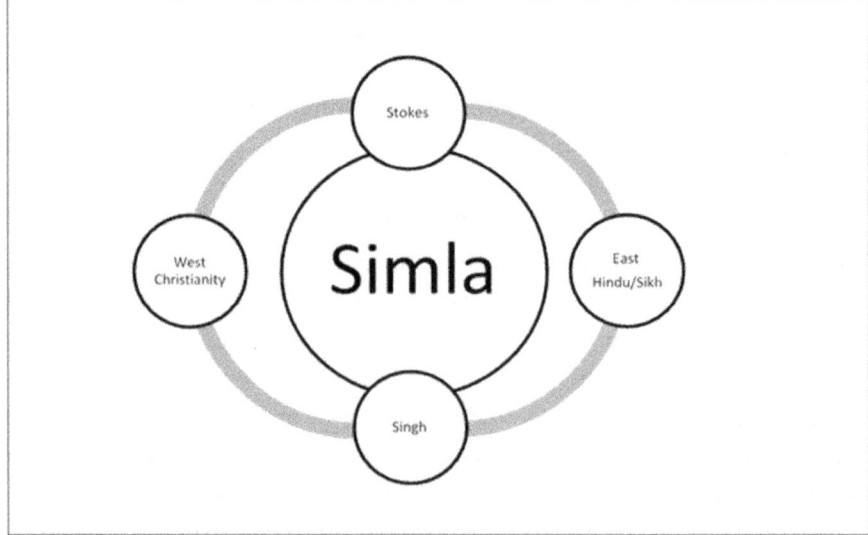

Figure 2.2 Categorizing Singh and Stokes.

In this chapter we have established that a certain kind of Christian material religion circulates around Himachal Pradesh and that this expression of material religion draws on both Western and Eastern aligned, yet distinct, traditions, which understand of the region as the Land of the Gods. Through Stokes and Singh we have seen how the Christian material religion worked with this traditional understanding, at the same time as adding to and transforming it, while also drawing into the weave significant actors from both the indigenous and colonial communities. Yet, as noted above, this tradition seems to have found resistance within the city of Shimla and in the next chapter we must therefore turn to explore further what the tradition of material religion within the city was. For, only then will we be in the position to fully comprehend how the movement from the periphery into the centre of Shimla of the sort of material religion described above, could act as the final trigger for Sita's tears.

3

Recreating Mount Olympus: From Shymla to Simla

Both Sadhu Sundar Singh and Samuel Evans Stokes engaged with a widespread and perduring understanding of Himachal Pradesh as an area that is constituted by sacred mountains. As we have seen (in the previous chapter) this understanding has rich mythological resonances that can be traced from the Vedic Mount Meru through to the twentieth century Shangri-La. For Stokes, this journey into the heart of the mountains and their associated mythology led him ultimately to a personal reconciliation with what may be viewed as indigenous Hindu doctrines (discussed in Chapter Two). For Singh, the mountains were a gateway to the higher plateau of Tibet, which many associate with the flat-topped Mount Meru (Sharpe 1990). Here, in a cave, he met with a 300-year-old Maharishi from the Middle East who was himself a Christian. Through this encounter Sadhu Sundar Singh therefore deepens his connection to an indigenous form of Christianity that comes direct from the Middle East, to the sacred mountains and allows him to root his Christian practice in a localised form of worship without fear of contradiction.

Stokes also reaches for a more indigenous form of Christianity, but through his politically engaged journey he is led from the realm of a Himalayan form of Christianity into that of a Himalayan form of Religion (albeit one that accords with certain Christian principles). Both Stokes and Singh however are alike in their desire to transpose a Christian ethic onto an indigenous sacred mountainscape and in so doing transform the materiality of Christian life. In Shimla city however the opposite process was in play: the desire to transpose a westernised mountainscape onto local mountains and in so doing transform the materiality of Himalayan life. For, even while Singh and Stokes were wandering through the Shimla countryside, at Shimla's heart a rather different form of Christian worship was unfurling. This worship had a markedly Western material culture that blended into a sacred mountainscape that the locals knew as Mount Olympus not Mount Meru.

i) Dùthchas, rain and replication

It is not hard to find accounts, from the very earliest days of the colonial experience in South Asia, that note a special sort of connection between the experience of the landscape of the mountainous regions of the subcontinent and the experience of the landscape of the writer's home (Kennedy 1996). Much of this is built upon highly stretched similarities that are perceived between the 'weather worlds' of the two places (Ingold 2010). By employing the term 'weather world' Ingold means to draw our attention to the importance of rain, wind, heat and sun in forming our everyday experience of the world, and our place within it (Ingold 2010: S126). Indeed, we may be able to go even further and suggest that weather is a key accelerator of people's impact on the environment, just as it is an accelerator of the environment's impact on the body. For example, in an environment wet and drenched with rain, such as the Kasi Hills, or the west coast of Scotland, the imprint of the movement of a person over such a landscape is quickened. We may imagine the rain transforming the earth in such a way that the imprint of the person is more readily accepted by the more malleable substance, and likewise excessive rain or sun will leave its mark in the accelerated processes of the weathering of the skin.

Now, one of the frequently commented features of the experience of altitude is that of wind and in particular of the kind of wind that is uncomfortably felt as it moves over the body and through the body (Miles-Watson 2016: 36). Again, we may turn here to Ingold, to understand how such experiences of wind can suggest transcendence, in a way that is either comfortable, or uncomfortable, depending upon the predisposition of the person involved in the experience (Ingold 2007d: S29–S32). For, wind bursts through the barriers of the human body, filling our lungs and reminding us of our connection to the beyond. For the many mystics, engaged with the Himalayas, this is of course a profound experience, tied to their searching for a connection to something beyond themselves, however, in layman's terms, it may be said to be simply exhilarating (Miles-Watson 2016: 37).

The early colonial actors in these regions, not only experience the weather as an exhilarating break from that of the plains, but they comment frequently on the cold, the wind, the rain, and the greening effect of these forces. What is more, they do this in a way that demonstrates a connection between the experience (and consequence) of these weather systems and the memory of the weather systems of the old ancestral homelands (either directly received or passed through families). This experience is summed up excellently by Fanny Parks, an early nineteenth century British explorer who describes her first experience of the Indian mountains with reference to the weather, writing 'how delicious is this coldness in the Hills! – It is just as wet, windy, and wretched as in England!' (Parks 1850: 239). In this statement we see that the strength of the connection and its uplifting properties, even in a figure who at other times could compare the land of her birth very unfavourably with the land of that she had spent twenty and four years on pilgrimage in.[1]

Once the connection between the landscape of the 'Hills' (read mountains) and landscape of home was made the colonist's actions transformed the landscape in a way that made the links ever more obvious. Through a process of schismogenesis, their every action can be seen as making the initial impulse seem more natural and the particular path taken the inevitable one (Bateson 1965: 175–178). The desire to be rooted in the land is perhaps best communicated by the Gaelic term *dùthchas*. The term has no direct English translation, but equates to something like the depth of relations that is built with humans and non-humans in a landscape of belonging. The idea is captured well in the poems of Sorley Maclean, which draw from his highly skilful and emotionally charged engagement with the landscape. This, sense of connectedness is clearly present in MacLean's most famous poem *Hallaig*. After opening with a stress on time, the poem turns chronology, bringing this dramatically together with geography to generate a sense of the haunting (yet deeply familiar) nature of the landscape:

> The window is nailed and boarded
> through which I saw the West
> and my love is at the Burn of Hallaig,
> a birch tree, and she has always been.
> ....
> she is a birch, a hazel,
> a straight, slender young rowan.
>
> MacLean 1992: 227

In the above extract we get a sense of both the persistence and transformation of the architectural environment. The window is still there, but now its function is transformed by the nails and boards that have been placed upon it, one set of past human actions overlaying on that of previous actors in a way that directs interaction in the present. This sense of consistency under change as the nature of human engagement with the environment is tied to a highly skilled ability to read those actions in the environment, and that this is deeply personal ('I saw the West'). This deep, emotional and personal engagement with the environment extends out of the purely architectural realm, in the passages that follow through the love that is expressed for the birch, the hazel and the rowan. But this does not extend to all trees, for, as we learn later in the poem, the pine trees 'are not the wood [he] love[s]' (MacLean 1992: 229). This is because the pine trees represent a different kind of engagement with the landscape to that which MacLean is intimately familiar. The pine trees represent the commoditization of the landscape and this contrasts to MacLean's more personal entanglement with the space. For the older residents of this region 'their daughters and their sons are a wood ... the girls a wood of birches', whose laughter is 'a mist' in the poet's ears (ibid). This is no mere act of remembrance, but a much more powerful joining of the then and now through the l landscape, its former residents are not only present they are active ('the dead have been seen alive' (ibid)), their presence shapes the landscape still.

In *Hallaig*, we see clearly therefore MacLean's connection with the landscape in the form of its human and non-human inhabitants, even its ghosts (these will be discussed further in Chapter Five). Ancestors are deeply tied to geography and despite the traumas of historic change this connection to some extent continues in a way that is poignant. But this idea of *dùthchas* is clearly linked to a land of birth and of ancestors posing the problem of what happens to *dùthchas* in the diaspora? How are diaspora communities, such as the Gaels and other Britishers in colonial India to feel at home? One way that this seems to occur is through a spatial equivalent of the temporal process that Bielo (2016) has termed replication. Following Coleman's later development of the concept of replication (Coleman and Bowman 2018, Coleman 2019) I want to suggest that a focus on this area usefully reveals the way that people create links, across space and through time by attempting to replicate an archetypal exemplar. The foundations of this process can be viewed through the reorientation of place through naming. It is, I believe, no coincidence that most of the world's mythology is highly toponymic (Miles-Watson 2019: 204). The power of association that is created by connecting places encountered in the here and now with places of significant historical, or trans-historical relevance is highly significant and will form an important part of a later discussion (located in Chapter Five). For now, it is important to note that the Shimla hills were filled with places that have European, largely British, counterparts. Even today, to walk around Shimla to move through Annandale, Stirling and Strawberry Hill, to name but a few. What is, however, perhaps most interesting here is the name Simla itself.

The name Simla does not have any particular colonial resonance prior to the founding of the city, although it interestingly was to develop into such an exemplar of a quintessential British city that it could be used as a template for names elsewhere, such as in the USA. In fact, the origins of the name Shimla are uncertain, but it is generally suggested that the name Shimla speaks to a pre-British significance of the site, perhaps to relate to the colour *shymla*, dark blue (Buck 1925: 243). We have, of course, tales of the light shining on mountains in a way that makes them seem blue, both in India and elsewhere in the world, and the origin of the name could be as simple as this. However, both in the historical record and in the contemporary mythology there are two other, far more significant, suggestions that have been put forward. The first of these relates that deep in the forest, at the centre of the town, there has stood since the time of the Gods a temple to Hanuman, known as Jakhoo (or Jaku) temple, which (it is popularly said) once had a blue coloured roof; the name Shimla, it is therefore suggested, simply comes from the location's association with the blue (roofed) temple.

An even more direct religious connection is given in the second origin myth. This states that these mountains were once the abode of a goddess called Shymla Devi and that when the British arrived, they took her *murti* (or physical representation) and threw it in a ditch. This, last understanding is perhaps the most commonly circulated origin myth today and it (intriguingly) also finds external historical verification in Edward Buck's 1904 account of the origin of Simla (Buck [1904] 1925: 243). It is also easy to imagine the Shimla hills, associated as they are with a plethora of different goddesses, having at their heart a (now lost) Divinity whose dark appearance would be in keeping with many Kali type depictions of the Divine (Kinsley 1998). Kanwar however cautions us against moving too readily to this assertion on the basis of one text, written at least half a century after the event (2003: X). It is also important to remember that mythology can move from the written to the oral tradition as readily as it can move the other way (Nagy 1986).

For our purposes, however, what is important is that in both of the above narratives there is a sense that the land was not entirely a tabula rasa, a promise that something pre-existed the colonial presence. The way that this presence is envisioned being engaged with by the colonial forces is however different in both accounts. In the Blue Temple mythology ancient Simla is allowed to continue, occluded by forest, but present none the less in the high peak behind the central colonial dwelling, which in a way mirrors the sitting of Simla within the wider land of the Gods. There is in this model a threefold division that is ideologically present in the city today and has at various times been a formative strain of life lived in and around these hills (see Figure 3.1A). The

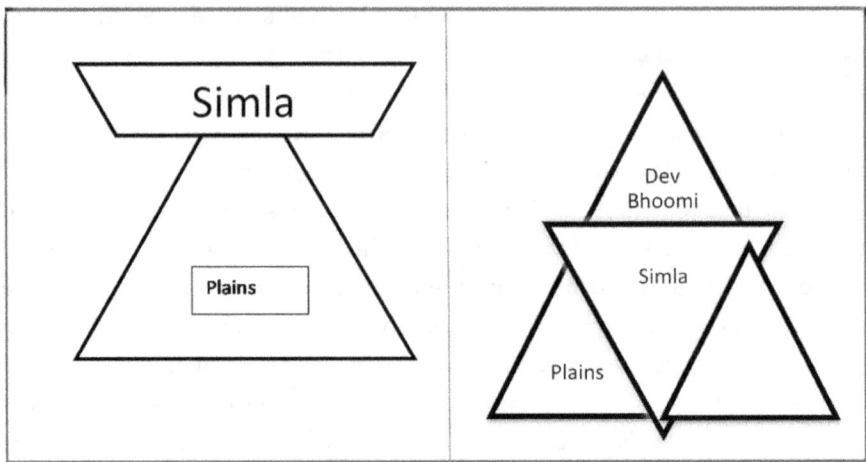

Figure 3.1A Simla as Mount Meru. **Figure 3.1B** Simla as vertically central.

second, perhaps more popular, myth however posits a less harmonious and more oppositional relationship between the colonial, precolonial (and even) postcolonial periods. This twofold model sees the old gods cast down from the hills to allow the (as depicted in Figure 3.1B) new residents to set themselves up as gods. The flat-topped ridge is no longer viewed as Mount Meru, instead a European mythological mountain is transposed, and it becomes Mount Olympus from which the colonials as self-styled divinities can rule the indigenous folk below, at the same time as maintaining a degree of ideological and physical separation.

For this sense of separation to take hold, the hills had to be transformed and an attempt at this was made that went far beyond acts of renaming. Natural deodar covered slopes may well have reminded visitors of the hills of Scotland and the Alps, but simply renaming the forests and clearings was not enough. Instead, species of trees, plants and flowers from Europe were added to the already rich vegetation of the region (Bhasin 1992: 96. And while the wildlife that lay within the forests was highly attractive to the early hunting parties, whose camps (in the early nineteenth century) were among the first more permanent colonial constructions in the region, with time new wildlife, from Europe, was introduced (Kanwar 2003: 15–16). Pedigree dogs, for example, were added to the monkeys and langurs who frequent the forest and even today it is possible to walk down Shimla Mall and see the monkeys acrobatically moving along the rooves, while along the Mall proudly trot packs of dogs, led perhaps by a giant St Bernard.

During my time in Shimla I had many encounters with these non-human peoples, both of whom had adapted wonderfully to their new urban environments in which they prospered. While langurs were a rarer sight, they were nonetheless visible from our tree top house situated on the edge of the town. They were however generally content to swing from branch to branch ignoring our presence. The monkeys, on the other hand, were keen to interact with us, our constructions, food and clothes (as illustrated in Figure 3.2). They were happy to climb Queen Victoria's Chinar Tree with gleeful irreverence and to humble those who walked to Jakhoo temple.[2] In general, I let the sleeping dogs lie in the sun, on the central roads, outside the churches and temples. On occasion, stories would circulate about these dogs becoming more dangerous and violent and I recall feeling more than a little trepidation when encountering a full pack of dogs in the forest on my own one day. We had a faithful local stray dog, called Kali, who would come regularly for food and water, until one night she was taken by a local leopard. These modern-day interactions are important in that they demonstrate both the ongoing entanglement of human and non-human, 'native' and 'immigrant', as well as the rich diversity of the colonial vision.

Figure 3.2 Shimla monkey.

In the nineteenth century, the colonists complexly sought to introduce non-human people to the region, hunting dogs, riding horses and even pet cats (Boyd 1922: 302). They did this partly out of sentiment, but mainly to use, for riding, ratting and hunting and at least two of these actions involve the subduing of the local non-human population. The Shimla hills are therefore presented as both places that are rich with wildlife and a place that is able to be uncomplicatedly reshaped, despite the existence of this 'wildlife'. Of course, there were also humans to be contended with in and around the Shimla hills. Particularly important here is the suggestion of one, or more sites of significant worship, but these were either hidden, displaced or dismissed. Moreover, the undoubtedly sparse local Pahari (hill-dwelling) population was understood to be less problematic than the dense population of the plains. This was partly an issue of pure numbers and partly an ideological positioning of Paharis in the category of the natural, unformed and receptive, rather than that of the potential corrupting civilization of the orient. This, problematic, yet formative categorizing is encapsulated in the British aristocrat Emily Eden's nineteenth century description of the people the of Shimla region as 'sort of vulgar Adams and Eves' (Eden 2010 [1837]: 231).

It is of course almost not necessary to mention, were it not of such importance, that statements like the one given above are highly problematic, resting (as they do) on a sense of cultural evolution, which posits an inexhaustible forward momentum of human development that is largely based around the categories of tool use and technology (Ingold 2000: 374). What is more, this idea of progress has tied to it the highly inaccurate (if persistent) assumption that not all people have moved forward the same rate; to travel through time therefore one merely has to travel through space (cf Davies 1804). Needless to say, such classifications are pure fabrications that not only occlude insight, but (more dangerously) intersect with harmful ideologically driven practices (cf Miles-Watson 2019). Nevertheless, these categorization schemes were undoubtedly a dominant formative concept in the first encounters of many nineteenth century colonists of this region. I highlight the concept here because it helps us understand why, when it came to the establishment of Simla, the chief concern of the colonial architects was not so much the assimilation and incorporation of their works into pre-existing social systems and structures, so much as the dismissal of the pre-existing systems, which were viewed as insignificant. This in turn led to a faulty understanding of the landscape as a suitable backcloth over which could be unproblematically layered visions of the old world. And so, as the nineteenth century progressed and Simla grew from a hunting camp into the summer capital, buildings were deliberately constructed in the style of the buildings of Europe, through a process of intentional replication (Coleman and Boweman 2018).

The first colonial houses were constructed in Simla in the early 1820s and by the 1870s a formal process of town planning had been instituted with organized roads, bridges and city planning zones (Kanwar 2003: 46). Between 1820 and 1880 a good number of houses and public buildings were constructed with obvious European influence (Bhasin 2009). These buildings can be described as mock Tudor, mock Gothic style, or Sveitserstil; at their grandest, they were made in the image of Balmoral, the Queen's residence in Scotland. These buildings were largely positioned on top (and along) of a flat ridge at the top of a series of summits connected by a smooth, broad, road known as the Mall (pictured below in Figure 3.3).

Simla was flat-topped, like Mount Meru, but its inspiration was less Hindu mythology than European mythology. Simla's colonial residents were therefore less likely to liken the place to Mount Meru than they were Mount Olympus (Fraser 1896, Geddes 1872, Millington 1898). The unknown author behind the pseudonym of Powell Millington captured this sense well when in 1893 he confidently proclaimed 'In India, as in Greece of old, there is a Mount Olympus; here the gods live . . . here, from their high seats above the clouds, they order the

Figure 3.3 Historical photograph of the Mall.

affairs of men' (Millington 1898: 362). Note here the sense of aggrandisement, power and control and yet also the ideological separation between the landscape of Simla and that of the rest of India. Simla is viewed as a haven from the plains, its city planning is essentially selfish and unsympathetic to its surroundings, but despite the talk of governing (or bickering) Divinities the architecture and sense of separation points to a desire for recollection and remembrance, rather than domination or imposition. Simla's landscape was therefore purposefully transformed by the colonials in an attempt to create a little piece of Europe in the Himalayas. Landscapes, however, are never simply backdrops and architects' plans are never simply imposed on place nor, are the local population so easily dismissed. The reality of Shimla was always more complex and hybrid than this vision and of course was all the richer for it.

ii) White robes and riding dresses: material religion in Simla

At the heart of this little European town in the Indian Himalayas, was placed a church, understood at times as the image of a typical parish church in the centre of a village, but also with grander ambitions that related to the great Cathedrals of Europe. The increasing population in Shimla and the ever-lengthening duration of stay, combined (after the advent of it is naming as the Summer Capital) with need for more formal rituals necessitated a sizeable, formal, Christian space, for the nominally Christian population. By the late nineteenth century there were three thousand three hundred and fifty-three self-identified as Christians in the town and the make-shift arrangements for spaces of worship could clearly no longer continue (Gazetteer 1889: 36). These Christians were largely not converts, the people identified as being of Christian ancestry and European ancestry, the heart of missionary activity in Himachal (such as it was) was always located outside of the city. particularly in Kotgarh. And so, this large, European, Christian population began increasingly to call for a space of worship that bared more resemblance to those that they were familiar with in Europe than the converted thatched, somewhat makeshift, building there had been in use from 1836 (Chug: 2004: 294).

It is commonly said today that the worshippers need for a formal, large space was met when Christ Church Cathedral was purposefully built in 1844, under the guidance of Major (later Colonel) Boileau (Buck 1925: 118). Boileau was an important local member of the Royal Engineers, who is credited with shaping much of Shimla's contemporary landscape (ibid). He was born in Calcutta, to a family of European ancestry and with strong connections back to Europe, but dedicated his life to India, taking particular interest in the development of (what was then) the fledgling Summer Capital (Cavendish 1995). Our house in Shimla was located adjacent to an area named after the Colonel, known as Boileau Ganj, which used to house a chapel of ease that has now fallen into disrepair (1904: 46). It is common to hear people today talk wistfully of the vision of Colonel Boileau and how contemporary town planning often compares unfavourably to it. However, despite the undoubted importance of the colonial to contemporary, collective, narratives of the historic construction of the city, Christ Church came into being through a long (ongoing), complicated process; this involved many different actors and materials who all left their mark on the landscape and it only when their actions are drawn together, across the years that we see something approaching the sacred site emerging.

The complexity of the process of Christ Church's becoming is pointed to by the many years that separate the advent of its construction (in 1844) and its consecration, or activation (in 1857), thirteen years later (Gazetteer 1904: 47). What is more, while it is tempting to see the date of consecration (1857) as marking a point of completion, it really only marks the landscape of the cathedral entering a new stage of engagement. In reality, long after its consecration, the Cathedral's landscape continued to be formed and reformed by those who moved around it, and this stretched throughout the colonial period and (as we shall see) beyond. This ongoing process of landscape formation brought together a diverse range of human and non-human actors as local materials blended with imported European materials and designs, while local craftsmen worked alongside Europeans. It was through this process of combined labour, spanning many lives, that the building began to take a recognisable shape (depicted in Figure 3.4).

This is not to suggest that the process of becoming was without symbolism or forethought. The deliberate process of design meant that the building held within it elements of universal Christian symbolism that have a particular European history, it is just that this symbolism is not the whole story of either the landscapes relevance, or formation. Therefore, while we find a traditional cruciform shape, stained glass (designed to communicate a theology of light) the materials that bind together to make this materiality are themselves traces of a mutual interlinking of a range of people and this place. The stained glass, for example containing stylized, clearly European renderings of classical Biblical themes that would, of course, have been familiar to Europeans, but are none the less the trace

Figure 3.4 Historical postcard of Christ Church Cathedral.

of the blending of European and South Asian actors (as discussed in Chapter Three). Similarly, the fresco of the sanctuary walls was designed by Lockwood Kipling, but painted by art students from Lahore (Gazetteer 1904: 46). Some materials in the Cathedral are local, but others were brought from Europe. These include the wonderful pipe organ, which was built (in 1855) by Morgan and Smith in England (at the behest of Lady Gomm) and the striking Steeple Clock (added in 1853) again from England (Carey and Wyman 1870: 44).

After the consecration of the Cathedral people continued to make and remake it through their daily lives as they moved around it, worshiped inside of it and marked their births and deaths on its walls (discussed further in Chapter Three). Favourite seats and positions in eth church became established as particular people became associated with particular areas of the landscape. The front of the church was associated with the ruling classes, with the Government of Punjab on one side and the Viceroy on the other. The back of the church with more recent converts to Christianity and the bulk of the Cathedral became constituted by the notables of the town, dressed in their Sunday best. The material dress of Christianity in this region of the Himalayas therefore couldn't be further from the enculturated material religion of Stokes and Singh. This sense is captured in a wonderful anecdote, preserved by Buck, which relates that one day the preacher is said to have struggled to find enough room in the church for all the people, arrayed as they were in their large dresses and therefore asked them to, as a special accommodation, come to church instead dressed in simple riding jodhpurs (Buck 1925: 118). This is indicative of a much wider trend for a certain kind of material religion and worship in colonial Simla, which is well documented in the archive (see especially Wilkinson 1903). We have then a clear picture of a pattern of worship in colonial Shimla that would have been highly familiar (in both sound and form) to that which took place in Episcopalian churches around the world at that time.

The material religion and living landscape of the Cathedral was therefore markedly different from the inculturated tradition of Christianity that circulated through the surrounding countryside. It is no coincidence that when Sadhu Sundar Singh visited Simla he was not baptised at Christ Church, not that when Stokes visited Christ Church Cathedral he didn't take to the style of worship at all. These issues will be explore more fully later in this volume (especially Chapter Eight) for now what is important to note is that the landscape of Christ Church Cathedral was markedly different to that of inculturated Himalayan Christianity and yet to view the one as Indian and the other as European is to deny the complexity of the relations that constitute both the landscapes of the city and the village.

Although Christ Church marked the centre of the colonial city, in terms of geography, spirituality and meaning making. There were other important religious nodes of action in colonial Simla (marked in Figure 6.5). From the late nineteenth century onwards a particularly notable entanglement of significance was St Michael's Roman Catholic Cathedral. This was built (in 1885) to accommodate an expanding Roman Catholic community by the then Roman Catholic viceroy, Lord Rippon (Buck 1925: 120). The Cathedral was situated further down the Mall towards the Viceroy's home and (rather than standing prominently on top of the ridge like Christ Church) St Michael's was tucked into the side of the Mall, below Scandal Point. It was constructed from local granite and left without render, which gave it the effect of blending with the rock of the mountainside that rose sharply up its Northern edge (Kanwar 1996). Just as Christ Church Cathedral had earlier been the result of long, ongoing processes of a complex of actors and materials, so too, St Michael's went through a series of iterations, only taking its current form in 1929. The overall style of St Michael's was mock Gothic and its shape (once again) cruciform, but many of the materials and craftsmen involved were far more rooted in the local context.

The process of the construction of St Michael's Cathedral was overseen by A. A. Rozia, a local engineer, who worked with designs drawn up in London by the

Matthews company (ibid). Through such collaborative efforts as these, the grey granite of the hills was mixed with bright marble alters, brought from Italy, brought together to create an internationally orientated, yet locally grounded place of worship. The stained-glass windows, depicting widely recognised scenes from Christian mythology were initially constructed in Europe and then dramatically reconstructed in India. The window behind the Chancel, for example, was originally designed in the late nineteenth century by a Bavarian company, however when, in the late twentieth century, the window fell into disrepair was lovingly restored by V. J. Kaushik, a Delhi-based craftsman (ibid).

A further centre of Christian worship in colonial Simla was St Andrew's, known locally as the Scottish church. It was visible only from several angles in the city, despite its central location (as depicted in Figures 6.2 and 6.3). Built of plain red brick in the Gothic style and as a cruciform, the current building was constructed around 1914 (on the site of the former Union Church) to cater to the Scottish population, although it was not to survive long as an active place of worship (discussed further in Chapter Five). Finally, it is important to mention St Thomas' Church, known as the native church in Shimla, even though it was not located on the central Mall. This was a consecrated space, developed by a Bengali Christian Rev. Thomas Edwards (formerly a clerk at Christ Church Cathedral) to provide a space for non-European worship, through both the mediums of Urdu and English (Negi 2002: 303). It was this church that Sadhu Sundar Singh was baptised in at and that Stokes felt more comfortable with. The church was located in an area below the formal city of Simla known as the Lower Bazar, a labyrinth style of wandering streets and market stalls that supported the many non-Europeans who were necessary for the maintenance of the European ideal above. St Thomas' opened in 1995 and closed in 1947 (Negi 2002: 304), however its legacy of worship continues to impact on the city today, as will be fully discussed later in the book (especially Chapter Eight).

At the heart of British Simla lay a complex sacred landscape woven together by distinct actors over a long period. For ease, we may understand the city as a place built in an environment chosen particularly for its weather, but with many implicit precolonial Hindu associations. Either through the Hidden temples located above the mall, or the many snowy peaks of the High Himalayas that are visible from the ridge on clear days. Colonial era constructions that are associated with the 'native' population (both from the plains and the hills) lie below, in the form of market stalls, churches and temples. However, dominating the skyline, we have a central Cathedralscape, a set of evocative European style, towers that extend upwards and connect above the many European styled houses and chalets that lie about them (illustrated in Figure 3.4). For many of the colonial population, this central band of the landscape was a set apart, special place, evocative of a homeland. It was also however landscape of aggrandisement in which they could live in an elevated status both literally and figuratively.

It is perhaps not surprising, if unfortunate, that there were, at various times, attempts to constrain the movement of non-European people across the central landscape, including the Churches. Restrictions such as these were not only morally flawed, but also impossible to maintain to any extent for any serious duration. The historical record shows that throughout most of Simla's history there were at least as many Indians there as Europeans. Indeed, the index of property registers reveals that, almost as soon as it had begun, Simla's local properties were owned by Indian born people of power, no doubt seeking to readjust to the shifting landscape of politics and keen to get some of the prestige that a house in the new Olympus would bestow on its occupants. What is more, the European population of Simla could not have engaged in such a substantial process of construction and maintenance without the skilled labour of many locals, which has (to some extent) already been indicated in the foregoing discussion.

It is true that in both secular and sacred rituals many residents of Simla attempted to connect with actions that are associated with Europe in general and Britain in particular. These took the form of plays, football matches, picnics and races. However, all of these actions were transformed by their relocation to the Simla hills. In particular, women seem to have found and largely enjoyed a different degree of agency in the colonies to that of their homelands. This sense is captured well by Emily Eden's letters, which give a wonderful account that captures both the sense of a distinct range of gender performance and the ever presence of Asia, in their imagined European enclave. First she notes the difference between life in India and life in England:

> We feel so certain that people [back home] ... would think us raving mad, if they [could see us] going galloping every morning at sunrise.
>
> Eden 2010 [1837]: 51

Later she captures well the degree to which the creation of a European landscape in the Himalayas is an obvious and unstable, perhaps ridiculous, fantasy:

> Twenty years ago, no European had ever been here, and there we were, with the band playing and eating salmon ... surrounded by at least 3,000 mountaineers,

who, wrapped in their hill blankets, looked on at what we call our polite amusements.

Eden 2010 [1837]: 293–294

It is perhaps also important to note that the simple binary of European/native did not hold out in practice in either direction. For, there were clearly Europeans, such as Samuel Evans Stokes, who were drawn away from the central European band of the landscape and enchanted from the beginning by older and more diverse forms of dwelling in these hills (as discussed above). Although it involves a less-profound engagement we can also see Rudyard Kipling's mention of the draw of the landscape of the exciting and exotic Lower Bazaar as having one foot on the path to a realization that Simla was never simply Europe in the Himalayas. At the other end of the spectrum lies Charles De Russet, a European who in the 1880s walked the paths above the Central Mall through the woods and into Hanuman's forest. There he became a mendicant of Jakhoo temple (renamed Baba Must Ram) and it was said that he came to understand the temple environment so much that like Hanuman he could converse with the forest monkeys (Sud 1992: 22–26).

The landscape then was always messier than formal, idealized, account of the colonial period allows. It is perhaps because of this that when Lord Dufferin visited for the first time his new summer capital he wrote home that it was not really an alluring landscape that reminded him of home, rather it was the sort of similar, yet different landscape that generated a haunting feeling of the uncanny (Pubby 1885: 15). Dufferin saw within the landscape a playfulness, as Emily Eden had before him, which bordered on the ridiculous and he described the landscape as resembling a pantomime stage set, designed by a child (ibid). Despite (or perhaps because of) Simla's playful references to a European ideal that it never truly achieved there were many who fell in love with place, precisely because of its strange familiarity. As time moved on Simla's landscape gathered a reputation as the Queen of Hills, the most exalted Hill Station and the place closest to refined European living in India. These dual notions of Simla as distastefully out of place and contradictorily exalting have carried into the present-day discussion of the landscape of Shimla and its relationship to old Simla. In 2018, the Vishwa Hindu Parishad (A politically right-wing organization) ran a campaign to change the name of Shimla to Shyamla as a way of erasing the legacy of the colonial period and its haunting ghosts (Bisht 2018). My own experience of Shimla is of a haunted city, yet I found these hauntings to be reassuring and in that, I was far from alone.

iii) Living in a ghost town: the materiality of spirits in Shimla

Shimla (as Simla was renamed after independence) is today a thriving state capital with a healthy tourist industry, nationally renowned schools (including Bishop Cotton) three Universities and (housed in the former Vice Regal Lodge) a dedicated institute for advanced research in the humanities (known as the IAS). The city is very much alive and continues to play an important regional and national role, however, the colonials, who took such care to craft a landscape of memory, have gone and new people have moved in. These people have both local (Pahari) identity and a cosmopolitan element. being drawn from both the surrounding areas and the opposite end of the country. Some of these people moved into the area immediately after the disruption of partition, which ushered in a new age of independent India. While others have come more recently for Shimla remains a migrant city attracting both residents and tourists (who double its population in peak season) from all over India and beyond. Residents are pulled to the city by the opportunities for employment that it offers in a wide-range of sectors, including renowned educational institutions, retail outlets, cafés, hotels and the substantial military and civil service Tourists are still drawn to Shimla by its weather world, but also by its haunting landscape, which bears so obviously the trace of past actions. For, while the city's population as swelled and many new postcolonial buildings have been added around the edges of its old colonial heart, that colonial heart remains. It remains central to life in the modern city and the key draw for contemporary tourists.

I, like many others lived in a more recent construction on the edge of the historic Mall. From there I would travel into its heart each day, along the winding cart road until I reached the smooth broad Mall, where pedestrians fill the road that is still lined by mock Tudor and Gothic buildings. These buildings house now anything from the globalized brands of the United Colors of Benetton to national chains, like Café Coffee Day, through to more local traditions and craft shops, such a Trishool. It is a general theory of landscape studies that massive population movement creates a disconnect between the built environment and the population. The traces of the past, as Harkin (2000) would have it become scars, wound that haunt the present. This only seems fitting for Shimla, the city is replete with ghosts and most of these ghosts are British.

Local residents would (unprompted) share ghost stories with me from time to time and I am sure that when returning home after dark I scared a few people in boileauganj, who thought I might be a ghost. Some of these ghosts are indeed terrifying, but many of them are in fact reassuring. The city then is haunted, but not necessarily in a wounding way. On the contrary the local population have been known to engage directly with ghosts at time of need and through practices that yield reciprocal benefits. Just outside the main city, lies a graveyard, where there are the graves clearly marked by (and marking) the lives lived in the colonial era. There are several such graveyards and more than one of them will make an appearance later in this book (Chapter Four). The one that I have in mind right now, contains within it a grave of the wife of a British civil servant, she died in labour and her mourning husband set above the grave an image of a woman, cradling a baby in its arms, as a commemoration the tragedy. However, long after the British left, this grave continued to be actively engaged with by the local population, many of whom believed that the ghost of this lady still remained in the place. What is more, because of her loss, she maintained the power to grant successful childbirth (and even fertility) to others. This it seemed, she was more than happy to do, provided the seeker appropriately propitiated her. The practice of postcolonial, largely Hindu, women coming to this colonial, Christian, grave to engage with it as a site of material religion, was so marked that (during my time in Shimla) the trace of their actions had worked to efface the original sculpture, so that it was barely recognisable. This situation has changed again, as I write the book, as will be discussed further in the next chapter. For now, I want to leave the memorial as it was when I was sat on a cold November day, in 2007, in a central coffeehouse, located inside a Tudor building, on Shimla Mall.

I was reading a recently published book a by Meenakshi Chaudhury, which aimed to collect together several ghost stories from the region (Chaudhry 2005). Ghosts were therefore my mind when I saw walking down the Mall Anup. Anup had proved to be a good conversation partner, having lived in Shimla for many years after moving from Lahore with his family, shortly after partition. Although he was a retired scientist, he had a great love for poetry and would often recite poems about the city. These were at times deliberately absurd and at time profound, but they always had an instructional purpose. I felt sure that Anup would have something interesting to say about Chaudhry's ghost book and so taking the last of my coffee I visited the shop and hurried to join him on his morning stroll along the Mall. After exchanging pleasantries for some time, I directed the conversation to the issue of ghosts:

"Anup", I said, "have you encountered many ghosts during your time in Shimla?"
"Of course,", he replied, " why the ghosts are all around us now!"

I stopped, momentarily taken aback by his directness, somewhat unsure if this was one of his characteristic jokes, before venturing:

"You mean to say that you can see the ghosts right now",
"Yes, he firmly replied, " I can see them there [pointing his stick] and over there".
"What do they look like they look like?"

Now it was his turn to show incredulity:

"Well, they are as they appear, scandal point", he said gesturing towards a covered stand at the crossroads ahead, "looks I suppose a bit like a giant umbrella, surely you know scandal point?"

I did know about scandal point, everyone did, it was a central place in the middle of Shimla, which locals were want to suggest had gained its name because in the colonial period the Maharaja of Patiala had defied a ban for riding on the Mall. What is more, he not only rode his horse his horse up to that point, but at that point swept up onto the horse's back the daughter of the British viceroy, before riding off with her into the hills. Although a favoured local myth it never appealed to me with as much strength as it seemed to appeal to others, although I could see within it a sort of useful logic about the ability of the local population (here represented by the Maharaja) to take from Shimla the fruits of her labour (the daughter) and with this addition return to the source (the hills).

My sense is that the above is not an entirely natural reading of the myth for those who recite it. This seems to be popularly understood as a romantic, if defiant gesture, rather than something approximating to an abduction. There is sense then that this a mutual love, which perhaps works well if we view the Viceroy as standing for Europe, the daughter as Shimla and the Maharaja as the newly independent India. From this perspective Shimla longs to be embraced by the people of India and through an act of brave defiance the Independence movement is able to take Shimla from the Europeans and unify her with Dev Bhoomi.

I also knew, from archival research, that there is very little in the historical record to corroborate this narrative. With the historical record instead pointing to a rather less glamorous creation myth, where the name simply derives from being a convenient place to stop and hear gossip about the various improprieties of the city's residents (Kanwar 2003: 4–6). On a different day I may well have chosen to push deeper into the history of Scandal Point, but on that day I was far too interested in the ghosts and I could not see how pointing to scandal point answered my question, could he see there now see the ghost of Maharaja (and perhaps his horse)? I decided to risk being an irritant push the point further:

> "You said the Ghosts are everywhere? Are they particularly around Scandal point? Did you see them further down the mall?"

I was relieved when Anup laughed at this line of questioning, before replying:

> "Don't you?"

And then, when I was silent, lost in thought, he filled the pause by going on to say:

> "I can even see the ghosts of our first meeting on this road".

It was at this point that I finally began to understand the simple message that he was trying to convey. The term that we were using, 'bhoot', here simply translated as ghost, was a wonderfully pliant term, which could be extended from the ghostly apparition all the way to the realm of memory.

Shimla is a place of memory and sometimes these memories take the form of ghostly apparition, but more often they haunt the landscape in less direct ways, through the way that they shape ongoing engagement with the landscape and alter the actions (even lives) of those who today join them in the constitution of this space. The ghosts were there in the very fabric of the place and the nature of the people whose trace so clearly could be felt, even as their absence was so obviously present. This feeling was indeed uncanny, disconcerting, for some, a sense of being part of something that stretched well beyond the confines of the self and challenged understandings of identity. Yet, for others, it was precisely a life lived amongst these ghosts that brought added significance to their lives. Lives lived in and around roads that have been walked by others in the past, shops and cafés with a long ongoing histories, and, of course, within the churches themselves, not least Christ Church Cathedral, the very symbol of postcolonial Shimla.

4

Churchscape, Landscape and Material Religion

The ancestors of Simla are gone, but not their ghosts. The postcolonial period saw a dramatic, somewhat traumatic and almost complete shift in the population that circulate around the city, as colonial Simla was reborn as postcolonial Shimla. It may seem logical that in the postcolonial period the colonial landscape increasingly diminished in relevance, as the old colonials who needed these places to connect with the land of their ancestors drifted away, and new people from all around India entered the city to make it their home. However, these grand colonial buildings were not simply bulldozed to be replaced by modern, utilitarian constructions. For sure, some of the retail operations within the Central Mall changed, but others remained and crucially the public and religious buildings retained both their form and (at least to some extent) their function. The modern city of Shimla is a place where the trace of the past is very present and demands integration into the lives of its contemporary residents. This provokes contemporary Shimlites to grapple with questions about nationhood, identity and belonging: How is old Simla, reconciled with new Shimla? How can the past in a modern city be integrated with the present? Why, according to a recent survey (Jutla 2000: 413), is such a haunted space associated primarily with home, peace and the familiar?

The answer to these questions lies in the way that the material and the immaterial are brought together in the daily life of the city. For, the Central Mall is not haunted in a way that is uncanny but rather, as the Maharaja of Patiala's Ghost shows (discussed in Chapter Three), reassuring. For, these haunted sites are nodes of meaning making processes for the contemporary population. Indeed, a recent survey of both tourists to and residents of Shimla placed the old central band of Simla Mall as the chief attraction to contemporary Shimla for both tourists and residents (Jutla 2000: 413). Within the Central Mall area Christ Church was singled out by both Tourists and Residents as the most important feature of contemporary Shimla (ibid) and this is not surprising for Christ Church Cathedral and its ghosts lie at the centre of this mystery. In this chapter we will therefore build upon the understanding that we have developed of the materiality of spirits within the city to approach the centre of the mystery of the city and in order to do this we will introduce and develop the concept of Implicit Mythology as a key device for unlocking the answers to these questions.

i) Displaced sacred space and implicit mythology

Back in 2006, heading up the Mall for the first time, I was drawn onward toward Christ Church, something about this sacred place was irresistibly attractive. Both the way that it seemed out of place to have a yellow, European looking church on a Himalayan mountain top and the way that it seemed so natural to the environment was enticing.[1] Even before reaching the city Christ Church Cathedral is clearly visible crowning the ridge of Shimla (Depicted in Figure 4.1). Over the years I came to Christ Church Cathedral from different places at different times of the day and during different seasons. On each occasion the building revealed something new about itself. Sometimes it would appear like a

Figure 4.1 Painting of Shimla by Aruna Mahajan.

lighthouse in the mist, at other times it sparkled in the sun, sometimes it was in dialogue with the mall, yet at others with Jakhoo forest, which holds (hidden within) Hanuman's temple. Sometimes Christ Church Cathedral was full of noise and life, yet at others it was still and possessed of great peace. After a year in Shimla I wrote in my field journal that 'despite its changing nature one constant feature of Christ Church Cathedral is its centrality – it is as if the rest of the city spirals around it'.

The sense of Christ Church as a contemporary axis mudi, or sacred centre of the contemporary city, is captured wonderfully by a local artist, Aruna Mahajan in the image above (see Figure 4.1). Aruna, now an ex-pat, describes her inspiration for her paintings as coming from 'having lived there ... to relive my memories, I paint'. This evocative painting clearly captures the sense of Christ Church as a core node of the landscape of the Shimla that is her home. It rises elegantly above the trees and houses below to dominate the skyline and unmistakably (when coupled with the Indian flag) mark this as postcolonial Shimla. In its role as a sacred centre or Axis Mundi, crowning the flat-topped ridge it seems fittingly reminiscent of the ancient and widespread association of the wider region with the mythological Mount Meru, which stands at the centre of Hindu cosmology (discussed further in Chapter Two).

Over the years I too have come to know Christ Church's rituals and learnt about its ghosts through a process of simply living life in and around this key node of the Shimla landscape. Both the haunting of the space and the significance of its present worship are brought together in my mind through a particular form of mythology, known as 'implicit mythology'. In what follows I will present these ghost stories, rituals, daily acts (and their role in emplacing the Cathedral) through the lens of Implicit mythology, which I have found to be both an insightful and important way to capture both the materiality of religious practice in this region and the importance of the (seemingly) immaterial elements of the landscape.

Mythology may strike some readers as an unusual way to attempt to approach something that I have already suggested is so central and sacred to life in this region, but I cannot but help see (and I will later demonstrate) that the category of myth is both a natural and enlightening way to engage with this material. Myth appears an awkward choice because it has gained, within the west, an unhelpful and damaging association with a lie (Miles-Watson and Asimos 2019: 3). This stems from a nineteenth century, European, conception of mythology as a category that contains explanations about the world, as offered by non-western actors (Tylor 1871: 286–187). These mythic explanations were viewed as largely inferior to Western scientific and historic explanations and so the categories of science and history became associated with truth (Segal 1999: 10). However, this dismissal of, or relegation of, the value of the insight that could be offered by material from outside of the Western academy runs contrary to the way the material categorized as Myth was understood by the people who produced it. For most of the global population, the material that was collected under the heading of myth was in fact understood as pertaining to a deep and sacred truth (Bascom 1965). What is more, there is an established trend for mythographers to apply the term in a way that means material containing truth, or a gateway to truth, through subsequent interpretation and analysis (Miles-Watson and Asimos 2019). By employing the term 'myth' therefore, both here and throughout this book, I intend to signal that we are dealing with material that is of the upmost importance and points towards a significant truth about life in this region.

Mythology is well suited to the exploration of the binding of person and place through the landscape. Indeed, this is the focus of the many toponymical myths that are told around the world as a way of connecting an individual (in a particular place at a particular time) with a collective identity (that connects time through place). I will however, in what follows, narrow the focus further from mythology in general to a particular kind of mythology, known as implicit mythology. This, often overlooked, aspect of myth lends itself well to the exploration of landscape, precisely because it moves mythology out of the page and into the world, where it is shown to merge and blend categories in the way that, as I will demonstrate (in Chapter Six), parallels the processes of Shimla's material religion. The idea of implicit mythology owes its birth to Lévi-Strauss (1981 [1971]: 668–669) who is better known for his analysis of explicit mythology. Indeed, his interpretation of implicit mythology has been so little discussed that many are completely unaware of it. This chapter therefore has the secondary aim of reintroducing to the study of material religion a core concept that has the potential to prove profitable both elsewhere and in comparative analysis.

There is, however, already a small, but significant, body of literature that develops the concept, which I will draw on (Galinier 2004, Houseman 1998, Hugh-Jones 1988, Kunin 2012, Asimos 2019). I will use this work inspirationally to fire the development of an understanding of implicit mythology that is unashamedly aimed at interpreting this field research. Through this process we will be able to decipher the messages of the ghosts and unlock the mystery of the continuing relevance of this colonial landscape to the postcolonial population. Viewing this contribution through the lens of implicit mythology will therefore be shown to be a useful way of moving the discussion of India's Christians away from the dominant, Dumontian, framework of caste (Kaufmann 1981, Mosse 1996, Robinson 1998, *et al*), as well as representing more accurately the way that ordinary Shimlites (As the people of Shimla are known) reckon with both sacred and secular environments.

Lévi-Strauss first introduces the concept of Implicit Mythology as a more disjointed type of mythology that often accompanies ritual action (1981 [1971]: 668–669, 1996 [1991]: 83). It is possible that, in origin he was focused on developing a disagreement with the ritual theorist Victor Turner (Peirano 2000: 7). Turner had suggested that ritual was the most important aspect of religion, which Lévi-Strauss (perhaps unsurprisingly) took exception to, countering that ritual was meaningless without it accompanying (implicit) mythology (Ibid). If we put to one side issues of academic territoriality and competition, then I believe that Lévi-Strauss' general assumption, that myth enlivens ritual, both highly useful and largely accurate (see, for example, Miles-Watson and Asimos 2019).

This idea also resonates with the insights of other theorists of myth/ritual, whose explorations on this topic both further support and develop the idea. Laycock, for example, presents compelling evidence for the connection between myth and ritual mimesis, which allows the participant to not simply hear the myth, but to enter the mythology (Laycock 2010). The same idea finds eloquent expression in the writings of Father Bede Griffiths, a pioneer of inculturated Christian worship in India and Indian style worship in the West, when he writes 'Myth is ... imaginative insight into ultimate reality ... [it] not only reveals the truth under a symbol but also enables those who receive the myth to participate [in it] (Griffiths 1982: 104). Here then implicit mythology suggests a mutual interlinking of the sacred and profound with the more limited lives lived by any given individual actor. The concept usefully links myth and ritual by abolishing the distinction between receiving and enacting, however it also has the capacity to go well beyond this.

If we take the concept of implicit mythology to the proving grounds of Shimla, then it yields a rich insight into the way that action, identity and mythology are fused in the landscape of the Cathedral through what we might call the 'technology of the imagination' (Sneath, Holbraad and Pederson 2009). For, if we do not so much construct meaning out of a chaotic world as we move along with a world of meaning (Ingold 2000: 98), then implicit mythology, anchored as it is to that movement through (and action within) the world, can reveal localised ecologies of being. This moves implicit mythology away from a cognitive model and towards a processual one in a way that mirrors the movement Sneath, Pederson and Holbraad's moving of the imagination from a cognitive backdrop to an Ingoldian process, or (as they would have it) 'technology' (2009: 19). In this understanding, implicit mythology is not a subsidiary category of explicit mythology; rather it is the other way around: explicit mythology forms a subsidiary category of implicit mythology, which folds together and focuses multiple areas of academic research in a way that reflects the lived experience of people in Shimla. By the term 'implicit mythology' then, I mean a shorthand for the narrativization that both accompanies and contextualises ritual action, as well as the trace of that ritual action.

I will demonstrate that implicit mythology can be found wherever there is a joining of meaningful material and action. This is crucial for the study of material religion because it means that implicit mythology can also be taken to mean art and architecture, as well as more obvious verbs such as eating and praying. This is because implicit mythology, like explicit mythology, can refer to at once something specific and something general. This ability of implicit mythology, this blurring of the boundaries of being, makes it a powerful tool for accurately reflecting the way that specific and general understandings interweave in Himachali people's daily life. In other words, just as we can talk about the myth of Tara and Himachali myth, so too we can talk about the implicit mythology surrounding a particular set of ritual actions and the implicit mythology of the church within which the actions are performed, and this captures the way that these levels of understanding cohesively fuse in experiential reality.

The development of the concept of implicit mythology, outlined above, draws inspiration from the work of Edmund Leach, who utilised explicit mythology, ritual narrative and religious material culture equally in his structural analyses (Hugh-Jones and Laidlaw 2000: 83).[2] I am also indebted to the writings Stephen Hugh-Jones (1988) and Christine Hugh-Jones (1979), whose analyses of the Barasana begins to open many similar possibilities. The opening of the potential of the category of implicit mythology can be clearly seen in Stephen Hugh-Jones' summary of his and his wife's now classic analyses of Barasana culture, which states that: 'in addition to the more usual topics of ethnographic enquiry, we ... paid particular attention to knowledge about the natural world, animals, plants, stars and seasons, and to the kind of 'implicit mythology' that is revealed in such things as hunting, fishing, gardening and food preparation, eating arrangements and manufacturing processes, as well as in ritual and ceremony' (1988: 14).

Hugh-Jones allows the concept of implicit mythology to move well beyond its explicit ritual context, where it is shown to give a sacred meaning to a wide range of activities and actions that we have become accustomed to associated with profane, everyday life. One of the most striking things about this work is its elucidation of the central role of architecture, alongside the suggestion that myth and ritual are anchored around key buildings. This of course resonates perfectly with what we have seen already about life in Shimla, which flows between and winds and knots around buildings. Implicit mythology ties neatly with the general turn to material religion and this book's emphasis on sacred landscapes, which are both constituted by (ritual) action and shaped by the trace of past (ritual) action. This is certainly my own experience; the importance of place has been a reoccurring theme in my discussion with people of all faiths in India, who have consistently highlighted that their faith is a source of relationships: relationships with both human and non-human people, the animate and the inanimate. This is clearly the sort of ecology of sacred landscapes that the concept of implicit mythology speaks to.

ii) The centre of the spiral: a key myth

In both the Raw and the Cooked (1994: 1–3) and From Honey to Ashes (1983: 30–47) Lévi-Strauss suggests that an analysis of (implicit) mythology should begin by locating a 'key myth'. This 'key myth' then forms the start of the analysis, which subsequently spirals out to incorporate new material that both is best understood in relation to the key myth and helps to further unlock the key myth's mysteries (ibid). Christ Church Cathedral is in many ways the key myth of this chapter and this chapter is the key saga of the book. ‚It is not, as Lévi-Strauss suggests (1994: 1–2). simply an arbitrarily chosen myth that reflects the analyst's logic; rather it is the sacred place around which the entire landscape turns. Christ Church's ghosts (and wider implicit mythology) are both literally and analytically central to our understanding of the contemporary landscape.

During my first two periods of fieldwork in Shimla (2006–2007; 2009–2010), Christ Church Cathedral was undoubtedly the city's most striking landmark: its yellow Gothic tower, like a beacon consistently called people to it. Most of the visitors to Shimla that I spoke to during these times reported that upon arrival in Shimla they would make for Christ Church Cathedral. Once there they would take a photograph of it, or have a photograph taken with them stood outside, for only then would they feel that they had truly arrived in Shimla. Similarly, many local residents would regularly walk the Mall until they came to Christ Church Cathedral where they would stop to enjoy the air and view before walking home.

Aruna Mahajan, whose picture is discussed above (see Figure 4.1) is not unusual in her placing of Christ Church at the heart of her memories of home. The visitor's book in Christ Church Cathedral records many local residents who describe the Cathedral as their favourite place in the city. Furthermore, when, at the beginning of this century, Jutla showed 266 photographs of Shimla to local residents (of 15 years or more) the vast majority chose a picture of Christ Church Cathedral as the one that best represented their home town (2000: 413). More recently, several social media groups have sprung up around a common interest in Shimla (such as We ♥ Simla and SHIMLA – The Queen of Hills) with thousands of members and these have featured Christ Church Cathedral heavily (at the time of writing Christ Church Cathedral is the Icon for We ♥ Simla).

It is clear therefore that Christ Church Cathedral has become synonymous with Shimla in both the minds of the majority of tourists and residents. It is striking that this colonial Christian landscape should be so important for postcolonial tourists, the majority of whom are Indian and Hindu (Bhardwaj, D. S. Chaudhary, M. & Kandari 1988: 235). However, it is even more counterintuitive and important that this colonial Cathedral is so bound up in the everyday lives and identity of the city's postcolonial population. The important role that churches play in the lives and identities of small-scale communities is well established (cf Whiting, 2010, Olney, & Burton, 2011, Miles-Watson 2015). It is however more unusual to see the church landscape maintaining such a central role in the unusually ruptured space of Simla. An exploration of the implicit mythology that surrounds Christ Church Cathedral will solve the logical problem of how this seemingly displaced sacred space operates, but before we can turn to this fully it is necessary to first explore more about the materiality of cathedrals in general, the relation of this to community identity and the way that this is particularly configured in the Shimla Hills.

iii) The materiality of myth in the Shimla Hills

Whereas once religion was commonly viewed as essentially the realm of beliefs today much has been written about the materiality of religious practice in general (Meyer 2015a, Morgan, 2010, Plate 2015 et al) and Christian practice in particular (Boylston 2013, McDannel 1995, Whitehead 2018). These studies collectively demonstrate the importance of what Graham Harvey has termed 'religion as everyday life' (Harvey 2013). Perhaps the most concrete working out of the issues of material religion in relation to identity can be found in Tim

Ingold's seminal exploration of the landscape of a typical European parish church (2000: 205–207). In his highly influential essays on perceptions of the environment, Ingold discusses a landscape painting of a rural churchscape, which he suggests possesses elements of a Bakhtinian chronotype (2000: 205). He argues that the church both resonates with (and helps to reinforce) simultaneously the human conception of linear time and cyclical time (Ingold 2000: 206). The church (or Cathedral) is the landscape that is always returned to at key moments of the year through a special ritual round of Harvest, Christmas, Easter and Pentecost; at the same time it is a landscape in which key rites-of passage are performed that move an individual through their life (birth, marriage and death). What is more, because the church bears the trace of action over lifetimes it creates an intergenerational link with the ancestors of the village, who are buried in the surrounding church yard and therefore both metaphorically and literally rooted in the church landscape (ibid.).

Ingold's theory works well for a settled, community such as the one imagined in the painting, but its emphasis on intergenerational links would seem to suggest that it would no longer be operational in Shimla, if indeed it ever was. Christ Church Cathedral was originally the Anglican Church in Shimla and the place where the Viceroy and surrounding dignitaries would commonly worship (ibid). It was therefore unashamedly connected with a particular type of European Christianity that was closely allied to secular positions of power. Over the years after its construction these people continued to leave the trace of their action on the landscape, such as through commissioning, or developing windows. The south wall of Christ Church Cathedral is punctuated by a series of bright, stained glass windows, depicting the Christian virtues of faith, charity, hope, fortitude, patience and humility. This was erected in memory of Lizzie Marion Walker who died in London in 1892. She was the owner of the famous Woodville Palace from 1882 until her death and the wife of Sir James Lewis Walker, who was the manager of the Alliance Bank of Simla (Buck 1925: 119).

From the light airy windows to the grounded stonework of the church, contemplation on elements of the landscape always leads us back to those who once lived and worshiped in this landscape, in the time before this time. The stone pulpit is a good example of this, for the church originally had a wooden pulpit, donated by the Governor of the North West province. However, when Bishop Milman died in 1876 the present stone pulpit was erected in memory of the sermons of 'unequalled eloquence and depth, filled with wisdom, earnestness and passion' that he delivered from there (Chatterton 1924: XVII). It is therefore possible, as Ingold suggests, to read the lives of the former residents in the landscape of the current building. For Ingold the most striking example of this is the graveyard, which the ancestors of community are literally rooted. Christ Church does not have an immediately adjacent graveyard, but even more strikingly its ancestors are woven into the walls.

What is instantly striking to everyone who goes to Christ Church is that the wall is lined with commemorative plaques (see Figure 4.2), but crucially these plaques commemorate a range of people who once moved around the church , but have little, if any direct intergenerational connection to most of the people who currently help to constitute the landscape (with a few notable exceptions discussed in Chapter Six). Like the haunting fertility ghost of the graveyard (discussed in the previous chapter) these plaques commemorate people whose lives, lived in and around this place, mostly originated elsewhere. Moreover, the trail of their ancestors often leads elsewhere and yet the relevance of the trace of their lives in this place both hauntingly remains and remains active in the lives of contemporary residents.

It is not simply in blood and birth but in the daily lives of many of the people woven into the walls that we can see a radical distinction to most of this landscape's current population. For, if Ingold's ancestors are tied to the land by

Figure 4.2 Rooting the Ancestors in the Walls.

Figure 4.3 Homans' memorial.

gathering the harvest in the way that the descendants do today, then we see no similar patterns of working with the land in such a direct way here. Many of these people are true internationalists who moved freely around the world, engaging more with warfare than agriculture. They are people like Caroline Homans (whose memorial is captured in Figure 4.3), a celebrated Boston socialite, daughter of a renowned surgeon, who moved to India after her marriage to Neville Priestley who had been awarded a job managing the Indian Railways. She died in Priestley's ancestral home in England and her husband's family understood her ties to Simla to be so strong that they commissioned a plaque in her memory.[3]

The visitor's book of Christ Church Cathedral shows that it is still (from time to time) visited by the descendants of those who once worshiped there, but this is the exception rather than the rule and during my time in Shimla I was so racially noticeable that I could be singled out in the congregation as 'our European Brother', by a visiting preacher. What is more, this radical change in the human constituents of the environment should (by conventional landscape theory) cause a rupture in the fabric of the environment that transforms this sacred place into a scarred place. A place that is a reminder of the traumas of history and that uncomfortably haunts the current population with discordant past memories. Yet, Christ Church Cathedral is still geographically and mythologically central – it is the mystery of this that makes it the ideal key for unlocking the wider mysteries of Shimla's implicit mythology.

5

Worshipping with Ghosts: Implicit Mythology in the Shimla Hills[1]

The Cathedral's first generation of Christian worshippers are now gone and so are their descendants, but the church is not dead. For, Christ Church continues to operate as an active site of worship, with two regular services a week and additional services at key points in both the circular and linear ritual calendars. A slender link therefore may be seen to remain with the colonial period through both this continuance of worship and those who participate in it that have links to the so called, 'native' Christians of Shimla Hills. These moved up from St Thomas' Church, in the lower Bazaar, to Christ Church Cathedral in the period immediately after independence (discussed further in Chapter Eight) and made the Cathedral their own. This, connecting, thread, established amid the turmoil of independence, remains today, anchoring the present congregation to past congregations of the city. However, it is no accident that St Thomas' church was located off the main (Europeanised) Mall, for it brought with it a different tradition of worship with both a distinct form of material religion and a strong association with key figures in the inculturated (Jesu Bhakti) Christianity movement (as noted in Chapter 2:2 and developed in Chapter 8:1).

The connection through colonial rupture that the movement of congregants from the native church on the lower bazaar to the Cathedral on the upper ridge represents an important link between these easily opposed time periods. The link that the native tradition represents is however too fragile to bear the weight of the trauma of change alone. Other processes are in play, which we will here uncover as a way of demonstrating how the Cathedral has retained both its centrality in the landscape and it sense of connection with the epoch that predates the present. For this sense of connection remains, perhaps in spite of as much as because of, the connection to inculturated worship in Shimla, which is a tradition that speaks to but a small part of the current congregation (see for example Chapter Eight). Today Christ Church Cathedral is part of the Church of

North India (hereafter referred to as the CNI), a loose Protestant coalition of churches that was established in 1970 following decades of ecumenical debates and discussions (Davis and Conway 2008: 136). Its mission was to allow for the existence of differences while moving towards a vision of a unified, distinctively Indian form of Christianity (Sahu 2013: 320). The Union of Churches in North India therefore sought to acknowledge both the global connectedness of Christian faith and the importance of the colonial period for the history of the development of the church in North India, while also highlighting the way that rooting that tradition in the fertile soil of North India had led to the present blooming of locally identifiable, suitably habituated, forms of Christian worship.

The congregation that I came to know there were drawn from a range of backgrounds, but many of them were immigrants from other areas. In a recent survey carried out by Usha Chug, 150 people self-identified as being a member of the congregation (2000: 135). In my experience this figure is somewhat higher than that at regular services and considerably lower than the number of people at special services and events (as discussed further in Chapter Eight). It is also a figure that does not account for the many people who are involved with Christ Church Cathedral to the extent of being bound up in its ongoing constitution, even though they would not self-identify as congregants (despite often being found within the congregation). These elements of the landscape are easy to dismiss as 'visitors', or 'casual members', yet to do so is to miss a key step in the processes by which this colonial Christian space becomes central to a postcolonial, largely Hindu, population.

i) Worshipping beyond the boundaries of faith

Christ Church Cathedral may be branded by the tourist board as a Christian holy site, but it is clearly not today a site that is exclusively reserved for Christians. Many local Hindus and Sikhs are no strangers to Christ Church Cathedral, many attended church services there as children and many as adults can be found at special services, such as those that occur around Christmas (this is explored further in Chapter Eight). This childhood connection with Christ Church Cathedral in many cases extends from either attending or knowing someone who attended one of the three elite CNI schools that exist in Shimla: Bishop Cotton's School, Auckland House and St Thomas' School. Most of these schools have long established connections with the colonial period of one sort or another. St Thomas, for example, was founded on the site of the old church of St Thomas by the notable British missionary (and founder of multiple mission schools) Helen Jerwood (Pass 2011). Bishop Cotton's School was founded in 1959, by the eponymous Bishop, a former assistant school master in Rugby, as a 'Thank-offering to Almighty God for the preservation of the British people during the Indian Mutiny of 1857' (Gazetteer 1889: 86) . Auckland House, which was in many ways the most important school for the contemporary CNI Cathedral, was founded in 1866 to provide high quality education to European and Anglo-Indian girls (ibid: 88).

Children who attend these schools today (and others like them) not only enjoy an educational link to the colonial era, but are also able to take advantage of regular engagement in CNI worship during their schooling, through this they become part of the life of the Cathedral. This is a pattern that is repeated throughout India where Christians form a minority of the overall population, yet a faith-based education is a powerful and prevalent feature of contemporary society. An education at Bishop Cotton's School, or Auckland House, is therefore associated less with formally belonging to the Christian faith than with being a member of the Indian upper middle class (Chug 2000: 136). The potential of those who move in and around these landscapes to share class, but not religious conviction is an important point that I will return to later. For now it is important to move from the realm of childhood and the schools to explore in more detail the adult constituents of the landscape.

Chug found that the majority of Christians who self-identified as belonging to Christ Church Cathedral also self-identified as being middle class (Chug 2000: 135). This fits with my own, more recent, experiences at Christ Church Cathedral. The most popular forms of employment for Shimla's urban Christians were unmistakably the civil service and education sectors, although a sizeable minority at Christ Church Cathedral (around ten per cent) were comparatively wealthy landowners (ibid: 135–140). The vast majority of the adult congregation that I came to know and that Chug surveyed were clearly marked as highly educated. Most were university graduates and Chug found that around forty per cent held postgraduate degrees (ibid: 141). The landscape of the Cathedral is therefore a complex landscape that is constituted by key actors who for all their differences are bound together by commonalities in education, class and occupation.

Most of Christ Church Cathedral's Christian congregation identified as being born into the faith and it is therefore not as surprising as it may at first seem that the majority of them were highly uncomfortable with the idea of conversion (Chug 2000: 199–200). During my time in Shimla I saw this manifested in the way that certain members of the congregation were unsettled by the presence of converts, especially those drawn from a different social background and with a different level of education. During focus groups, I had the opportunity to explore this, sensitive, issue further and through these I learnt that the perceived discomfort stemmed from a belief that these groups were not sufficiently aware of the history and tradition of worshipping in a place like Christ Church Cathedral, which it was suggested led the converts to behave in way that were inappropriate. I understand this as a highly insightful comment around the relationship between skill, belonging and worship. The concept of religion as a skill will be explored and developed further later in this book (especially Chapter Seven) for now, it is important to note that the congregants located their own unease at certain forms of behaviour as arising from a lack of appropriate skill, although they would not have termed it quite this way. If we move even further away from emic and towards analytic, etic terms, we may argue that what they were communicating was a sense that the converts lacked sufficient fluency in the implicit mythology necessary to imaginatively enter into the mythical field and creatively engage with the ghosts of the Cathedral.

ii) Engaging with the material trace of past worship

When I first wound my way up the Central Mall and entered Christ Church Cathedral my eyes were drawn to elements that I could recognise: the crucifix shape, the pews, clearly designed for prayer, the noticeable altar and the chancel window (depicting scenes from familiar biblical passages). I therefore began to interpret both the space and how to properly engage with it through reference to similar sacred spaces that I had a history of engagement with elsewhere. However, I had little knowledge of the particular history of this sacred space and how it was used today. Over the years I came to know that specific history through members of the Cathedral's generous sharing of folk memories of the place. Oftentimes, someone who I was in conversation with would point out certain features of the cathedral that were relevant to the general topic of the conversation and therefore direct my attention to the trace of past historical action in this place. Because of this process, today, when my eyes roam around Christ Church Cathedral, I no longer simply see universal patterns of architecture; I see the particular histories that have resulted in Christ Church Cathedral's contemporary form.

Through attending worship in Christ Church Cathedral, I increasingly became skilled in the practice of observing the trace of certain past (historical) action in the present (contemporary) sacred space. Therefore, when I look today at the chancel window, I do not simply see it as a depiction of particular biblical scene, set for abstract architectural reasons in a particular place; rather I associate it with a particular set of historical events and particular historical characters. These would include Caroline Homans, Lizzie Marion Walker and Bishop Milman whose lives, as lived in around this space, we explored in the previous chapter (Chapter Four) . In this I am not alone, conversations with the many migrant members of the congregation revealed a similar journey to my own.

The ability to reckon with the church environment that I arrived with, as well as that which I subsequently developed, may be seen as two subcategories of implicit mythology, discussed in Chapter Four, which Lévi-Strauss suggests properly accompany ritual action (1981: 668–669). The first type of implicit mythology described above can be seen as a form of 'standardised implicit mythology', for it refers to widely held international understandings of Christian rituals in general. The second type of implicit mythology is a form of 'vernacular implicit mythology', in that it refers specifically to historical ritual and devotional action that has occurred within Christ Church Cathedral itself (Miles-Watson 2019). Vernacular implicit mythology is in keeping with Lévi-Strauss' examples from small scale societies, whereas the standardised implicit mythology is a logical development of Lévi-Strauss' thought when applied to an international religious organization. There is also a third kind of narrativization that surrounds Christ Church Cathedral, this is a form of implicit mythology that contextualises both the sacred space and the action that unfolds there. This 'reflexive implicit mythology' is even more personal and powerful than the two types of implicit mythology that I have discussed so far and pushes the concept of implicit mythology well beyond Lévi-Strauss' sketch of the concept.

The first service that I ever attended at Christ Church Cathedral generated for me a sense of belonging that was striking in both its emotional impact and its ability to rapidly, profoundly, transform my sense of connection to the place. This may have had something to do with elements of worship that reminded me of those that I had previously experienced during my childhood in the United Kingdom. These somewhat familiar elements included the traditional form and decoration of the church and the relationship of the service and hymns to those found in the Book of Common Prayer. Of course, the service was also quite different to anything that I had encountered before. Phrases of liturgy that I recognised blended with other, more vernacular expressions and the congregation that I joined with was entirely unknown to me, even as something about their dress, actions and mannerisms was deeply familiar.

Looking back at my field journal entries for those early encounters is both embarrassing and enlightening. Today I am well aware of the inadequacies of early reflective statements that nonetheless capture something of my own, naive and biased, engagement with the place. Statements such as that I had 'found the community in the church', or worse, experienced 'an alluring blending of the familiar and the strange'. This, last statement, was not to stand the test of time and over the following years I developed a very different appreciation of worship at Christ Church Cathedral. Although it is embarrassing to open my own lack of understanding in this way I do so because my own journey of development here illuminates excellently more general processes by which people move from a model of Christ Church Cathedral as alterity to one in which it becomes home. Drawn to Christ Church as seemingly a place out of place, it became somewhat familiar to me at the same time as allowing me to feel the gratitude that comes from the embrace of a community of strangers, before finally moving to a position where I myself know what it is to be part of that community and to welcome the stranger.

One early morning, at the end of a hot summer, I found myself called to the front of Christ Church Cathedral by a minister who had been, for some time in deep conversation with a young woman wearing tattered, yet not inexpensive clothes. As I approached, he introduced me, "this is Jonathan, a member of this church from Britain" and then turning to me he said, "Jonathan, this girl is from the west and is feeling confused, perhaps you could talk to her, to try to help her". And so I found myself in conversation with a rather disillusioned young lady who had been wandering India in search of a peace that had continued to elude her throughout her travels. In this moment the loop that opened when I first entered Shimla became closed. No longer the wandering outsider, drawn to the Shimla Hills by its welcome, I was now the insider welcoming the wandering stranger into our midst. What is more, it was my past status as an outsider far from detracting from my value heightened my ability to act as a mediator.

The above outlined shift from outsider being welcomed to insider welcoming is made possible through a shift in my own relationship to the landscape of Christ Church Cathedral. In contrast to my first, embarrassing, impressions of the landscape, the sense of the exotic has dissolved to be replaced entirely by the familiar. What is more, I have developed an understanding of the landscape in a way that is both deeply personal and tied to my own sense of self. The people in the congregation are now no longer simply demographics to me, rather they are individuals, who I know well and with whom I share many collective memories and understandings. Clearly, my own sense of self is now connected to that place and when I talk to people about Christ Church Cathedral, I can see a similar line of development in their own understandings. Many have similar tales of migration and welcome and all that I have spoken with share narrative of worship that are deeply personal and rich with emotional resonance. In these accounts we see a coming together of a dual awareness of the trace of general historical, sacred, action and personal historical sacred action, which may be extended to that of known individuals. This analysis of reflexive implicit mythology therefore demands, despite Lévi-Strauss' recommendations to the contrary (1981: 668), that the analyst engage with the messy realm of emotions, which both initiate connection with the landscape and resonate through the landscape.

We are now in a position to understand why the seemingly colonial Christ Church Cathedral offers postcolonial Shimlites as a key to resolving the tensions of the colonial past and the postcolonial present. When a postcolonial church organist sits at the nineteenth century pipe organ, they join their skill, as a postcolonial musician, with the skill of colonial craftsmen to generate a soundscape[2] that both evokes and inspires worship. The organist also remembers, while playing now, past recitations and simultaneously is aware that all of their performances are but the latest in a long line of human engagement, a line that stretches back well beyond the lifetime of the current performers. Indeed, during my time in Shimla I learnt of an organist who was so aware of these past elements that when they played, they often sensed that the ghost of an old colonial pianist playing along, sometimes sounding extra notes and adding to the resonance of the composition. Quite clearly, despite the suggestion in landscape theory (Palang, Printsmann and Sooväli 2007) that massive population movement leads to ruptures in the landscape of worship and the recent trend in the anthropology of Christianity to view Christian institutions as rupturing agents (Engelke and Tomlinson 2007), Shimla's Christians population speak to a different reality. One in which the contemporary Christian population have the capacity to anchor themselves in the past of the city through the church, even though most cannot claim to have families that worshipped at the church before independence. Thus, the church neither becomes a separated history, nor a dead space; rather, the processes of modernity and migration heighten the importance of the church as an anchoring device and situate it as the arena within which space can be transformed into place (De Certeau 1984: 117).

The colonial building is transformed into an arena for the anchoring of the postcolonial population, through the flows and traumas of history, precisely because, emotionally charged, reflexive, implicit mythology, is interwoven with vernacular implicit mythology. This results in the blending of the memories of the individual and the collective in a satisfying way. Of course, the contemporary Christian does not experience these as separate categories in the way that I have displayed them here, rather they engage with Christ Church Cathedral in a way that effortlessly weaves the standardised, vernacular and reflexive implicit mythologies just as they continue to weave the implicit mythology of the building by continuously engaging in devotional practices that further alter the mythic landscape. Here, somewhat ironically, the utility of the term implicit mythology becomes manifest: the unity that the term conjures accurately captures the way that emotion, place, memory and space are unified in the lived experience of any individual. What is more, as the next section will demonstrate, the term also has the ability to bridge from the sphere of the individual to that of the collective, wherein the individual actors themselves become part of the myth.

The discussion so far has highlighted that at the centre of our mythic spiral stands Christ Church Cathedral. It is a site of powerful implicit mythology, which operates at three levels in the lives of many of Shimla's Christians: the global, the local and the personal. Yet, Shimla's Christians are a minority group, who can hardly claim to be representative of the overall population, we therefore still have to solve the mystery of how our key site of implicit mythology can unlock the wider mystery of the city. In order to do this, I intend to summon evidence from the ghosts of Shimla, who can be found throughout the city as well as within Christ Church Cathedral. Shimla is full of ghosts, as are many hill stations in India, and people are always ready to discuss them. Shimla's ghosts range from corporeal manifestations to more abstract yet equally experientially real agents (Chaudhry 2005).

iii) Churchscapes, material religion and ghosts

As we have seen, Shimla's central Mall came together (at least in part) through Europeans in India's longing for a landscape that resonated with an (imagined) homeland (discussed more fully in Chapter Two). At the heart of these imagined villages were Churches and so it is not surprising that at the heart of Shimla mall's mock Tudor and mock gothic constructions we find a series of interconnecting churchscapes, crowned by Christ Church Cathedral. In the colonial period this had the added sense of meeting the practical needs of the city's more formal residents, the majority of whom were (at least nominally) Christian. We have seen how the small minority that identify as Christian today have maintained an important link with the thread of the past through a continuing worship that connects them with the ghosts of the past. A connection that allows them to transform the haunting spirits of the past in reassuring ancestors of a place that the postcolonial Christian community now claim as their own. However, the landscape of Shimla offers a far greater insight than simply the survival of a minority culture in changed times. For, as we shall see, it points to the possibility of a focus on landscapes to dissolve preconceived boundaries of all kinds (religious, racial and temporal).

At the entrance to Shimla Mall there is a sign, erected in the postcolonial period, which proudly proclaims 'our built history is our heritage' (see Figure 5.1). The sign claims, unproblematically, a shared heritage (it is ours) and positioned where it is suggests an appropriation of the Mall (and the key heritage symbol that lies at its heart) by the postcolonial, largely Hindu population. There is nothing inevitable about this widespread sense of attachment to the built (sacred and secular) environment of a former colonial population. In Tallinn, Estonia, for example there sits a Cathedral at the heart of the old town that was constructed during the Soviet period and remains active as site of worship for the city's now marginalised Russian Orthodox population. While it is popular with tourists, it

Figure 5.1 Heritage and identity sign.

is seen as a scar on the landscape, a reminder of a traumatic history, by many of the city's largely atheist, Estonian residents. As Veronica Della Dora and Helen Sooväli succinctly put it 'Estonians do not like it [the Cathedral]. And yet there it stands, restored in all its provocative ... grandeur' (2009:17).

By contrast, in Shimla the Cathedral is largely loved by tourists and residents alike, despite its rupturing potential. Christ Church Cathedral is not understood as a problematic other within, so much as an essential part of the postcolonial population's own identity. At worst, Christ Church Cathedral is seen as Bhasin would have it 'a dearly loved adopted child'(2009: 95), at its best it overcomes Bhasin's 'mine but not mine' (ibid) problem to become unproblematically mine. Indeed, this seems to be the view of the vast majority, who identify it as the central motif of contemporary Shimlite identity (Jutla 2000). The landscape is therefore not shunned, but embraced, held close and affectionately – its ghosts far from being a symptom of rupture are a loving and reassuring presence. For, to engage meaningfully with this landscape inevitably involves engaging with ghosts and the Hindu population are in my experience) as likely to talk lovingly of ghosts as the Christian community.

The range of responses of the wider postcolonial population of Shimla to the colonial ghosts of Simla tells us something important about the ways that the contemporary population are able to meaningfully engage with the rich and highly visible traces of past action in this landscape. We must therefore turn our attention now to the relation of the postcolonial Hindu population to the (at least nominally) Christian ghosts of the colonial period. Fortunately, in our exploration we have already encountered two, highly revealing, accounts of Hindu engagement with ghosts, those of the dissenting Maharaja (discussed in Chapter Three) and the fertility granting Memsahib (discussed in Chapter Three). Both the Maharaja's and Memsahib's hauntings point to the importance of historic European actors for the present postcolonial population, yet each takes this understanding in different directions. The Maharaja seems to enter the landscape through a defiant love for it. In so doing he offers an Indian, non-Christian, connection to this heritage that predates the contemporary population. It is as though the trace of his actions both guides and sanctions that of the postcolonial Hindu population. The fertility ghost of the graveyard offers a more direct engagement with a tangible trace of colonial action in a deliberately liminal, sacred, landscape. Here the colonial ghost is not malicious but benevolent, she has turned her own tragedy into a blessing for the contemporary population that (quite literally) ensures their fruitfulness. This second incarnation although it takes place well away from the Mall points us towards the way that the wider postcolonial population are able to engage so successfully with the sacred heart of the mall, Christ Church Cathedral. While the wider context in which Anup (in Chapter Three) raised the ghost of the Maharaja, reminds us of the important connection between ghosts and collective memory (Carsten 2008: 3), which in turn points us back towards the concept of implicit mythology.

iv) Ghosts, ancestors and myths of becoming

I have been fortunate enough to learn from an elderly, Hindu, female, resident of Shimla something of the way that she understands her own entry into the implicit mythology of Christ Church Cathedral. More fragmented discussions with others and my own observations (having lived embedded in a Hindu community) suggest that while elements of the narrative might be particular to her own life (reflexive implicit mythology) at a deeper structural level the myths unlock what I have termed the central mystery of the Shimla hills. They act as a key for our key myth and open important insight into the mystery that stands at the heart of this postcolonial landscape. These implicit myths all involve ghosts of one sort or another. I am extremely grateful for the generous sharing of this important information, which in anonymized and summarised form provides the basis for the next movement of this analysis.

Although the chronology of the narrativization is retrospective, rather than drawn from a longitudinal study, the chronology of the events as presented is valuable as an idealised account that is reflective of the informant's structuring of their own history. This structure highlights the transformative abilities of implicit mythology and the way that entering imaginatively into the weave of these mythologies answers wider questions of nationhood, identity and belonging.

a) First memories

> I remember as a child being drawn to the Cathedral. I would look up at it from the lower bazaar and think how wonderful it looked. Yet, whenever I expressed my desire to visit my grandparents would rebuke me saying that I should not travel up there, because the ghosts of Britishers could be found there. These ghosts were said to be very violent and to dislike Indians: if they caught you they would cut off the top of your head and hang you upside down. Despite my grandparents' warnings I did not stay away from the cathedral and I would join

a group of children who would venture up to the Cathedral to play a game around the outside the building ... when it started getting dark we would nervously hurry down the hill ... the ghost of an English woman, who had died inside the church, haunted the place and she would get angry if children were too noisy or rowdy near the church.

This narrativization of early interaction with the Cathedral by a young Hindu is clearly a kind of reflexive implicit myth, for it relates to actions undertaken around a sacred space and (while that action is not strictly speaking ritual action) it is surrounded by ritualistic features. Perhaps more importantly, these stories act as a pre-myth for the main implicit mythology that follows by creating dramatic tension. When the child encounters the cathedral it first appears as a strange place, yet one that has to be reckoned with. The young Shimla resident is inescapably, almost against their will, drawn towards it. Like countless, classical, mythological landscapes, the place is at once central to the landscape and forbidden. What is more, as the grandparents warn, this is not only an alien place but a place of unreasonable aggression and perilous danger. The problem that the landscape presents, and that the mythology will seek a resolution to is set. It is a problem that still potentially exists today: how does this imposing colonial, Christian, landscape relate to the life of a postcolonial Hindu?

An attempt to resolve this problem is found in the second movement of the reflexive implicit mythology. Here we see an attempt to claim the sacred central space, represented by the colonial Cathedral. This attempt involves interlacing personal memories of childhood games around the outside of the building, yet this resolution is only partial and the place is still one fraught with danger and hostility, albeit now of a slightly more reasonable kind. For, a second ghost now emerges, that of the easily irritated female Britisher. Although she is less antagonistic than the head cleavers, she is hardly welcoming, especially as she seems to view the young Indian's engagement with the space as inappropriate (id est noisy/rowdy).

I have also learned, from a young Anglo-Indian Christian, a complimentary myth, which states that this ghost was an English lady organist who loved to play so much that she was in the church playing on a bitterly cold evening. Then suddenly, in the middle of playing, she died of the cold. It was too cold for a proper funeral at the graveyard and so she was buried in the backyard. But this woman returned to the church as a spirit and would continue to play. Several contemporary congregants have related to me that they have heard the ghost practicing when the doors are locked and I have been informed that sometimes contemporary organists are accompanied by ghostly ones (as discussed earlier in this section). This related narrativization from a distinct personal set (or group of sets) shows a different understanding of the ghosts that is perhaps to be expected from Christians. However, remarkably, in the second narrativization of their life's engagement with the space (and by extension its ghosts) our original Hindu resident arrives at a similar understanding.

In this second narrativization we move within the church and clearly into the realm of both reflexive implicit mythology and vernacular implicit mythology. Indeed, although directly absent from the narrative the account indirectly also suggests a familiarity with relevant elements of standardised implicit mythology. This narrative also shows the resolution to the problem posed by the first narrativization. Through increasing familiarity with the implicit mythology of the space, it is transformed from a foreboding realm of alterity into a comfortable and familiar realm. The ghosts have moved from first being violent, to then being angry, before becoming reassuring presences – all this is achieved without conversion or the compromising of a Hindu, Indian identity. The completeness of this movement (and its relevance for wider Shimla life) is brought out in a final narrative.

b) School days

> During school days I attended ... services at the church ... The first time that I entered into the church it was a revelation ... it was so peaceful to be there and be part of the worship. When I spent more time in the church it became more familiar and I came to know of all the people who had worshiped there before ... To be honest, I became a bit angry with myself, I felt a bit foolish for having thought of it as a place of danger.... When we sang, I liked to imagine ... [that] the former choir girls [were] singing along with us ... [We] talked ... about a stained-glass window [the Chancel window], designed by Lockwood Kipling, the father of Rudyard Kipling ... that felt good.

In this second narrativization we move within the church and clearly into the realm of both reflexive implicit mythology and vernacular implicit mythology. Indeed, although directly absent from the narrative the account indirectly also suggests a familiarity with relevant elements of standardised implicit mythology. This narrative also shows the resolution to the problem posed by the first narrativization. Through increasing familiarity with the implicit mythology of the space it is transformed from a foreboding realm of alterity into a comfortable and familiar realm. The ghosts have now moved from being violent, to being angry, to being reassuring presences and all this is achieved without conversion or the compromising of a Hindu, Indian identity. The completeness of this sense of fusion and its relevance for wider Shimla life is brought out in a final narrative.

In this second narrativization we move within the church and clearly into the realm of both reflexive implicit mythology and vernacular implicit mythology. Indeed, although directly absent from the narrative the account indirectly also suggests a familiarity with relevant elements of standardised implicit mythology. This narrative also shows the resolution to the problem posed by the first narrativization. Through increasing familiarity with the implicit mythology of the space, it is transformed from a foreboding realm of alterity into a comfortable and familiar realm. The ghosts have moved from first being violent, to then being angry, before becoming reassuring presences – all this is achieved without conversion or the compromising of a Hindu, Indian identity. The completeness of this movement (and its relevance for wider Shimla life) is brought out in a final narrative.

c) **Homecoming**

> I returned [to Shimla], I immediately went towards ... [the] Cathedral ... I wanted to feel connected with the city once more. It seemed to have changed, there were new shops and stalls on the Lower Bazaar and Mall and the whole place seemed busier than I remembered. I wanted to see something that had not changed, that I could relate to now, as I had done as a child and I thought that ... [the] Cathedral would be the place for that. At first, I could not see it clearly, there were too many crowds of people in the way, but I found my way through to Ladies' Park and standing there I looked up and saw it again, just like I looked at it as a child. And I remembered everything: my childhood days playing there, the fear of the ghost ... singing ... how [Lockwood] Kipling had designed the chancel window, even my Grandmother's tales ... I knew then that I had come home.

This final offering in many ways reflects the informant's view of their own relationship to the Cathedral at the time of narrativization and clearly displays the high degree to which the implicit mythology has become internalised, or part of their own identity. Through this process the implicit mythology of the Cathedral on the Ridge has become a key for understanding the wider landscape of Shimla. When taken together, these narratives show a movement in the chronology of the implicit mythology. In the early ghost stories the Cathedral is clearly the realm of the other:

Cathedral : Unreasonable Violence : Alterity :: Lower Bazaar : Safety : Home.

If we simplify these relations to two primary categories (and map the content of those categories) we can see that Cathedral, along with Unreasonable Violence and Alterity, falls into one category (A) and the Lower Bazaar, Safety and Home, are united in a second (B). The two categories have little content overlap and movement from one to the other is problematic. This suggests an underlying structure of negative qualitative valence, which can be transcribed as A − B, or, A/B. As the narrative progresses the young girl tries to reckon with the environment and engage with the outside and this has some success in rehabilitating the place, but the resolution is clearly incomplete:

Cathedral : Reasonable Violence : Somewhat Familiar :: Lower Bazaar : Safety : Home.

These mythemes possess a more mediated structure (A = B), yet the underlying equation is still a weak form of opposition (A − B). Movement between the two categories is attempted, but is severely restricted and fraught with danger. Some of the categories' mythemes have a degree of overlap (Somewhat Familiar and Home), but others are more oppositional (Reasonable Violence and Safety). However, by the final set of narrativizations, a transformation has occurred, which results in category overlap between the world of the Lower Bazaar and that of the Ridge and potentially an inversion of positioning. This effectively rehabilitates the Ridge by overcoming the perceived difference between the colonial Christian and the postcolonial Hindu worlds:

Cathedral : Timeless Peace (Safety) : Home :: Lower Bazaar : Safety : Home (estranged).

It is possible to read this final set of mythemes as suggesting that the movement between the two categories (and locations) is unproblematic and the content of the two categories has become almost identical, suggesting that the two categories have now dissolved into one (A + B). However, it is also possible to read this as an inversion of points where it is that which was originally other (the Cathedral), which now is home, whereas that which once was home (the bazaar) has now become somewhat strange (mapped in Figure 5.2). We could dismiss this inversion of structural position as simply the result of what Lévi-Strauss (1967: 42) calls the aperture effect: as the detail focuses in the oppositions become blurred only to become clear again in an inverted form. However, elsewhere Lévi-Strauss develops a sophisticated theory of inversion, known as the canonical formula, which suggests that inversions can be central to the meaning making process of mythology (1955, 1988, 1995). In particular, it is useful to note that in his seminal piece ('The Structural Study of Myth'), Lévi-Strauss suggests that myth raises certain problems, or contradictions before moving towards their resolution through a process of inversion, which he maps (through the canonical formula) as operating through the play of two opposed terms, with two opposed, corresponding functions (Lévi-Strauss 1955: 228). This gives the formula:

$$fx_{(a)} : fy_{(b)} \cong fx_{(b)} : fa^{-1}_{(y)}$$

If we map the mythemes that we have uncovered above onto this formula then it does indeed reveal something significant about the way that the implicit mythology of Christ Church Cathedral demonstrates awareness of a problem and moves towards its resolution. In this case the problem is the centrality of the trace of colonial action to life in the postcolonial present with its potential to generate a sense of the uncanny. The resolution is the transformation of these violent ghosts into benevolent ancestor spirts that generate an important sense of comfort and home in the face of the ongoing transformation of the landscape. We may therefore map the mythemes onto the formula in the following way:

$$\text{Home}_{(\text{Old Bazaar})} : \text{Other}_{(\text{Cathedral})} \cong \text{Home}_{(\text{Cathedral})} : \text{New Shops}_{(\text{Other})}$$

When the mythemes are expressed in this way, we are able to clearly see the way that the function of providing an anchoring presence of home is, in the early myths, provided by the category of the Old Bazaar (fx(a)). However, in these myths there is also a problem (represented by fy(b)), which exists in opposition to the category of home(fx). This, second, element is the prestige site of the Cathedral((b)), which is viewed as problematic to the extent of being life threatening (through decapitation). By the end of the mythic set (fa $^{-1}$(y)) however the lower levels of Shimla provide less comfort (it seemed to have changed, there were new shops and stalls). The new shops (a^{-1}) are a source of discomfort, a reminder that landscape making processes continue after individual human actors have departed. To put it another way, the landscape that was so central to her identity reveals how little of its identity was dependent on her, as such, its function is inverted and it becomes a source of discomfort, categorizable as an alterity ($_{(y)}$). However, Christ Church Cathedral ($_{(a)}$) now comes to the rescue, by providing an anchoring point, a living memory of home (fx), which seems to transcend the noise of history to offer communion with timeless peace. The mythic set has therefore resolved the issue of Christ Church Cathedral being a disruptive marker in the landscape of home (fy$_{(b)}$), by

Colonial Landscape	Own	Other
M a		X
M b	X	
M c	X	

Figure 5.2 Mapping myth's journey.

transforming it into the centre of home (fx $_{(b)}$). In this, new, position the landscapes ability to stand outside of the here and now, far from being a problem, is essential for the generation of continuous meaning across a life that was lived through turmoil and change.

By exploring the nexus of relations that wind around the Cathedral through the concept of implicit mythology, we are therefore able to see the way that transnational (standardised), vernacular and reflexive accounts are woven together through the lives of both contemporary Christian and Hindu residents. This suggests that binary categories of Hindu and Christian, colonial and postcolonial are of limited use in this context. For, we see people existing along a continuum that cuts across faith and time and relates to the level of the individual's engagement with the implicit mythology of the place (discussed further in Chapter Seven). For sure, the accounts that I have presented are representative of people who have a reasonably high degree of engagement, but they are by no means isolated cases. In Shimla, I lived embedded within a middle-class Hindu community and my neighbours were extremely proud of Christ Church Cathedral, which they considered to be as much their church as that of the Christians.

I have over the years been fortunate enough to receive many more narrativizations of childhood experiences at Christ Church Cathedral. Indeed, this was the case with every long-term resident of Shimla that I have ever encountered. What is more this personal, qualitative, perception of the landscape is supported by the findings of quantitative statistical data. For, Jutla's statistical data not only demonstrates that Christ Church Cathedral is the picture most residents would choose to represent Shimla, but also shows that the words most commonly associated with it are 'familiar', 'peaceful' and 'home' (2000: 413). We have also seen how the paintings of 'home' produced by the Hindu artist Aruna Mahajan place Christ Church at its heart (Chapter Four) and we will later (Chapter Nine) learn that Christ Church Cathedral is the key identifying icon of home for both ex-pat and resident social media groups. It is also important to remember that many Hindus are active in the generation of rituals within Christ Church Cathedral. Many continue to attend Christmas services (as discussed in Chapter Five) and it is common for people of all faiths to treat this site as meaningfully sacred, or to borrow a term from Sheldrake (2007), awesome. Indeed, it is hard to find anyone in Shimla who will suggest that the church is not central to the life of the town. I have here suggested that this centrality can only partly be explained by its physical location, for its real worth lies in the way that it creates a connection with the past through the implicit mythology that is associated with the landscape.

v) Beyond binaries: landscapes, myth and history

One consequence of viewing the landscape through the lens of implicit mythology is that it highlights both the interreligious power of the landscape and its ability to move beyond the confines of history by focusing on historical action. For, it is a widely commented (Eliade 1963, Griffiths 1982, Malinowski 1926, et al) feature of mythology that it folds historical time, trans-historical time and present action together by inviting participation in a symbolic truth, it elevates the individual from the realm of time-bound, limited life, into communion with seemingly eternal communally held truths (Griffiths 1982). This is indeed the process that seems to be at work in the implicit mythology that I have here explored, moreover we have seen that implicit mythology is remarkably robust and has the capacity to obviate the traumas of history in a way that is reminiscent of how both Eliade (1963) suggests mythology in general functions and Lévi-Strauss suggests a certain type of structuring mythology, known as 'cold', operates. However, Lévi-Strauss' thought is perhaps more subtly and reflexive than that of Eliade, for he implies that so called history is also a form of structured mythology, albeit one that is the opposite of 'cold', which is to say that it is 'hot'. The notion of 'hot' and 'cold' cultures, like that of implicit mythology, is an area of Lévi-Strauss' work that he tantalisingly raises without fully developing (1977: 28–29). However, unlike the concept of implicit mythology the idea of 'hot' and 'cold' cultures has captured the imagination of Lévi-Strauss' critics, who in their hurry to condemn the concept often seem to miss its potential (Hugh-Jones 1988: 139).

Lévi-Strauss stresses that these types are ideal rather than actual, yet it is broadly possible to say that a 'cold' culture is one which is like a small clockwork device: it has systems in place which enable it to resist entropy (1969: 33).

Whereas a 'hot' culture, in contrast, is said to be like a steam engine: it constructs a presentist myth which incorporates a linear sense of progression (ibid). This is no doubt what Lévi-Strauss has in mind when he says that the myths of the Americas act in such a way as to annul the effects of time (1994: 16, 1981: 606). They contain within them systems which act as shock absorbers for the changes brought about by historical analysis and allow for time to be focused on the present (1966: 68–69).

This theory, while in itself controversial, is quite different to the crude evolutionism often attributed to Lévi-Strauss. Lévi-Strauss himself states that the Structuralist 'should not draw a distinction between societies with no history and societies which have histories ... [for] every human society has a history' (1969: 39). Furthermore, the idea of 'coldness', of resistance to entropy, does not apply to the supposed state of a society's myths but rather to the way that the myths function (Gow 2001: 127). Thus, Lévi-Strauss does not claim, as is often supposed, that the myths are somehow frozen and resistant to change: rather they resist change by being dynamic and open to historical events. Indeed, as Gow has noted, based upon Lévi-Strauss' writings the last thing we would expect of myths is self-identical reproduction over time; 'instead, we would expect them to be marked by extreme openness and lability'(ibid).

It seems that Lévi-Strauss may have seen in the Amazonian explicit mythologies that he was familiar with a way of dealing with the traumas of history that has resonance with the Himalayan implicit mythology that we have been exploring. For, the implicit mythology of Christ Church Cathedral has the ability to overcome the traumas of history, not by remaining static but precisely by being open and incorporating the trace of historical action. It is precisely the visibility of the trace of personal and non-personal histories that gives Christ Church its ability to heal the ruptures of colonialism, postcolonialism and globalization. From this perspective we move beyond the binaries of myth and history, the colonial and the postcolonial, as well as those of Christian and Hindu, into an understanding where these divisions are overcome not by ignoring them so much as embracing the richness of their entangled natures.

We have seen how amidst all of the flux of Shimla; Christ Church Cathedral can be an anchor that is associated with both personal history (home) and timeless peace. The reason for this sense of stability and timelessness, this ability to obviate the traumas of history, was precisely the sacred landscape's ability to display the traces of historical trauma and historical action that the implicit mythology directs attention towards. By viewing the ethnographic mystery presented by Shimla's Christians from the perspective of implicit mythology we have been able to go beyond the dominant discussions of caste, spatial economics and political rupture. This has opened a door into the answers that Shimla holds for the modern globalizing world and allowed for a more experiential understanding of certain aspects of the religious life of a key group of Shimla's residents in the subsequent sections of this book we will move across this threshold and further explore the tangles of meaning that surround this sacred landscape.

6

Materiality, Heterodoxy and Bonding at The Hidden Cathedral

We have in this book, up until this point, presented a (perhaps too neat) synthesising picture of the way that the landscape in Shimla is made and remade by its contemporary residents. The remainder of this book will now complicate that picture by picking at certain individual threads and demonstrating the tensions that bind them together. In this chapter we will begin that process by focusing on the other major Christian community on the Mall, the Roman Catholic community and particularly the way that they engage with an important sacred node, which is known as St Michael's cathedral. To explore this, we will bring together two areas of theoretical discussion in a way that complicates our understanding of each, separate, area. Initially the ideal of Churchscape will be narrowed to that of Cathedralscape, a term employed here, as far as I am aware, for the first time, at least in an academic context. Distinguishing the Cathedralscape from the Churchscape allows us to consider if there is something distinct about Cathedrals, as nodes of power in the landscape and to draw in both historic and contemporary reflections on Cathedrals. Our newly formed concept of Cathedralscape will then be engaged with the now more established work on religious capital as a way of both capturing the contribution that Shimla's minority community make to the environment and pushing the theory into a new area of landscape capital, which in turn leads us to understand the importance of what I am terming Cathedralscape capital.

The second movement of the chapter puts forward a major new understanding in the exploration of religion that moves it from the concept of believing and belonging towards the positioning of it as a skill for reckoning with the environment. This idea draws from the reality of participant observation with Christian Communities in the Shimla hills and is shown to have the potential to reconfigure wider understandings of religion in India and beyond. It also points, however to a darker side of religious landscape capital and introduces the concepts of power, hierarchy and division into the more idealised discussions of communitas, social capital and heritage. The chapter concludes with a reflexive consideration of my own role in the Cathedralscape and the implications of the shift from belief to landscape, belonging to skill, for a claim to methodological agnosticism. For, the very highlighting of this landscape through this book and the positioning of it as a Cathedralscape is far from an innocent task. Rather, it is one guided by a local political imperative and an academic sense of the need to intervene, to engage in sort of 'prophetic anthropology' that acts to change the presence of these Cathedralscapes in the overall saga that is the ethnographic record, adding my voice to others in an attempt to shift the melody from diminuendo to crescendo.

i) Cathedralscapes[1]

The heart of Shimla's colonial Mall is a landscape dominated by cathedrals to such an extent that I believe it is useful to view it as a churchscape, or Cathedralscape. Cathedrals are undoubtedly the most potent site of meaning making and very few places (perhaps we could here count scandal point) have anything approaching the rich implicit mythology that we find in and around the cathedrals. I employ this term here as a way of highlighting the centrality of the church, broadly conceived, and indeed the cathedral, in its widest operational sense, as well as allowing us to shift the focus of our understanding of the Central Mall away from a presumed encompassing urban and Hindu, character. I would not wish this definition, however, to be tied too closely to earlier uses of the term churchscape such as (Greenagle 2001; Leppman 2005), which have used it as a way of describing the architectural presence of churches within particular landscapes. To the contrary, I want to demonstrate the way that the Cathedrals operate as key nodes within an ever-moving, always flowing, landscape, which contains within its architecture, to be sure, but also people, sound, light and wind. For, Shimla's cathedrals are ever changing yet seemingly constant features of the landscape that reveal different aspects of themselves at different times. What is certain, is that regardless of if we are perceiving the Cathedrals from far, or happening upon when turning a corner, there are always dramatic revelations in the landscape to give it a sense of transcendence and unity, unity of space but also unity through time.

Simon Coleman and Mariam Bowman have recently (2019) suggested that there is something special about the way that Cathedrals both shape and draw people into the landscape. In this they are not alone, there is now in Europe an emerging field of Cathedral Studies that has demonstrated the ability of what I would like to term the Cathedralscape to maintain its vitality even as the number of those who would self-identify as Christians dwindles (Guest 2007: 68). In extending the concept of churchscape to that of Cathedralscape I am making, I believe, a largely new move. This is certainly the case with regards to the academic literature, which scarcely talks about churchscape, but does not directly consider Cathedralscape, although it may spend a good deal of time considering the architecture of Cathedrals (Braun 1972, Emery 2001, Macaulay 1973, *et al*).

Outside of the purely academic sphere, the most notable user of the term 'Cathedralscapes' was the American artist John Serafin, whose colourful pictures both present the vitality and aliveness of Cathedrals, as well as their connection to the people that flow around them. In an exhibition, entitled 'Cathedralscape' (held at Syracuse's Delavan Gallery, in 2005) Serafin presented a wonderful range of landscapes that all were united by the way that they centred on colourful and vital Cathedrals. I find the ability of these paintings to communicate both the movement that is integral to the Cathedralscape and the emotional charge of the landscape strikingly resonant with the situation in Shimla. Perhaps the best example of these dual traits of movement and emotion, for our purposes, is the painting 'Cathedral Village' (depicted in Figure 6.1).

In Cathedral Village we see a range of human and non-human people moving around, through and between a series of Cathedrals, and this has great resonance with the situation in Shimla. In particular, The picture is dramatically in accord with my description of Shimla in the way that one Cathedral centres and grounds the landscapes, while others give depth to the picture through a sympathetic resonance, which extends the eye away from the Central Cathedral at the same time as reinforcing its centrality. The colourful Cathedral sets up a sympathetic contrast with the vegetal tones that surround it, in a way that is strongly resonant to what we have seen of Christ Church Cathedral (and Aruna Mahajan's painting of it – Figure 4.1). Serafin's painting however contains a crucial element that we did not see in Mahajan's representation of Christ Church, even though it is strongly stressed in this ethnography, this is the notion that a Cathedralscape is as much constituted by people as architecture. If we look at Cathedral Village for any length of time, then we cannot but help become aware of a diverse range of human (and non-human) people moving around, through and between the Cathedrals. These actors constitute the Cathedralscape through a range of actions that may be termed sacred or profane, but are always carried out in reference to the Cathedralscape, at the same time adding to and transforming the picture.

John Serafin, "Cathedral Village" 06/03, acrylic on canvas, 52"x 78"

Figure 6.1 Cathedral Village by John Serafin.

The strong parallels between the Cathedralscape presented in Serafin's vision and that which we have explored in Shimla suggests that it is useful to consider further how viewing Shimla's landscape as a Cathedralscape may place it in dialogue with wider patterns of engagement with global Cathedralscapes, which arise no doubt out of the complimentary nature of their historical engagement and the phenomenology of their present incarnations (cf Coleman and Bowman 2019). The theologian Phillip Sheldrake has suggested (2001: 59–60) that historically Cathedralscapes , were one of the key resources for creating social harmony in the medieval European city and he has called for contemporary urban planners to consider the power of these landscapes to liberate the local population from a sense of fundamental estrangement (Sheldrake 2007: 255). Sheldrake later, rather delightfully, describes these Cathedralscapes *as truly awesome landscapes*, which he defines as landscapes that inspire both reverence and awe (Sheldrake 2007: 252). Such landscapes, Sheldrake (2007: 256) argues, will be both transcendent and grounded, gifting a sense of the Divine at the same time as a reverence for the environment and other people. The Cathedralscape then, for Sheldrake, was a key resource of the medieval city, both providing a source of wellbeing to the population and linking them in a sort of 'harmonia', or Divine order (Sheldrake 2007: 247). He, however, seems to suggest that something is broken in the Cathedralscape today and that the fault is to be found with the people who have entered into the landscape, especially around the issue of if their presence regenerates or disrupts the landscape. We shall see that this resonates well with the accounts of some of my interlocutors from Shimla's Cathedralscape.

ii) In search of The Hidden Cathedral

In Shimla, the Cathedralscape stretches across the Central Mall and acts as a unifying system for interconnected nodes of action, meaning and symbolic resonance. It is in many ways like the painted Cathedralscape of the American artist John Serafin (discussed above and depicted in Figure 6.1). Christ Church Cathedral is almost certainly the most central and visible of these nodes of significance, but it is important that it is set in the context of the other great cathedrals of this landscape. The Cathedralscape as a whole, has a lapidary effect, which creates an ongoing conversation between people, buildings, the weather and trees. When the Cathedrals are looked at in relation to each other, they speak of roads not taken, as well as the vibrancy of the future. Christ Church

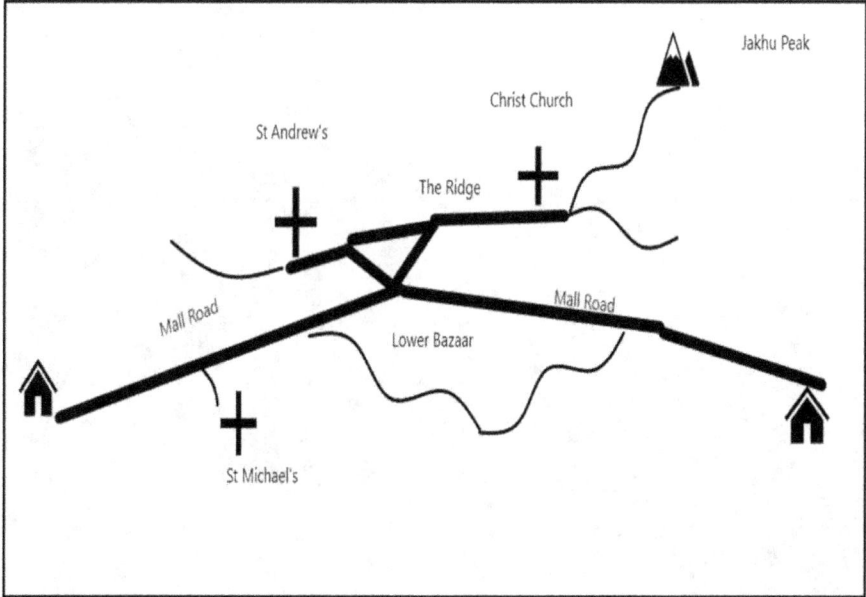

Figure 6.2 Sacred nodes of Shimla.

Cathedral stands out as the most prominent node of activity precisely because it jars with preconceptions about the postcolonial city. The other two important nodes in this Cathedralscape (St Andrew's and St Michael's) are less jarring and more blended. They are however highly important for the maintenance of the overall Cathedralscape even as they both (figuratively and literally) sink ever more into the mounts cape that they are embedded within.

Opposite the ridge, located at the beginning of Kali Bari road, lies the crumbling edifice that was once known as Andrew's Church or the Scottish Kirk. A red brick building that is perhaps less remarkable in design (depicted in Figure 6.3). It was appropriated in the 1970s by Himachal Pradesh University who use space today as a centre for evening studies. The ongoing use of this area of the landscape allows it to retain its importance as node of operation despite the diminishing number of people who could use it as a space of worship. The building is in bad repair, but while it still stands it is a key link in the churchscape, a reminder of the presence of other kinds of Christianity. What is more, through the ghosts of this building, a connection is formed between those that frequent it now and those who did in the colonial past.

Figure 6.3 St Andrew's Kirk.

There is however little doubt that St Andrew's loss of the capacity to operate as an active site of ritual practice, combined with the radical transformation of contemporary engagement with the landscape has undoubtedly the lessoned it and transformed its emotional charge. It has changed from a landscape filled with the sounds of religious worship, to one filled with the sounds of rustling papers. It has also lost something of its prestige and in both my personal experience and the statistical data there is no indicating, whatsoever of it being a symbol of individual and group identity in the way that Christ Church Cathedral is. It will not therefore overly delay us and we shall explore it as a site that is moved past, rather than dwelt within, which is how it is understood by the vast majority of people in the Shimla Hills To walk along the Mall is to briefly pass and be confronted with St Andrew's Kirk as I have done on many occasions, however the first time it really struck me was as a place of transit between two nodes of serious significance, Christ Church Cathedral and St Michael's Cathedral. This happened at the very beginning of my time in Shimla in a period before I even understood it as a site of fieldwork.

December 2006, −2 feels cold without central heating, a dusting of snow has fallen overnight, and the wind shakes the branches outside my window. I wake early and fight the urge to stay in my cocoon of relative warmth under the blankets. I am motivated to wake early this Sunday morning, before the shops on the Mall have swung into life and the dogs found their patch of sun to lie in. I am drawn up and out of my room by the call of a large Cathedral, positioned on the ridge at the top of the town. I am not drawn by research plans, or the dictates of a submitted proposal. In my understanding, I am simply passing through the region and have been drawn to Christ Church Cathedral by its phenomenology: its commanding position in the landscape and the sweet saltiness of its strange familiarity (as discussed in Chapter One). As I get closer the building changes, it no longer seems to me as like childhood memory that I have of a fondant cake topper sprinkled with icing sugar, rather it seems more substantial, more other, aged and imposing. The hills around are unusually silent, apart from the sound of crows cawing to the slowly rising sun, which carries in that particular way that sound moves in the hills, the building is also hushed, no music spills out of the doors, no bells peel, the doors are closed.

Then I notice a man, smartly dressed, appearing from the side of the building. He is not wearing a uniform, but something about the way he holds himself makes me think that he is a member of the Indian Military. Seeing me, staring at the barred front doors, he turns and walks briskly towards me, as he nears, he looks at me in a familiar way and then speaks in English:

"I think it's closed"

"Oh dear, I expressively reply, "I was rather looking forward to this"

The man thought for a second and then smiling spoke:

"Challo [let's go] there's another church"

And then we are moving, walking silently, breath fogging the clear air, as we move along the ridge and then turn away from the red bricked St Andrew's and move down the Mall further. St Andrew's momentarily, dramatically towers above us on the right-hand side, as wind ever down, and then it disappears lost behind a dramatically rising mountainside, with a large picture of a harvest scene on it. On we walk, the shops and houses begin to thin out then the large and long Axis Bank building gives way and trees fill either side of the Mall, we turn off the Mall, moving further down the mountainside and there, almost immediately I see something, something substantial, a large unmistakably ecclesiastical grey stone structure, peering through the pine trees (depicted in Figure 6.4). The road twists once more and we face the breathtakingly beautiful

Figure 6.4 St Michael's Cathedral.

dressed stone building, which has a large square tower to one side and an inviting, open, arched wooded door, on the other.

A quiet murmur of hushed, respectful voices drifts out of the gleaming white, brightly lit, interior and my companion speaks again, for the first time since we left Christ Church Cathedral behind.

> "Yes!" this is the place, actually . . . I think this was the church I meant to come to always, this is a proper church"

I am struck by the sentiment 'proper church' and what he means to imply by this. Is he suggesting that the Cathedral on the ridge is too prominent to cater to the needs of worshippers, is it instead a tourist church and what does this mean for its ministry? But I have no time to put these questions to my guide as we already now passing a glowing statue of Mary and into the surprisingly warm interior of the grey stone, mock Gothic building. It is noticeably larger than Christ Church Cathedral, spreading out and broadening at the end into a rounded, almost basilica like chancel, which is spectacularly lit by the newly risen sun refracted a large, stained glass window, at the far end over a marble altar in the Basilica like roundness to the end of its cruciform. Under the window is a brilliant white, marble alter surmounted by a cross, whose luminescence is enhanced by a string of electrical lights running around it. Here then amidst the old and the new, the silence of the stone and the quietly bubbling effervescence of the congregation I experienced a sense of grace. Returning to my sense of self I look around for my guide to this place, but I cannot see him anywhere and it was the same both when the service ended and evermore. I never did get chance to thank him, for guiding me into this landscape, which I was to become so bound up in over the years.

In this first journey of many to St Michael's Cathedral, I passed from one end of Shimla's Cathedralscape to the other. Beginning at the heights of the old Anglican Cathedral (Christ Church) and moving past the shell of St Andrew's Kirk, before finally winding down to St Michael's Cathedral. This end of the Cathedralscape is the most concealed, probably even more so that St Andrew's and it is the end at which the Cathedralscape is most blended with the natural environment. However, St Michael's, like Christ Church (or even more so on this occasion), is seen to be still alive with worship. Both St Andrew's Kirk and St Michael's Cathedral have serious structural problems that see them crumbling into the rocks upon which they stand upon and yet the continuing the continuing loving care that obviously surrounded St Michael's ensured that instead of being place of decay, I experienced it as filled with warmth and life. My first experiences

Figure 6.5 Entering St Michael's Cathedral.

are of course far from the whole story, as we shall see later, yet I would place on them enough significance to suggest that the implicit mythology that surrounds here had found a way to be mailable enough to incorporate the stranger without losing its central narrative.

The sense of St Michael's being open to change, while being rooted in tradition, is perhaps facilitated by elements of the implicit mythology that surrounds it, particularly the blended nature of both the human and non-human elements of the Cathedralscape. We will discuss the mix of congregants more later, but for now it is important to note the way that the Cathedralscape draws into its very fabric elements of the past and present, Europe and Asia. The light filtering through the stained-glass window mixes with the electrical lights across the alter and around the Marion statues. The dark Burma teak wood of the roof contrasts to bright, white, marble Italian floor. The modern drum kit stood next to the historic pipe organ. This blended focus gave the Cathedralscape a sense of 'being a real cathedral' rather than one somehow stuck in time, as I would take the words of my guide to imply.

iii) Heterodoxy and harmony in the Cathedralscape

When considering the relation of the various nodes of Christian significance in contemporary Shimla, the concept of Cathedralscapes finds added utility, for there emerges strongly from the literature a sense that Cathedrals in Europe (and beyond) are of increasing value precisely because of their ability to act as performative landscapes, which imaginatively capture and uplift the lives of those that engage with them (Bowman, Coleman 2019). In Chapter Five we explored the imposing Alexander Nevsky Cathedral, in Tallinn, particularly in relation to the way that its performative place in the landscape continued to attract tourists but was actively rejected by the majority of the local population (as discussed in Chapter Three). This rejection was not complete, for the Cathedral was always in the landscape needing reckoning with, it is perhaps is better phrased as a movement from seeing it as a sacred centre in the landscape to a scar, or even an unhealed wound. This is in part the result of the way that contrasting narrativizations of the site create a clashing landscape – home for a minority, but an occupation for the majority. This is because the Cathedral is viewed as the preserve of a (now isolated) once hostile minority, by contrast, in Western Europe, we see the growth in the importance of Cathedrals being tied strongly to an understanding of the Cathedralscape as a less exclusive place than the average church. A place that people of all backgrounds are free to enter into, join with, and exit from without question (Coleman 2015).

If we turn the same logic, of openness equalling increased vitality, to Shimla then we are able to see an important correlation in the importance of the Cathedral as a wide-spread, ongoing, centre of becoming. For, in the Cathedralscape of Shimla, St Andrew's Kirk is the least open of any of the three Christian nodes that we have been exploring. This is because St Andrew's Kirk is restricted to authorised visitors only and the select members of the night school (who form less than 0.005 per cent of the overall population). It has therefore, through these restrictions, lost something of its significance for the wider community, whilst undoubtedly remaining important, albeit in a transformed way for the select few who frequent there. Christ Church Cathedral, by contrast is the most open node in the Cathedralscape with many more people frequently engaging with it than are classed as official members of the congregation. Locals of all professions of faith and tourists enter into the Cathedral reasonably freely and exit from without commitment. Indeed, one of the most difficult aspects of carrying out fieldwork there was the lack of a formal after service gathering at many meetings. This added to the sense that it was a place that people could simply drift in and out of, which is in keeping with what we see in the most dynamic and alive cathedrals in (what we may call) post-secular Europe (Knott 2010). It is perhaps unsurprising therefore that the role of Christ Church in the Cathedralscape is highly vital.

Although geographically St Michael's lies at one end of the Cathedralscape when placed on the continuum of openness that we have been exploring then it clearly lies in the middle, somewhere between the extreme restrictions of St Andrew's Kirk and the openness and anonymity of Christ Church Cathedral. We can see it as positioned between the performative open space, which attracts more tourists and non-Christian residents, and the closed space of requirement and commitment that is the university. St Michael's Cathedral is not listed in the results of Jutla's survey as either one of the 10 most important landmarks for either tourists or locals (Jutla 2000). Yet my own experience shows that it gathers around it a Christian community that is both larger and more diverse than Christ Church Cathedral, at the same time as being considered a place of significance, from time to time, by both members of the local population and the occasional travelling tourist. St Michael's Cathedral is important therefore to those who live the centre of this Cathedralscape and its significance extends out to others at the cathedralscape's periphery.

7

Ritual, Materiality and Skill

When I think today of St Michael's Cathedral I think of a warm community that I was privileged to join with for the time that I was there. It is that sense of community, my acceptance by it and subsequent connection with it that radically transformed my own understanding of Shimla. Through this connection I was emboldened to engage in a more directed form of Anthropology, one that did not simply follow the field but actively sought to shape our understanding of it (at least within the academy). The vibrancy and life of St Michael's community, both in formal rituals and through the less formal gatherings that occur in and around the cathedral are a powerful operationalisation of its mission statement. These activities undertaken within the Cathedralscape while also extending beyond it are perhaps best approached through the now well-trodden ground of social and religious capital theory. For, of all the Christian groups in and around Shimla my experience is of St Michael's one of the richest generators of a form of religious capital that operates to bond the community. By employing an extended version of this theory in the following section I will both capture the essence of the activities of these Christians within the wider landscape and develop the concepts of Cathedralscape and religious capital.

Over the past thirty years a considerable amount of literature has developed around the concepts of social capital and cultural capital (Bourdieu 1983; Coleman 1988; Putnam 2000 et al.). While these concepts have their problems (Morrow 2008) they have proved to be useful tools for a wide range of people, including academics, policy makers and faith-based institutions. Social capital has thus become a common term across a range of discourses, providing a common language for diverse actors and has become a familiar way to describe the value that various nongovernmental groups bring to both their members and wider civil society (Baker and Miles-Watson 2010). The concept, therefore, for all its restrictions, is well suited to the task of helping us explore the value that the minority that is Shimla's Christians bring to the wider community. This occurs in a setting where the Christian community's value is implicitly understood by the majority population, yet always open to question from the political right wing.

There are commonly said (cf Field 2003) to be three main schools of writings about social/cultural capital, which are formed around three foundational figures): Robert Putnam (2000), Pierre Bourdieu (1983) and James Coleman (1988). These three thinkers have considerable differences in their conceptions with, broadly speaking, Bourdieu emphasising the way that cultural capital benefits the individual and Coleman and Putnam focusing more on the way that it benefits the group (Baker and Miles Watson 2010). There is however a further important distinction between Coleman and Putnam's theories: for Coleman the social capital generated by a group, such as the family unit, benefits that particular group, whereas Putnam expands the benefits of social capital to suggest that it can be generated by a group for the benefit of wider civil society (Putnam 2000: 25). When the language of capitals is used by academics, NGOs and religious organizations to describe their work it nearly always draws from Putnam's definitions of social capital and very rarely uses Bourdieu's definition (ibid.). In what follows we will think with all three definitions in mind as we move through some of what I know about life lived in and around St Michael's Cathedralscape we will first however need to complicate these foundational understandings to equip them for an exploration of the action that occurs within religious communities, before making the move to explore the value of sacred landscapes.

In doing this I follow a wider trend in social capital theory, which has seen academics, policy makers and practitioners develop, often seemingly independently of each other, the idea that religious groups are not only excellent generators of social capital (Putnam 2000: 300), but that they also make a distinct contribution to civil society, which has been termed religious capital or spiritual capital (Baker and Miles-Watson 2010). Baker and Skinner (2006) have influentially combined the descriptors spiritual capital and religious capital to suggest that they are not simply mutually interchangeable descriptors, but are actually terms to describe different aspects of one overarching process. They suggest that spiritual capital should be used to define the (often personal) process of energising, which allows for the completion of social good that occurs through religious engagement, whereas religious capital represents the communally held tangible social outworking of spiritual capital (Baker and Skinner 2006). This pulls apart the categories that are held together by both the concepts of implicit mythology and the Cathedralscape and we will therefore have to find a way to maintain an understanding of the value of Shimla's Christian landscapes at the same time as reintegrating the here divided landscape elements of place, identity and person.

There is, however (before we can turn to the task of bringing person, action and landscape back together again), first a question that needs to be addressed, about how far the religious capital is 'outworked' from its point of origin. This is of direct importance to Shimla, where we have seen a continuum, or range of approaches, to the closed, or openness, of certain nodes of operation. It also links well with Putnam's (2000) development of social capital, which distinguishes between intragroup bonding capital and intergroup bridging capital. This leaves us therefore with an understanding of the activities undertaken by religious communities as developing an energising form of spiritual capital that can be used to either bond the group or bridge out to other communities. If we remove the language of capitals (which in this instance I believe is useful) then we are left with something similar to the perhaps more familiar concepts of energising effervescence (Durkheim 2001: 164), bonding communitas (Turner 2012) and bridging anti-structure (Marriot 1966).

If we turn these concepts back to St Michael's Cathedral and stay for a while in December 2006, with the example of the first engagement that I had with this node of significance, then we can already see some of these ideas in play through the sense of grace that I felt during the service. After the rituals had finished I looked once more for my mysterious guide, seeking to thank him for bringing me into this arena where I felt genuinely energised. I did not however find him, but instead encountered an elderly male member of the congregation, smartly dressed in a suit. He approached me and seemed keen to talk, appearing genuinely interested in why I was there, where I had come from, and, where I was going next.

These questions could have appeared intimidating, but I recorded in my diary that night that 'I had enjoyed a most pleasant conversation and had made to leave feeling pleased about this interaction.' Although I do not recall it clearly now, there must have been something welcoming and reassuring about his manner and this welcoming feeling was to continue, for I did not at that point manage to extract myself from the landscape that I was becoming ever more entangled in. Just as I was saying my farewells and preparing to leave, the priest approached me and firmly grabbed my hand, before shaking it in what was a warm and welcoming gesture. He then insisted that I walk with him to the outer courtyard of the Cathedral where people were gathered drinking milk-tea and sharing stories with each other. After chatting with me for some time the priest moved on to talk with others, but not before first insisting that he introduced me to a professor from a local university and his former student, who was also a member of the congregation. Talking to these two was as easy as talking with an old friend, yet had all the excitement of reading a new novel and I was delighted to accept their invitation to return later that evening for a special carol service that was taking place. I did indeed attend this carol service where there was a wide range of different performances of Christian carols, ranging from more traditional to what we might call a more inculturated form of worship. I felt embraced and accepted and was back there again a few days later where tea and carolling were followed by bingo and a conversation that ran out of the Cathedral and into a nearby coffeehouse.

I offer the slightly unorthodox above autoethnography, which took place through a form of engaged participant observation before I understood even that it would be any way valuable as what we might call research, because subsequent more formal research has shown me that this autoethnographic account communicates so well why St Michael's Cathedral feels so alive. At its heart are highly eloquent and warm people who are happy to engage both with each other and (at least certain) strangers. We see in effect here a strong form of bonding capital arising from a sense of spiritual capital that is only (at best) in part generated through the formal rituals and mainly thrives in the more informal rituals that surround tea drinking. This bonding however does not arise from a breakdown in order, such as we would expect to see through communitas (cf Turner 1993), but instead is to be found in the maintenance of order, manners and restraint combined with a willingness to allow others to enter, what feels like a privileged family. Here the lack of liability that St Michael's has operates as a strength for the capital of its members at the same time as it weakens its ability to engage in other forms of bridging capital. This will be explored further in the following section. For now however it is important to note that St Michael's appeared (at least at first) rich in bonding capital and I myself feel that I have been the recipient of that as well as hopefully someone who has helped (in some small way) with its continuation.

My first impressions were of course reinforced by subsequent protracted fieldwork, interviews and focus groups. Through these I learnt about the origins of many of the features that were at first so striking for me, as well as the tensions that exist beneath them. One of the most striking things that I noticed when I first arrived at St Michael's Cathedral was the tea drinking activity, which was so intensified my own experience of uplift. Several years (and cups of tea) later I was sat one day with the priest in charge talking while the monkeys chattered and musicians strummed in the background, when he revealed to me that he first introduced the practice of taking tea not long after moving to Shimla from the South so that he could 'increase the interaction [of people] with each other

... [and] let people who come on transfer feel welcome'; this clearly works as nearly everyone does stay for tea. Similarly, during focus groups held with the congregants they repeatedly echoed the sentiments that their earliest impressions of the Cathedralscape were of it as a site of bonding capital. In the following exchange I present the responses from two community leaders. The first, who I have here called Rose is an elderly female, who is educated to degree level and only converted to Catholicism (from protestant Christianity) after marriage. The second respondent that I have chosen here to highlight I have named Simon, he is a highly educated, long-standing member of St Michael's.

JM-W What are your earliest impressions of St Michael's, ones that have stayed with you through the years?

Rose I was CNI and moved after marriage, what I liked is that we were all very close here...

Simon I first remember here as a small and wonderful community, with lots of Anglo-Indians...

These memories, interventions and experiences all help to reinforce the picture that is emerging of St Michael's as a landscape in which people can feel a great bonding, or communitas, not through a levelling of status, or a repeal of norms that exist outside of the ritual landscape, so much as through an intensification and reinforcement of pre-existing status, understanding and skill. We need to now consider how the actors within the Cathedral are drawn further into its landscape – how capital may reside in the tangible Cathedralscape, rather than the less tangible arenas of society, or culture. For that we need to move beyond religious capital through landscape capital and towards a notion of Churchscape capital.

Although it is rare to read of landscape capital I am not the first to try to ground the concept of capital in the landscape. I am however, as I understand it, the first to develop this concept into the realm of the sacred and to move it beyond a limited understanding of the term landscape. Most contemporary uses of the term 'landscape capital' trace it back to Harold Brookfield (1984, 1986, 2001a, 2001b), who used the term to capture the value that can be stored in the land by agricultural labourers, in small scale societies (Blaikie and Brookfield 1987). This understanding of landscape capital can be seen as a development of Coleman's social capital theory in that, alike to Coleman, Brookfield imagines the capital as being generated by a group and stored to be used by later descendants, only here the capital is expressly stored in the land (Blaikie and Brookfield 1987).

If I believed that the concept of landscape capital had to remain this limited then I would find it of little use as a way of describing and mapping the kinds of diverse processes that concern this volume. However, the term landscape is here being used only in one very specific way. If the term landscape is broadened, as we have done throughout this book, then the concept of landscape capital is correspondingly broadened and it is here that it becomes useful for understanding the way that Shimla's Catholic and wider Christian communities generate as specific kind of landscape capital, which we are terming churchscape capital. For if landscape and by extension Cathedralscapes are a polyrhythmic composition of processes, then it stands to reason that the concept of landscape capital has to refer to something far more complicated than simply a value that can be stored in the land. What is more, from our new perspective there is clearly no need to restrict the notion of landscape capital to small scale, rural, societies. For, we are all surely, in one way or another, capable of both generating and accessing landscape capital. I therefore here employ the term 'landscape capital' to refer to the social and personal development that arises from the continuing historical interrelation of human and non-human, in any given (somewhat artificially) bounded place. From this perspective landscape capital is something that is both historically developed and continuously renewed, it is not something that is held in the land alone; rather it is generated at the interface between the mind and the world. Being constantly engaged in a historically determined process of renewal, it can never be something that, as Brookfield suggested, is simply developed by one generation to be exploited by the next. What is more, as it is not something that is constructed or found and then used, or underused, it cannot be developed by simply diversifying the action that occurs in any given place. Indeed, as I shall demonstrate, in the subsequent section, such diversification of action can be of benefit for one group at the expense of another.

When, eleven years ago, I first presented these ideas, at an international symposium in Estonia (Miles-Watson 2008), the geographer Edward Soja remarked that the paper would read better if I replaced the term landscape with the term space. I have however in this instance deliberately chosen to avoid the perhaps more fashionable term space and the corresponding concept of spatial capital. This is because I believe that the notion of landscape captures better the processes that I am trying to describe than the term space. Both historical and contemporary uses of the term landscape make it a natural choice to describe the phenomena that I am concerned with, viz, the way that human and non-human actors engage in the mutual constitution of something tangible (Olwig 1996). In contrast, the term space suggests to many a rather vague area that something is done within (Ingold 2011). It therefore has a separation between action, time and area that landscape etymologically folds together more neatly. Of course, the term space can be used in a sophisticated and multifaceted way (Lefebvre 1991, Soja 1996); however, such usage typically results in a complication of the discourse that simply using the term landscape avoids.

If we turn to examine the currently emerging academic definition of spatial capital then it is clear to see that the dividing of actor, action, time and space continues. The emerging field of spatial capital scholarship has to date been led by the Swedish architect Lars Marcus (2007, 2010). His approach to spatial capital is neatly summarised in a recent discussion where he defined spatial capital as the measurable effects of urban design on urban living (Marcus 2007). The space of the city is seen in this equation as designed apriori and only once completed is it inhabited by people, whose ability to act within the space is helped or hindered by its historic design (ibid.). It is clear then that to describe the dynamic processes that are the topic of this book, the term space and the associated discussion of spatial capital is inadequate. To distinguish my position from these approaches I have therefore deliberately chosen to term the theory that I here develop landscape capital, for it is this term that seems best suited to capturing the valance of the complicated set of processes that are here under discussion.

Although Christians are a minority group in Shimla, who have received little academic attention, they are part of a central Cathedralscape that is rich in a certain kind of landscape capital. We have seen in the previous chapter the value of this resource as an anchoring device through the potentially traumatic process of history. The rich implicit mythology transforms the Cathedral from the site of a potential scare to a sacred healing centre and this is the key capital that these Cathedralscapes have to offer to the wider society. They anchor and act as winding points for the increasingly distinct threads of human action that gather around it. Here the human and the non-human continue to be drawn together along with past and the present and this creates a sense of stability against the ravages of history, not by ignoring them but by incorporating them. The Cathedralscape's capital is not hoarded by a minority group but rather presents a sort of cypher to the wider civil society and therefore acts to bridge out to other communities.

If, however we turn to look more closely at St Michael's Cathedral as a key node of action within the wider Cathedralscape then we can begin to complicate this model. For it is instantly clear that while the congregation suggests the appeal of carols and the priest talks about Christianity not being about ritual so much as your heart's conviction, it is not as free a landscape to move in and out of as Christ Church Cathedral. You do not enter anonymously and while that connectedness helps it generate a strong bonding of some within the landscape it can be a deterrent for others. Moreover, both Christ Church Cathedral and St Michael's Cathedral, seem to require a certain knowledge of relevant implicit mythology, or ability to reckon meaningfully with the environment if you are not to be viewed as a disruptive agent within the landscape.

i) Skilful worship

The previous chapters of this book have clearly demonstrated that as people move through and within the Cathedralscape they add to its constitution at the same time as they allow their lives to become entangled with it, to be shaped by it and their very identity formed as what Halbmayer has termed a multi-vidual personhood (2012). That is to say an understanding of the self that moves beyond the limits of an individual body and acknowledges the importance of other actors for identity formation. Most of the individual strands of this Cathedralscape that I have chosen to highlight in the first half of the book engage in this multividual vision, while demonstrating that there is, within the Cathedralscape, a rich resource of ritual and mythological wisdom. When operationalised I have termed this implicit mythology (in Chapter Five). There is a certain degree of skill involved in the meaningful engagement with and generation of this implicit mythology and this is tied strongly to the ability to reckon in a considered (considerate) way with these environments. In the following chapter, we will go on to develop further the idea of religion as skill, or rather as a process of enskilment. This, I believe, is highly useful, not only for our understanding of these communities, but also for an understanding of how religion operates elsewhere in the world. I am certain that the historical movement to fix religion, as a given and bounded identity, is responsible for a great deal of human (and non-human) suffering in the world today; I believe that viewing religion as a process of enskilment has the capacity to act as a corrective, to replace the sense of a religion as a prescriptive noun with that of religious practices as descriptive verbs.

This concept has been one that I have been playing with (in various ways) for over twenty years, but it is particularly through engagement with religion in South Asia, in the new millennium, that I have been able to concretise my early ideas, at the same time as becoming increasingly aware of the need for intervention around this issue. I first began to develop the idea of religion as skill in the late 1990s when I was fortunate enough to benefit from regular lectures by Tim Ingold. He was at that point developing and refining, somewhat through his lectures, ideas that would go on to form his seminal essays on livelihood, dwelling and skill. Engagement with these ideas, transformed my own worldview and have stuck with me ever since. It struck me then, as it does now, that it was strange that more people were not discussing religion through the lens of skilful practice, although of course the idea was implicit in many early texts (Ames 1928, Nelson 1982, Pye 1978). I therefore took it upon myself to explicitly develop these notions by integrating them with material from other areas of embodied action, particularly mythology, first publishing on this topic in 2006. It was not, however, until four years later, in 2010, that I published a clear rationale for the value of exploring religion as skill, or rather as a process of enskilment. This was particularly interested, at that point, in exploring the way that an understanding of ethnography could help those grappling theologically with issues of happiness, belonging and homemaking in the world (Miles-Watson 2010). Here, I argued that central to these processes were relations – relations of all kinds, with human and non-human, animate and inanimate, people (ibid).

While I have developed my understanding further over the last 10 years, particularly in relation to the landscapes of Shimla, I still hold now, as I did then, that

> "the religious process is not so much one of world formation as world discovery. It provides us with a framework for engaging with that which flows from existence. Religion enskills us in ways of being attentive to certain aspects of life.... This enskilment is crucial for our ability to weave meaningful relationships, which are essential for ... wellbeing".
>
> Miles-Watson 2010: 127

What I meant by this, is that the dominant theories of religion of the last millennium, particularly those drawn from the likes of Berger (1967) and Geertz (1966), are fundamentally flawed. In that they suggest that religion is still, to some extent or the other, generated through the human attempt to grapple with existence, which is subsequently projected onto the world to create a view that seems uniquely real. If however, as Ingold (2000) has suggested, humans do not engage with a world of their own making but rather are made by the world as they move along with it, then religion is clearly a process of discovery (or at least engagement) not creation. This idea of course lies at the heart of the definition of landscape that we have developed and used in this book to further our understanding of material religion in the Indian Himalayas. We can, however, I believe, go further, and argue that religion makes most sense as something that we receive through the guidance of a more experienced practitioner. The material that we have explored in this book does suggest that this is indeed the case in Shimla's Cathedralscape. We are seen how most of the congregants at St Michael's and Christ Church self-identify as being raised within the church, as well as how they frequently describe coming to know the Cathedralscape as they grew into it, not in a haphazard way, but rather in a directed way – acting and engaging with an environment that they themselves inhabit.

It is, of course, not just the Christians who skilfully engage with the Cathedralscape and one of the most developed accounts that I have presented of the process of this kind of enskilment occurs in the context of a series of implicit myths, narrated by a Hindu (as discussed in Chapter Five). Hindus then are similarly able to benefit from a more guided engagement with the Cathedralscape as they move from childhood to being adults. This process chimes well with my suggestion (made in 2010) that religion is a skill that is developed typically in youth, under the guidance of a caregiver, as a way of engaging meaningfully with other elements of the environment (Miles-Watson 2010: 131).

The understanding of religion's capacity to enskill humans that I presented in the publications (from 2006–2015) outlined above has more recently (2015, 2017) been picked up (and taken in slightly different direction) by the theologian Sigurd Bergmann (2015, 2017).[1] In both his book chapter on religion as climate change (2015) and his book length exploration of religion and the environment (2017), Bergmann echoes my engagement with Ingold's work on skill. However, rather than engaging this theory with information drawn from participant observation, he takes the concept in a different direction and brings it into dialogue with a range of historical, theological, material, especially the German concept of Beheimatung, which I understand as a form of sheltering (Eigler 2014). Through this engagement Bergman is led to suggest that it is best if we see religion as a category containing 'substantial cultural skills for ... locate[ing] believers in the world and at a place, which is inhabited by the Divine' (2015: 187). In his later (2017) work on this topic he further develops this definition to present religion as a skill of orientation in times of change (2017: 35). Much of this resonates with my earlier (2006, 2008, 2010, 2011, 2012) suggestions of the value of religion for reckoning meaningfully with the landscape, however there is a slight difference in focus that it will prove profitable to explore. In 'Ethnographic Insights into Happiness' (2010) I focus on religion as a process, what I am here terming enskilment, whereas in *Religion and the Environment* (2017), Bergman focuses on religion as a quality (that is to say skill).

It is important for my development of this concept that religion is understood primarily as a process of becoming skilled, as well as admittedly, potentially the demonstration of skilful practice. I am however, unashamedly more interested in religion's potential for the former, as a process of coming to be able to reckon meaningfully with the world, or a process of enskilment. I take the concept of enskilment from Pálson, who has defined it as a mode of learning which 'emphasizes immersion in the practical world, being caught up in the incessant flow of everyday life and not simply, as many cognitive studies have assumed, the mechanistic internalisation and application of a mental script, a stock of knowledge or a cultural model' (1991: 901). This focus on practice and application of religion is as Vasquez argues (2011) more helpful than a focus on it as a series of abstract philosophical reasonings. Moreover, Pálson's definition captures the concepts of flow and ongoing development in a way that is particularly useful for its connection to the ideas of landscape and Cathedralscape (as ongoing processes), which we have been developing in this book.

In the final consideration, it is clear that viewing religion as a form of enskilment when engaged with the concept of the Cathedralscape, leads us back to the ongoing development of meaningful relations with the environment. This, I have suggested in the case of Shimla (and indeed other places (cf Miles Watson 2010, 2015)) is best approached through this process of guided engagement with the real and lived in world. A real world of complex actors and entangled agencies that is nonetheless engaged with in a far from innocent way. For, our history of engagement and the practices of enskilment that surround us do indeed guide our present and future interactions. This much our understanding shares with more traditional homo-centric symbolic theories of religion (Geertz 1966 , Berger 1967, Freud 1918), however the crucial distinction is that we do not see religion, so much as a filter that obscures, transforms, or filters out aspects of reality, as a history of skilled practice, which leads us to engage with our environments in a particular, directed, way.

One of the first books that I ever consciously read as an authorised ethnography was *Make Prayers to the Raven* (1983), written by the American anthropologist Richard Nelson. It was one of those texts that sparks a love of Anthropology and *Make Prayers to the Raven*, along with the later text *The Island Within* (1989), have remained with me as guiding texts for the sort of engaged evocative ethnography that I, at my most ambitious moments, aspire to. It is a gift that Nelson has given, but which I never have had the opportunity to thank him for, nor now will I, for he left this life in November 2019. Throughout his career, but perhaps especially in *Make Prayers,* Nelson explored the way that Koyukon mastery of what I am terming 'implicit mythology', gave them the skill to engage with their environment in a way that was deeply meaningful, productive and sacred. What is more, although he does not use the term, Nelson's successive publications open his own experience, as a way of sharing the processes of enskilment, which lie at the heart of the Koyukon landscapes. In a particularly powerful passage, taken from the beautifully evocative *Island Within,* Nelson captures the sentiment of this wonderfully when he writes:

> I've often thought of the forest as a living cathedral ... If I have understood Koyukon teachings, the forest is not merely an expression, or representation, of sacredness, nor a place to invoke the sacred; the forest is sacredness itself..... Whoever moves within the forest can partake directly of sacredness, experience sacredness with ... [their] entire body, breathe sacredness and contain it within [themselves]
>
> Nelson 1989: 52

If indeed we were to substitute here the term forest, for cathedral, or perhaps Cathedralscape, (and teachings for implicit mythology) then I believe that we would approach a description of Shimla's Cathedralscape that would capture much of our discussion of it to this point with perhaps a slight twist at the end. Something along the lines of, the Cathedralscape is not merely an expression, or representation of sacredness, not a place to invoke the sacred, for the Cathedralscape is sacredness. Whoever moves within the Cathedralscape can partake directly of sacredness, experience sacredness with their entire body, breathe sacredness and be within it as it is within them. Later, in the same text, Nelson will go on to add that he is never alone (note the firm assertion 'is', not the weaker 'feels') in 'this forest of elders, this forest of eyes' (ibid). Here again I am struck by the connection between Shimla's ancestral Cathedralscape of ghosts and the importance of the trace of past action in the northern forest for meaningful engagement with it in the present. By suggesting that the forest is full of eyes, I understand that Nelson means to communicate the sense of mutual becoming that his now comparatively skilled engagement with the landscape draws attention to, while (of course) every action becomes a practice of further enskilment. (cf Ingold 2000: 55). Nelson is therefore, guided into an ever more skilful interaction with the environment and a core part of that process is the development of his awareness of his own interconnectedness with what I would like to term, following Bateson (2000), a wider ecology of being.

Having established firmly the process and value of enskilment I now want to return to my earlier suggestion that one particular practice of enskilment might be distinct to another. If we simplify the discussion by placing it in a more prosaic and undisputed area of enskilment then we can see that the approach to the technique of striking a ball may differ, depending on the history of coaching that an individual has had, combined with their own ongoing relationship with the ball. I do not believe however that this needs to imply that new techniques cannot be encountered and learnt that will broaden the range (and potentially the level) of enskilment. I have discussed elsewhere (Miles- Watson 2011) and will do so later in this chapter, the possibility that having our skill honed too narrowly, or adapted in a rigid way, say to the performance of one particular technique, to the exclusion of all others, will lead us away from skill by limiting our range of ability to respond to the environment, which can have serious consequences when we experience things that fall radically outside of our experience.

It is possible to therefore put forward an argument for a sort of religious multi skilling, but this is perhaps a lazy use of language. To be more precise, I would like to propose that enskilment should not be seen as the repetitive pursuit of one technique to the exclusion of all others. Ingold has suggested that a skill which is not able to respond to changes in the environment is not a skill, but rather a habit (2018). To view religion as habit then is to see it as something that is repeated almost to rote without sensitivity or engagement. It is not what I think any active member of a religious community would describe their practice as. Religion as enskilment by contrast opens understanding and possibilities for engagement with the environment and practice. At the broad level I would therefore like to suggest that we view active religion as a process of enskilment and dogmatic adherence to a closed set of religious performances as habit, or technique.

My experience of a process of enskilment in Shimla and most other places that I have ever spent time is of the sensitive development of skilful practice that does not heed artificial boundaries on the range of action. Globally and historically in most places throughout time, we do indeed see an approach to the sacred that is focused on enskilment rather than the narrowing of response through prescribed restrictions of religious exploration and faith. This is not to deny the weight of literature describing cultures that have precisely fallen into the trap of forsaking skill for habit and openness for adaptation. Rather, it is to seek to set those accounts in the long and diverse history of human life on this planet. This, I argue, is also how children, freed from the confines imposed upon them by institutions, naturally grow into the world.

My own experience of mixed faith families tells me that the children naturally (and beautifully) develop their religious skill in a way that is not conscious of supposed boundaries of faith – they use what works for them at any given time, without any conflict or problem. This occurs up until the point that they are asked that inevitable question, perhaps at school, or some other external organization, 'which religion do you really belong to?' I truly find this a poisonous question that aims to destroy the natural process of living in the world by imposing unhelpful limits on a child's growth. For it is inevitable that such questioning, pursued often and aggressively enough will begin to place a false notion of two opposed camps that the mixed faith child is unhappily fixed in a no-man's land, between. However, in reality, the mixed faith child is not between, but rather at the centre, the centre of a valid and rich, skilful, engagement with the environment.

Before marriage and children, I first began thinking about the notion of enskilment through the medium of my own understanding of enskilment in the in martial arts. Cox (and others) have subsequently (2011) done this in a far more complete way than I ever achieved, but rather than dwell on the fascinating insights developed by this literature here, I want to return to my own ground of understanding as a way of exploring why I believe enskilment should not be overly concerned with purity and lineages. It is not uncommon in the practice of martial arts today to hear people talking about preserving purity of style, or trying to discern if a particular move is an interloper from another lineage. Yet, my own experience of martial instruction, is of an environment where, when troubled by purity of style, my guide would simply reply that "in the old days they were not concerned if something was Bagua, or Kung Fu, they simply took what they needed to stay alive on the battlefield the next day".

Life may not be a battlefield, but it is a place for serious engagement and if humans are to operate skilfully, especially in this age of crises it is crucial that we are not overly concerned with maintaining the purity of the boundaries of various religious communities, but instead allow ourselves to be guided through a process of enskilment to engage meaningfully with the world around us, using whatever is most effective. It is crucial that we are free to do this without fear of condemnation for polluting a religion's (or denomination's) purity and ideally without the sneers of those who dismiss what they see as a 'pick and mix' syncretism. This I believe is the wider gift that religion as enskilment has to offer to the world. An understanding of religion as a gateway to a serious reckoning with landscapes, all of which can be made sacred by their engagement with an understanding of the divine potential within. This is then a Batesonian

(2000:128–130) form of grace, which is felt so strongly in the dissolving of false boundaries between individual and action, as well as the merging of the self with the other, the human and the non-human, the past and the present, the infinite and the finite.

ii) Weaving material religion

Most people would agree that it is good to be skilful and that in general that engaging in one process does not destroy our understanding of the other, rather it broadens our enskilment. If I learn to ride a bicycle, for example, it does not mean that I have now destroyed my ability to ride a horse. Rather, my range of possible ways of moving over the landscape (and subsequent experience of it) is broadened and I am more (not less) enskilled in forms of locomotion. So too, I believe it is with religion. Indeed, it may well be helpful to cross-train as it were and gain a wider range of tools for engaging with the sacred. There is however, I believe, a danger in the opposite direction that over-specialisation, or even adaptation, can blind us to other alternatives. To put it another way, a high level of a particular implicit mythology can guide us to such an extent that we miss other unseen potential revelations of the Cathedralscape. This also points to a further issue with the idea of Cathedralscape capital in particular, and social capital in general, which is the cosy (and rather simplistic) use thus far of the idea of the group as a bounded, unified, identity. For sure, we have noted the way that levels of social capital can be reflected in differing levels of investment in the community's capital, but at no time thus far have we been aware of the possibility of competing capitals, or indeed the issues around those who have capital and those that do not. In what follows we will now aim to rectify this, complicating our understanding of churchscape capital, particularly through engagement with the concept of enskilment.

Putnam's early (2000) model of social capital is remarkably optimistic, especially in its sense that the capital generated by various groups will naturally benefit the wider society. In this it contrasts sharply to the more cynical appropriation of the concept of cultural capital that Bourdieu developed, with its focus on the cultural power that individuals might levy over others (Bourdieu 1983). Having thought for quite some time now with a strand of theory that commences with Putnam, somewhat supplemented by that of Coleman, I want to switch tracks at this point and think more with Bourdieu. This will lead us into an exploration of the way that capital may be to the benefit of one community, at the expense of another.

It might be remembered that at the entry to the Mall there is a signpost, which proudly proclaims 'our built heritage is our identity'(as can be seen in Figure 5.1). The term heritage, like the word capital, is of course not uncontested and while I will ultimately argue that there is some justification for exploring the landscape as a collective, I want to begin with a problematising of the term. Heritage of course is frequently naively employed in popular discourse, in South Asia, Europe and beyond. In this imagining it is used to suggest an appeal to a shared present bounty that can be found in what are deemed by an elite to be significant objects, ideas, performances and buildings from the past Such employments of the term 'heritage' , as Hall (1999) has shown, are always lacking the question of whose heritage? Who is it who will benefit from this heritage claim? Whose stories and narratives are being privileged? Whose are being excluded?

This book began with a sense that the heritage of Shimla's Christians, the stories and narratives, their contribution to the society, is precisely that which is being excluded in more general discussions about the heritage of India. But if I am to grant this, then I also have to consider that within the sphere of Shimla's churchscape we potentially have a heritage that is inclusive of Christians but excludes, or denies the heritage of other communities. In the previous chapter, I have gone some way to addressing these fears, by demonstrating the way that a large number of middle-class Indians, who self-identify as Hindu, are able to access (what may be seen as) Christian landscapes of worship. What is more, they do not simply enter these landscapes, but they benefit from direct engagement with them, folding their own lives into the landscape to the extent that we can clearly see how closely tied the heritage of the Churchscape is to wider senses of belonging to the landscape of Shimla. There are however more exclusionary processes at work, both at Christ Church Cathedral and at St Michael' s Cathedral. These forces do not seek to operate across not so much lines of faith as lines of skill or rather skill for mastery of the ability to reckon with the complex postcolonial church scape that is Shimla.

December 2010, I am sat in St Michael's Cathedral for the first time, but not the last. The service is underway, the first hymn begins and I am struck by the juxtaposition of this old, Gothic styled, Cathedral and the music. There is a dusty looking pipe organ, but it is silent. Instead we are drawn to praise by the jazzier sounds of a young three-piece band consisting of keyboard, guitar and a full drum kit. The music is undoubtedly not what I would call an inculturated performance and yet it is also dissonant to my expectations of the soundscape of this clearly historic building. Behind the young band, sit a group of people all smartly dressed in their traditional Sunday best. The men are turned out in suits and shirts, the women modest dresses. Amongst them are also sat a sizeable number of youths, suggesting a degree of intergenerational connection. I cast my eyes around the Cathedral further and notice another distinct group sat on the opposite side of the cathedral, towards the back. They seem to embody a different kind of material religion, being dressed in what appears to be the sort of clothing that I would expect to find in a village in a rural area of the plains. Some of the women have their heads covered and hold young children, who squirm in their mother's restrictive grip. The men are dressed in simple, kurta style, untucked shirts, or open neck polo shirts despite the cold winter's day. There are far fewer of this camp than the Sunday Best group, but there are enough of them to form a clearly distinct group and to suggest to me a potential divide.

The service moves on and after three hymns sung in English we now move to a Hindi hymn, which I engage with as enthusiastically as my language skills will allow. But while the song is going on my concentration is slipping away as I move towards a realisation of the significance of the fact that the priest has been alternating his service, speaking sometimes in Hindi, and then immediately afterwards in English: "Hey Hamare Pita" (our Father) and then, "who art in heaven". This pattern repeated throughout, the words, or phrases, did not repeat in each language, rather they followed on from each other, in what was a wonderful act of code switching that spanned the entire service. This had at first suggested to me a remarkable sense of blending, a truly balanced, religious service. With, perhaps, one foot both in the colonial past (and the globalizing future), while the other foot was fixed family in the postcolonial present (and a past that existed beyond the sphere of colonial activity).

As the service progressed, I increasingly began to doubt my initial reaction. I began to wonder if the code switching suggested a join, or a divide, in the Cathedralscape. During the Hindi hymn, I noticed the priest glancing at the group at the rear of the Cathedral and it came to me that throughout the service, he would shift his stance to the effect that when he spoke in English, he was facing towards the Sunday best group and when he spoke in Hindi he was projecting towards the back of the church with its distinctly attired community. What is more, while I was no Master of Hindi, it was clear even from my knowledge, that Hindi was not a language of natural choice for the priest, suggesting that this was something of a deliberate policy or practice.

I later learned from the priest himself that the community sat at the back were a smaller, newer, group of converts to Catholicism, who had come from Rajasthan to work as migrant workers, recently. The other group I soon got to know well and understood that these consisted of more established, middle class, members of the landscape. Further, when I questioned the priest directly on his code switching, he claimed it was not a clearly premeditated plan, for he was simply led by the Holy Spirit when speaking in the Cathedral. However, on a later occasion he (somewhat confusingly) also suggested that he was particularly keen to bring the entire community together, which was why he felt holding a single service that blended Hindi and English was better than holding two separate services: one in Hindi and the other in English.

Later, I also learnt from the same priest that he had instituted the idea of post worship tea, as a deliberate attempt to bring all members of the church community together. However, he confessed, that many of the more recent converts "will not automatically engage, even at tea, but if you go to them, they will speak to you". In this communication I sense a degree of ambivalence in the exact effectiveness of the tea mornings as a way of bridging this divide. It was suggested to me on more than one occasion by members of the congregation that this was not necessarily the case. In one particularly dramatic example of this, a few months into my fieldwork proper, I was told that the Catholic community was not as united as it seemed, by a young engineer who was frequently part of the Cathedralscape. "There are churches in Himachal Pradesh where they still worry about caste even though it is against the church teachings ... even here", he went on dropping his voice conspiratorially, "you may feel the effects of such things". Caste of course has dominated South Asian Studies historically and it continues to be a marked feature of many recent accounts of South Asian Christianity. These focus particularly on the role that Christianity has played in helping those from low caste backgrounds gain a degree of status in wider society, what we might term, following Patulny (2009), a form of linking capital.

It may be remembered, that I earlier stressed the importance of a focus on landscape for overcoming the obsession with caste, which is itself is a sort of habitual reference point that blinds us to other potential realities. I do not wish to recant that position at this point, for, it seems to me, that although I could have chased the concept of caste for the rest of my time in Shimla. that would not have been a natural way of following the filed. For this was but one fleeting comment, made by one member of the congregation, at one point in time. Instead of talking about caste, the congregations at both St Michael's and Christ Church Cathedral were keen to share with me what they perceived to be a division based not on skill. Again, and again people talked about the ability of others to engage with the landscape in what can best be described as a skilful way as one of the key criteria for being a welcome element in the landscape. This came through in conversations, at both cathedrals, as well as more formal focus group meetings. It was clear that to act meaningfully within the environment, required that a certain degree of enskilment should have already occurred. To blunder into the Cathedralscape and move around unthinkingly was to risk disrupting, maybe even destroying, its fragile ecology.

The congregation of St Michael's Cathedral gave me a clear sense of this in the focus groups that I ran with them as the following extract demonstrates in discussions between Simon, an elderly highly educated Catholic male, Rose an elderly female Catholic, educated to degree level, Mary a young female Catholic school girl and Amy, also a young Catholic school girl:

Simon When I first came it was a small and wonderful community with lots of Anglo Indians . I Loved the Latin services, but then it all changed they started using English or Hindi, it was a problem and we had two mases (small masses).

Mary There used to be many English people, but now there are less.

JM-W Really you have seen that in your lifetime?

Mary Yes.

Amy Yes, and then the church was strict and now it is not, the new children, they run around, even during the mass, there are less English to keep everything as should be.

Simon I tell you, when we opened the window, we let in the Devil.

Rose The Church Schools and Universities do not look after others, they do not give our own girls and boys opportunities, like they used to.

Simon Our priests and sisters care more about other communities, look at our schools, look at our colleges and tell me how many of the jobs there have gone to the faithful?

Amy They are not so strict not now though and in some ways that is not so good, but also you don't want it too strict.

[Laughter]

Simon Some people come to the church and the schools just for what they can get from it but do they observe Catholicism, no! And then those of us who have been here all along receive nothing.

We see here how the cultural capital of bonding, which has been so prized within the St Michael's community is seen to be under threat by disruptive agents in the landscape. Strikingly this, to some extent, would include the clergy, who seek to deny the transference of religious capital into the realm of economic capital. The priest is at St Michael's for his part was always clear with me that it is not the rich that need help, but the poor. But I understand this debate as not simply revolving around economics or social prestige, in the comments of both Simon and Amy I see a suggestion that those who are perceived as lacking the skill to engage correctly with the landscape, risk are being dangerously indulged. Particularly in Simon and Rose's view it seems that the new elements introduced into the landscape are at risk of destroying it by their very presence within it. This again, however was countered by the clergy at St Michael' Cathedral who see the situation as an opportunity to improve the ability of recent converts to engage effectively with the sacred landscape. They also feel that they can control any potential failure, as one priest related to me: "all are not experts, but when I am there, and I control it, all will go well".

The discussion above demonstrates that St Michael's Cathedral is viewed by the clergy as a landscape in which people can engage in a process of profitable enskilment with the potential to radically transform the capacity to engage with the wider environment outside of the Cathedralscape. A priest in charge related to me (on a separate occasion) that whilst coming from South India to Shimla he had noticed a difference in how people behaved. Before going on to say that "the way people relate to their environment comes from their religion, in Shimla many people engage in one way that is not so helpful, but there is another". On a further occasion, he suggested that "being Christian is not about being baptised, it is about following a path, a path that starts in your heart". The strong suggestion here is that Christianity is an ongoing process of learning, carried out within a supportive community and with the capacity to radically transform the wider ecology of the world.

This transformative, processual vision stands in direct contrast to the idea of the Cathedralscape as an arena for the performance of a highly skilled engagement. This is not a simple showing off, but rather seen as a necessary task, in way that perhaps resonates with Grace Davie's (2007) theory of vicarious religion. There is however a genuine fear in Shimla that without this ongoing performance the landscape may well lose its ability to generate religious capital, or entirely disappear. As one congregant bluntly put it, "if we keep going like this then this church has no future!". Perhaps we can follow Ingold in suggesting that these people have shifted from being skilful practitioners of their religion to merely habitual ones, unable to reckon with a changing. But I feel that is too harsh a condemnation, for it misses the emotional driver behind all this – the threat of the disruption to the Cathedralscape is a threat to a key part of each individual's identity, which is so bound up with the Cathedralscape. A radical transformation in the Cathedralscape equates to a radical transformation in their own identities and it is these that are more fixed to. For, it is these that have connected them with the ancestor of the past and gives them a sense of fulfilment today. As one elderly male congregant put it: 'When the Muslims look at the Taj Mahal, they say we built that and they are proud, I am proud of this Cathedral, proud that something so beautiful has been made by Catholics'.

The Cathedralscape therefore presents a challenge, it is clearly not a neutral environment and is prized by many as a landscape that links through the trauma of the movement to the postcolonial period. Yet, counterintuitively this place that has acted as a harbour against the storms of change is itself viewed as a fragile ecosystem. This requires very definite forms of interaction to maintain the fragile balance and of couse any disruption to this ecosystem is seen to threaten the entire fabric of the wider Cathedralscape. This disruption also operates on a very personal level, as a threat to the identity of those who operate within it (as will be explored further in the next chapter). At the same time, it is clear that this sense of service of landscape maintenance works against the natural dynamism of landscapes and places great restrictions, binding the type of action that can take place within it and creating barriers to engagement with the landscape.

iv) Becoming one with the landscape

Tourists do not always blend neatly into the Cathedral landscapes, as will be explored further in the next chapter. I personally witnessed, on one occasion, a rather aggressive exchange between a tourist visiting Christ Church Cathedral from the plains. He wished to take several photographs during the service and was forcibly moved to the back of the church, where he would be less disruptive. At the end of the service it just so happened that there was a distribution of photographs, which had been taken by a professional photographer at an event held in the Cathedral a few weeks before. Upon seeing this the tourist angrily marched down the aisle to demand why these photographs were ok but not his. It was explained that this was special Church-authorised photography where all expected to be photographed and indeed expected to receive the photograph of themselves. They were not photographs of the congregation, so much as photographs for the congregation. Still annoyed, the man replied that he wanted to buy some of these photographs only to be told that they were not for sale. At this point, I stepped forward to receive my photograph and he looked angrily at me. "Well how come he gets one?" he roared. Calmly the priest replied "brother

Jonathan is a member of this community" – I too was in that landscape shaping it at the same time as it shaped me.

The line between personal life and professional practice in anthropology is perhaps inevitably difficult to draw. The prolonged nature of the time that most anthropologists spend in the field means that they build up relationships with people and places that are as much personal as they are professional (Hendry 1992: 163–174). Through these relationships some seek personal transformation and acceptance (Hugh-Jones 2007). Thus, the practice of anthropology can act as a facilitator for our personal desires at the same time as generating information of wide-ranging social significance. Given this, it is not unreasonable to question if attempts to divide our lives into the realms of the academic and the personal, the scientific and the religious are desirable?

This well attested (Hendry 1992, Hugh-Jones 2007, McLean 2007 et al) blurring of personal and professional activity in anthropology has taken on a new impetus recently in the emerging debates surrounding the anthropology of Christianity. Many of the people central to this debate (Bialcki, Coleman, Leurhmann, Robbins et al) led a well-attended and lively discussion at the 2010 meeting of the American Anthropological Association, which addressed the usefulness of blurring the relationship between researcher and believer in the anthropological exploration of Christian worship. This debate drew both upon personal fieldwork and the increasing body of literature that supports a position of methodological theism (Engelke 2002, Howell 2007, Turner 1993, et al). Overall, there is a notable trend towards taking a research position that just a couple of decades ago would have been viewed as on the margins of acceptable practice (Ewing 1994: 571).

For an anthropologist of Christianity, a position of methodological theism involves engaging with Christian worship as a new member of the congregation and as such being open to accepting the reality of accompanying spiritual experiences. Of course, if the anthropologist is naturally embedded within the congregation a different set of issues, surrounding distance and authority come into play (Narayan 1993). Rather than dwell on this here I would like to pursue the ethical consequences of the way that methodological theism can blur the boundaries between scientist and subject, rationality and faith, internal and external worlds. Following Ingold (2000: 200), I would suggest that the collapsing of these divisions more accurately reflects the processes through which we all move along with the world.

An interesting consequence of this is the complication of anthropological codes of conduct. The widely discussed (Castenada 2006, Mäkelä 2008,

Monchamp 2008, et al) American Anthropological Association's code of ethics clearly has a division in mind between the researcher and the research subjects. Similarly, its Brazilian counterpart distinguishes between the researcher and the researched and demands that research be strictly objective. Given this, is a research strategy that deliberately blurs personal emotion and scientific activity inherently problematic? Many who argue for clearer frames of research activity suggest that this carries with it the ethical assurance that research subjects are always aware of when they are being researched. However, if we are not so much researching people as researching with people then is it always appropriate to interrupt religious activity in order to remind both the researcher and ourselves that we are present not as devotees but as researchers? Some researchers describe a moment of pulling away from Christian groups when they feel that faith is starting to get to them (Bielecki, Coleman, Csordas et al 2010). This moment is often spoken about as a point of reassertion of identity as an anthropological researcher rather than member of the faith community. But what if we follow Turner's (1993) suggestion and allow ourselves to crossover that threshold? Do we pass beyond the limits of anthropology and into the realms of theology? Do we have to abandon anthropological codes of ethics so that we might engage fully with the lived ethical frameworks of those we work with?

It should be clear by now from what I have already stated in this book that during my fieldwork with Christians in Shimla, I adopted a position of methodological theism. I remember clearly a moment that caused some consternation in my fieldwork and initiated much reflection over countless cups of coffee. It was a sign that I had reached a sort of breakthrough being seen as an integral part of the Cathedralscape and yet also something that made me acutely aware of my own, rather unusual place within it. This event happened long before the photograph incident at Christ Church Cathedral, on a delightful summer afternoon, during the after-service tea at St Michael's Cathedral. I was introduced by a regular and influential congregant to a passing tourist and in her introduction, she casually stated, "this is Jonathan, he is one of our key parishioners". I was not sure what it meant to be a key parishioner, but it sounded like something I should be happy about for a number of reasons and yet, there was something about the statement though that was also troubling. I wrote later in my field journal that I was 'worried that despite my constant attempts to remind people that I was in Shimla to carry out research with the Christian population, people often found it hard to reconcile the church as a dual space of research and worship'.

I quickly discovered that people had their own accounts of why a British man happened to be living in postcolonial Shimla. Those who did not look blankly when I explained that I was an anthropologist could not shake the feeling that praying in church was not what anthropological fieldwork should entail. Nevertheless, I believe that these attempts to rebrand my positioning in Shimla were also a statement of the congregation's view of me as someone who was far more involved with the life of the church than the researcher/researched dichotomy suggested.

Sometime after that memorable summer's day it was obvious that most of the Christian congregation and clergy were now relating to me as though I was a member of their congregation. Yet, this was neither a deceit nor a misunderstanding, for through adopting a position of methodological theism I did become a member of the congregation. I prayed with my fellow congregants, sang hymns of praise, designed leaflets to help promote the church and even dressed up as Father Christmas (discussed further in the next chapter). I never experienced a period of pulling away from the faith that surrounded me. I never reached the sort of breaking point described above and yet I had moments of questioning and self-rationalisation of events that I found to be in keeping with the experience of the majority of the congregation whose positioning was far more fluid than may be supposed.

Much of this has to do with whether we view religious belonging as a key fixed idea or a process of enskilment into particular Cathedralscape. I was not a formal convert in any sense, but I did not go forward in the sort of process of enskilment that the priest at St Michael's suggested to me makes you a Christian and I was throughout careful not to overly disrupt the fragile ecosystems of the Cathedral. Yet of course, by entering into the landscapes I transformed them, but my presence, perhaps as an almost visible ghost of the now vanished, and fondly remembered, English, always felt like it was viewed as a welcome augmentation of pre-existing system rather than a radical disruption. Indeed, the entire research exercise can be viewed as resulting from an invitation by the congregation to engage in what I may term a form of prophetic anthropology. An anthropology that speaks to those in power with the voice of the people and acts as a check, or balance, against other dominant forces.

From a position of religion as enskilment I also do not need to see my own identity as compromised in some way. Rather, I hope that I have been able to demonstrate (in the way that echoes Nelson) how my own processes of enskilment have left me with an enhanced capacity to engage (not only with Shimla) but with the environment. In *Make Prayers to the Raven*, Nelson demonstrates clearly how what we may call an approach of methodological theism results in a personal transformation. He never becomes Koyukon, or loses his own identity, but he does clearly come to an enhanced understanding of how to reckon with his environment. By the end of the text he is juggling two identities and is not entirely happy with this situation, he feels he has lost certainty and thus he concludes his ethnography by musing:

> 'I ... watched a raven fly above me, vanishing and reappearing as it passed behind the treetops. And I wondered what, or who, it really was. Certainty is for those who have learned and believed only one truth. Where I came from the raven is just a bird ... But where I am now, the raven is many other things.... It is a person and a power, God in a clown's suit, incarnation of a once omnipotent spirit. The raven sees, hears, understands, reveals ... determines. What is the raven? Bird-watchers and biologists know. Koyukon elders and their children who listen know. But those like me, who have heard and accepted them both, are left to watch and wonder'.
>
> 1986: 248

In this conclusion Nelson argues for a classical symbolic anthropological interpretation by suggesting that the bird can be interpreted in different ways due to the cultural framework imposed upon it: for a western biologist the raven signifies a certain subspecies of bird, yet for the Koyukon elder it signifies a host of other things. But from an enskilment perspective, he was not so much learning a new set of codes, which can be applied to a chaotic set of data, as uncovering a new side to something, by interacting with it in a new way. Indeed, Ingold suggests that whilst Nelson may claim that the way he gained his new understanding was by passively listening, thus being enculturated, his own ethnography suggests that the way in which he gained this new knowledge was through enskilment (Ingold 2000: 55). And, a close examination of Nelson's ethnography shows that whilst he does draw much of his knowledge from stories about other people's experience with ravens, he also has his own experience with them and things associated with them (such as Dotson k'idltsina). It is therefore by learning a new skill of how to perceive the environment that Nelson is able to shift his view of the raven.

Thus, we are presented with an image of the anthropological project as a process of enskilment that broadens our ability to reckon with the environment. From this perspective Nelson has not so much lost a concrete vision of the world as entered into it. As an anthropologist, he is now positioned to be able to act as a facilitator for future enskilment through his evocative ethnography. Similarly, my engagement with the Cathedralscapes of Shimla was transformed through the relationships I fostered there, yet this did not mean that I forgot, or worse abandoned, anthropology and my responsibility to the wider research community. For sure, I could not describe my view at all times as objective, but I was subjective in an important way, being aware of the way that the experiences I was having fitted into a wider body of ethnographic and anthropological material. In my case then there was no point at which being an anthropologist was limiting. I was able in an honest and open way to accept being both a parishioner and a research active anthropologist, just as the congregation and clergy were able to accept me as both researcher and parishioner. I was able to go on a journey into the life of the churches that paralleled the journey that many of those around me were on in this immigrant city (Korpela and Miles-Watson 2010). I found that, far from taking me beyond the limits of anthropology, methodological theism took me to the heart of it.

8

Pipe Organs and Satsang

This chapter explores the ways in which the landscape of the Shimla's churches, what I have previously called the Cathedralscape, has new performances wound around it that speak to the fears of those at both Cathedrals. The chief of these fears is that their landscape (and hence their identity) is in some way being threatened. Here, at this far end of the book, we will therefore return to Sita's tears, which both began our exploration and my own journey into these Cathedralscapes. These new expressions of faith enacted on the landscape through explosions of music and dance are a visible reminder of the tensions that lie at the heart of the community that congregates around the churches. The rifts between the historical and the local, the European past and the postcolonial present are enacted through these performances. We also draw firmly back into focus here the material religion of the Maharishi of Kailash, Stokes and Singh and this leads to questions around the nature of enskilment that is occurring in the Cathedralscape. The landscapes that this inculturated worship brings point back to precolonial connections and therefore attempt to deal with the trauma of the colonial period by denying its existence. In doing so, they expose hierarchies and how the various groups of churchgoers identify themselves in relation to each other.

In the previous chapter we were keen to particularly explore the congregation of St Michael's Cathedral and their church as a contest site of meaning making in the contemporary landscape. This section develops the theme of contestation further and stays with the congregation of St Michael's Cathedral, but now we travel with them, back up the Mall to the ridge and Christ Church Cathedral. Here, we discover whether the confluence of South Asian Satsang and Christian worship creates harmony or dissonance. These themes mirror wider discussion about the nature of Christianity in India (see for example, Raj and Dempsey 2015). Through this exploration we will see how this inculturated form of worship when brought to Shimla may be viewed as an enactment of bridging capital but actually ends up both threatening and generating bonding capital. Particularly, I will explore the way that contrasting visions of Christianity in the region are drawn together into a single landscape and the consequences of this for the identity formation of all involved.

i) Tensions, tears and ruptures in the landscape[1]

Many memories and stories of the past direct my senses when I visit Christ Church, however, there is one particular story that always comes to the fore as I approach the courtyard. In the winter of 2008, I topped the Mall Road and saw Christ Church Cathedral transformed: alongside the familiar looking tower was a strange, festooned, courtyard. Normally the church has a neat and unremarkable fenced off courtyard, which stands between the Mall Road and the side entrance to the church. The back wall of the courtyard is provided by the church hall, which has the appearance of a large Tudor house. On that December afternoon, however, this usually quiet corner of the ridge was alive with people and the air was thick with noise. The church hall was barely visible through the throngs of people, gold coloured bunting and brightly coloured banners that filled the courtyard (see Figure 8.1).

Figure 8.1 Christmas worship at Christ Church Cathedral Shimla.

A small stage had been erected at the church side of the church hall's front door and stood there in saffron robes, was a long haired and bearded Christian guru from the surrounding countryside. He was a contrast to the usual priests and congregants at the church nearly all of whom had neat short hair, with either clean shaved faces, or neatly trimmed moustaches. Furthermore, the customary dress at Christ Church was either shirt and trousers or a full suit and tie. The distinctly dressed guru, accompanied by what can be termed a Christian qawwali band, proceeded to lead the worship through a series of bhajans for Jesus, which is a relatively new and irregular style of worship at Christ Church Cathedral. Although I had experienced this style of worship here before, the transformation from the usual landscape of worship at Christ Church was so dramatic that I nevertheless felt somewhat unbalanced by the experience.

Although such a style of worship is relatively novel for Christ Church Cathedral, it has a long history elsewhere in India (Bauman 2008). What is more, this style of worship is also well established (as we saw in Chapter Two) in the countryside immediately surrounding Shimla. It is important here to return, before proceeding further, to the tale of Samuel Evans Stokes. also known as Satyananda Stokes. In particular it is important for our purposes here to recall that Stokes famously lived as a Christian renouncer, abandoning the pleasures of life and embracing a humble life of suffering in order to get closer to God and the life of Jesus (Emilsen 1998: 97). He also drew inspiration from Hinduism and particularly the Hindu tradition of the wandering ascetic, before eventually converting to Hinduism (Hausner 2007). He therefore copied the material culture and style of worship of local Hindu holy men and spent time wandering the Himalayas as a Christian sadhu, sometimes alone and sometimes with another remarkable, and often locally discussed, historical character, Sadhu Sundar Singh.

Sadhu Sundar Singh, of course, moved in the opposite direction and after starting life hostile to Christianity had a dramatic road to Damascus conversation that saw him become a wandering sadhu in the Indian tradition, following the teachings of Jesus and spreading the message of the Gospels (Thompson 2005, 45). Crucial for this section is the earlier stated fact (in Chapter Two) that while he was formally baptised in Shimla, this did not take place at Christ Church, but rather at St Thomas' also known as the 'native church' (Buck 1925, 123). Neither Stokes, nor Singh felt comfortable with the environment of Simla, with Christ Church at its heart and both found their ministry elsewhere. As such, it is perhaps not surprising that Sadhu Sundar Singh's Christianity, which is associated more with rural Himachal Pradesh than Shimla, finds an association with the city in the area of it that spoke to so many of something other than the dream of Simla.

Sundar Singh later travelled with Stokes, the pair sharing together certain ideals of Christianity. This in part drew from a shared belief in the inspirational value of the life of St Francis (Thompson 2005: 53–57) and in part from a shared belief that the most appropriate form of Christianity for India was one that engaged with wider patterns of religious practice in South Asia (Chug 2000: 65). Therefore, it seems reasonable to assume that both Stokes and Singh would have been in favour of the kind of Christian worship that I entered into, outside Christ Church Cathedral, one December morning, in 2009 (depicted in Figure 8.1). Furthermore, it is possible to view this worship as a continuation and development of a certain kind of Christian worship that has over a century of distinguished history in this region.

At the same time as Stokes and Singh were wandering the Shimla hills as Christian Sadhus, a rather different kind of Christian witness was of course occurring in Shimla, this time actually at Christ Church Cathedral itself. This is the mainstream worship that we have been exploring throughout this book, but especially in Chapter Four, a kind of worship aimed to evoke the worship that was occurring at that time in mainstream Anglican churches in Europe. It was, as will be remembered, also an issue of maintaining authority, being attended by the Viceroy and surrounding dignitaries. It is therefore only natural that it used English as the main language and followed the Book of Common Prayer, priding itself on having a choir and pipe organ to rival those of Europe (Buck 1925: 118). Far from adopting saffron robes, or local forms of dress, the congregants dressed in the fashionable clothes of Europe at that time.

There are then, as we outlined in Chapter Three, two different traditions of worship within the Shimla region and both have rather different contexts, for while one allows for the maintaining of a minority group status the other invokes personal transformation as a way of reaching out to the population's majority. One may be said to be rich in bonding capital, whereas the other is rich in bridging capital (Putnam 2000, 25). One belongs to the high hills and the rural areas, the other to the city. One draws from the east and moves to the west, the other comes from the west and aims to replicate it in the east.

It will be remembered that when Simla became Shimla and part of the independent Indian nation state, the city experienced a massive transformation in its population. In the colonial period the majority of its congregants had been Europeans, however today its congregants are exclusively Indian, or Anglo-Indian. The Church has 150 people who self-identify as members, of whom

10 per cent claim to be upper class, 80 per cent middle class, 8 per cent lower class and 2 per cent labouring class (Chug 2000, 7). I understand that class in India is a problematic category (Sen 1982) and that it is more common to talk of caste in India, both generally (Bayly 2001, Dumont 1970, Srinivas 1962, et al) and in relation to Christians (Fuller 1976, Mosse 1996, Kaufmann 1981, et al). However, as we saw at St Michael's Cathedral (in Chapter Six) members of Christ Church Cathedral do not like to talk about caste and while this does not mean that issues of caste do not implicitly play out in the church it means that it is not a category that they ever openly use for self-categorization. What is more, they are happy, on the whole, to talk in terms of class, although what matters most for them in their self-definitions is their level of education and to some extent historical connection with Shimla and its institutions or others like them. Issues of geographic origin also from time to time emerge as a way of groups within the congregation distinguishing themselves.

The church landscapes of worship often also consist of Christians who identify themselves as primarily belonging to other congregations in India. The majority of these worship regularly at the nearby St Michael's Catholic Cathedral, which has a similar history to Christ Church. In addition to the self-affirming Christians, Christ Church Cathedral is of course always frequented by large numbers of Hindus. These range from adult local residents, who like to particularly attend special events, to young school girls, who sing in the choir, to tourists from the plains, many of whom are entering a church for the first time. Given this eclectic mix of people and the transformation from a largely European to a largely Indian congregation it is not unreasonable to assume that the scene of worship I presented at the beginning of the chapter is fairly typical. However, such worship is actually a very rare event, which can only be experienced a couple of times a year. Ordinarily worship, inside Christ Church Cathedral, shows a thread of continuity through the rupture of the colonial period. Every Sunday for most of the year it is possible to still hear services at Christ Church held entirely through the medium of English, with a liturgy that is based upon the Book of Common Prayer, punctuated with the singing of Victorian hymns, which are accompanied by a choir of school girls and a deftly played pipe organ (as illustrated Figure 8.2).

It is not only regular worship, but also the special festivals that many Hindus attend, which maintain some sense of connection with how things were once thought to be done at Christ Church. Indeed, the Christmas celebration that I have been describing was preceded, only a few days earlier, by a celebration in the Church Hall, (located behind the stage in Figure 8.2) where the people

Figure 8.2 Christmas at Christ Church Cathedral.

dressed in their ordinary formal clothes (shirts, ties etc), Father Christmas distributed sweets, the children made a nativity and all sang such old favourites as the Holly and the Ivy. One of the ministers at Christ Church also took children from the local orphanage door to door carolling around Shimla, something that was almost universally appreciated by those he called on. Therefore, the kind of worship that I began by describing is not the staple fair of Christ Church Cathedral, despite its strong history within the wider region.

Returning now to the opening scene of worship (illustrated in Figure 8.1), with swami ji and the Christian qawwali band of Gundu James, singing passionately repetitive praises of God, it is possible to understand more fully some of the dynamic tensions that are present in the landscape of worship. The landscape that I described may at first appear to be a fusion of the two distinct strands of Shimla's history of Christian worship: the saffron robes and Tudor buildings here come together. The style of worship that in the colonial period could only make it to the lower bazaar has now moved up the Mall, onto the ridge and into the church courtyard itself. Here, we stood at the threshold of the old colonial church building, praising Jesus in a very vernacular style. Yet, we were only at the threshold, we did not make it inside of the church. It is as if the church building, forged out of a dream of churches in Europe and pregnant with the memory of European acts of worship, was too powerful and restrictive a space to entertain this kind of worship. I was aware of the strong feelings that some in the church had about preserving a sense of continuity of worship in this space and so I turned away from the stage and began to search the faces of my fellow worshippers, most of whom, but not all, I knew well (as depicted in Figure 8.3). The first thing that was noticeable was that although the Guru kept urging people to dance, the vast majority of the crowd were stood still, some swayed silently following the movement of the bunting in the languid wind, but none seemed to be responding wildly and spontaneously to the quickening drum and driving, passionate, vocals.

After a while, an old woman, who I did not recognise, with covered hair (which was strikingly unusual) stepped out of the crowd and began to dance. When I talked to people in Shimla, who were from more evangelical backgrounds, they often claimed that the liturgy and hymns at Christ Church were not lively enough. One lady who had been raised in the Baptist church of North East India lamented that, although worship was supposed to make you want to shout, jump up and dance, the old plodding Victorian hymns at Christ Church never did.

Figure 8.3 Shimla crowd.

Figure 8.4 Mixed responses to ecstatic music.

However, that December there was an opportunity to dance to vibrant and unrestrained music yet, in the entire crowd, there was only one stranger who answered that call. Even the lady from the Baptist background remained rooted and stationary throughout the ceremony (illustrated in Figure 8.4).

It may be argued, following the line of thought developed by Douglas (2002: 44) that the kind of evangelical, vernacular, expressions of worship that we are discussing were in this landscape out of place. Furthermore, it is possible to draw further inspiration from Douglas to suggest that the free form expression that was being called upon by the leader of the worship was too much in the realm of elaborated code, that it required too improvisation, to be appreciated by a congregation used to operating in the realm of restricted code (2003, 57–71). To put it another way, the congregation is so used to generating a landscape of worship that speaks to those of the past that when asked to improvise and exist purely in the moment they are bound to reject the challenge. However, this is only, at best, part of the story. What actually was happening was a complex becoming of a landscape of worship within which distinct forces merged uncomfortably.

As I turned and looked at the faces of those I knew, I could see a range of reactions, which was neither surprising in its diversity, nor in the specific way those different congregational groups, reacted. Some looked on with dismay and concern, while others had their eyes clasped tight in prayer, hence remaining more reserved than the carefree dancer, yet nevertheless clearly being moved by the event. In fact, what was instantly notable was that most people were being emotionally moved, in one way or another, by this event, for very few was it insignificant. As I gazed at the crowd, gazing past me towards the stage, my eyes caught a set of eyes looking at me. Behind the gaze I saw Shimla's younger Christians, stood slightly apart from the main crowd with some of their friends under a tree. I made my way back through the crowd towards her to discover what they thought about the event. They informed me that they found it interesting enough for a change, but said that they were already a bit bored and that she would hate it if worship was always like this. Some of the older children later related to me that they felt that pressure even more. As we found when we explored (in Chapter Six) the focus groups that I ran in St Michael's there is a great resistance there to an inculturated form of worship which would undermine the congregant's own identity. It is perhaps not surprising then that both on this occasion and when I attended a similar style of worship at Christ Church in 2006, I witnessed strong emotional outpourings from normally reserved Shimlites.

The first occasion was of course Sita's dramatic outpouring of tears that we began this book with. The scene in 2006 was not so distinct from that which I described in 2009, the same band led the same kind of worship and although the air was a little colder and the crowd a little less dense, the same mix of local Christians, local Hindus, local Sikhs and tourists (of all religions) were gathered in the courtyard. The group I was with were very disparaging of the event that was unfolding and I was tempted to think that this was a case of rivalry between the two churches. However, the reasons that they gave for not enjoying the service, were not that it drew attention away from them, but rather that it caused people to think about them in the wrong way We have spiralled back to this at a point in which we can now fully appreciate the depth of her sentiment and its relation to the concepts of skill, enskilment and the Cathedralscape.

At the first pass it seemed clear that what we have been confronted with here was a complication of the general crusade to present Christians in India as distinct from European Christians and therefore true Indians (Hedlund 2000, Schmalz 2011). Rather we see a post Vatican II Indian Catholic arguing against what may be termed inculturation (Collins 2007), because it destroys traditions that developed during the time of British India. What is more these traditions are viewed as both closely tied to personal identity and compatible with an

Indian national identity, they are argued to be as valid as any others. This perception is striking yet far from unique and many people in St Michael's congregation expressed similar concerns to me at varying points during my time in Shimla. Nearly all the people who expressed these views were middle class, highly educated adults, who had a comparatively long family connection both to St Michael's and to Shimla. This demographic constitutes around 50 per cent of the 500 people who self-identify as being congregational members of St Michael's Catholic Church in Shimla (Chug 2000, 3).

On the second pass we are now in a position to see that these are feelings of persecution that stem for a wide range of factors and are fears, which are only ever partially materialised. Indeed, far from St Michael's Cathedral transforming to a fully indigenised form of worship it has developed (as we saw in Chapter Six) an uneasy fusion of styles to give birth to a truly vernacular form of Christianity. Religious meetings today fluidly mix traditional English songs and more modern Hindi songs. Although it will be remembered that the Hindi songs are sung to rock and roll tunes rather than qawwali style music. This style of worship has so far managed to bring together an eclectic mix of Catholics. As well as labourer class, poorly educated, recent converts and highly educated, middle class, families, with a tradition of Christian worship. Yet, it will be remembered that at St Michael's Cathedral, as at Christ Church Cathedral, there is a tension that both lies behind and helps to form these inclusive landscapes of worship. This tension stems from the understanding of action as an expression of being, coupled with competing ideas of how a Shimlite Christian should act. For these reasons I argue that a focus on landscape here, rather than the dominant trope of caste is more revealing. It is the landscapes that are generating varying levels of bridging and bonding capital.

In 2009, as I stood listening to the qawwali band play at Christ Church, I once again saw the landscape of worship move a Shimla Christian powerfully. This time there could be no doubt that the reaction was sparked by something other than a sense of rivalry, for this response was manifested in a long standing, and important, member of Christ Church. This man that normally stood at the centre of the church during worship could not bring himself to remain at the event, which he saw as too painful a destruction of the church's traditions. This attachment to the traditions of the space is fairly typical of a strand of thought that can be found at the heart of Christ Church Cathedral's contemporary landscapes of worship. Put baldly, this is a belief that by creating landscapes of worship that are sensitive to Shimla's past the Church performs a powerful form of civil service (Miles-Watson and Korpela 2010, 73).

ii) Landscapes of group expansion and group maintenance

When I ran focus groups with Shimla's Christians a reoccurring theme was the sense of duty to preserve past traditions, combined with a feeling that, despite all efforts to the contrary, standards were slipping. A common complaint was that things were not being done today as they were when the Europeans were still here. There was also a general lamenting of the gradual drifting away from Shimla of Anglo-Indian families and the moving in of migrant labourers. I heard on several occasions, from a range of well-established upper class, or middle-class Christians in Shimla that the introduction of migrant labourers was part of the decline of the church. The new converts were said to lack theological sophistication and the knowledge of how to behave properly in Church. This may of course be tied to the suggestion that if all Christians are judged together by association, then replacing government officials with labourers devalues the status of belonging to the Church. Yet, behind this rhetoric, lies a real concern about the way that the landscape of worship is being altered by the constituents of its congregation, the sense of worship as being something that protects the group identity and maintains links to the past is being undercut by the desire to create a form of worship that is capable of communicating the Christian message to a wider range of people. On the one hand a certain degree of education in what it means to be a Shimla Christian is needed, sensitivity to reading and interpreting the signs of the past. On the other side all that is needed is an open heart.

This second view is captured perfectly by a key member of Christ Church Cathedral who draws from an evangelical form of South Indian Christianity. In many ways he stands at the opposite end of the spectrum to one of the other key church members, who is a long-term Shimla resident and an Anglo-Indian. The two would often clash on ideas of what the church is and how it should operate. The first would often lament the weight of engaging with a heritage building like Christ Church. For him worship could be held anywhere at any time, the building was not important, rather it was the message. And of course, he would argue that the church should be embracing the legacy of local heroes such as Sadhu Sundar Singh more and looking less to the practices of former Viceroys. He told me on many occasions how he felt the standard CNI liturgy to be far too restrictive and the hymns of Christ Church Cathedral to be too formal: 'People go through the actions of worship but it is more important to feel the power of the Holy Spirit', he told me over tea, one stormy afternoon in Shimla. For him, it transpired, there were two main differences between being a Christian and being Hindu (as the majority of his family are):

a) The way that Christianity encourages practical good deeds for the betterment of society and the mobility of the poor.
b) The way that Jesus empowers people to do these good deeds and has more power than Hindu Divinities to bring about healing of all kinds of disease.

On another occasion he told me a story of a Christian woman from a humble background, who lived in a nearby village, and had walked from there for many hours to attend the Church service at Christ Church. Once there she began to dance with joy, but to his alarm, the other congregants far from seeing the Holy Spirit at work complained that this was not proper behaviour. For this man (and those like him) the power of Christianity is something that is practically and personally felt through the miracles of the Holy Spirit; therefore, he would often relate such miraculous tales. He is not alone in thinking this way and there are several members of the congregation who, at other times, have echoed his views. However, these views also contrast sharply with other members of the church for whom Christianity is different from Hinduism fundamentally in terms of custom. Therefore, during focus groups the majority of people stressed that the key difference between a Christian Church and a Hindu temple is the sense of peace and timelessness that the church brings. This they would contrast to the noise and clamour of more popular Hindu devotional spots. For them a key element of Christian practice was silent meditative prayer, which leads to the freeing of the spirit, not through actual healing of the sick so much as through providing insight into the nature of sickness.

These issues play out wonderfully in the dilemma that tourists pose to Christ Church. Internal tourists flood to Shimla from the plains during the hottest summer months, swelling the streets and guest houses to beyond capacity. At the height of summer many travellers can literally find no room for them in the city and have to turn their cars and jeeps around and head back down to the plains of Punjab. Christ Church is a spot that tourists of all religious backgrounds are instantly drawn to and if they happen to be up early enough to be there during a service then they are happy to attend. Some of these tourists slip quietly into the blend of the service with little noticeable impact. This is especially the case during the winter season or when the majority of tourists are western. But in the summer months the tourists can have quite an impact on the service. Many of them are delighted to see what to them amounts to some sort of living history as the traditional service plays out before their eyes. Like most tourists, when the tourists in the Cathedral see something that they like, they attempt to capture it on camera or video camera, standing in the isles to take the best shots and excitedly talking to each other in often not so hushed voices.

When I was there many in the church became so frustrated by this intrusion that they had a security guard attempt to first bar the outsiders from entering the church and then, if they managed to enter, located them and ask them to leave. Many tourists would fight their forced departure, trying to get one last camera shot, as they were removed from the church. Just prior to this system a more inclusive system had been tried, where outsiders were incorporated into the worship more, but it was said that they were far too disruptive and kept doing the wrong things at the wrong times. One of these wrong things is to attempt to receive communion. I have seen a priest in Shimla question a man at the altar who professed to be a Christian before refusing him communion. I later asked the priest why this had happened and he explained to me that this was necessary to tell the true Christians from those who only pretended to be a part of the church. Here then we see an emphasis on bonding capital and group maintained overriding that of bridging capital: because these tourists were not in the group, they were not part of the Shimla Christian identity.

There was also a point where Christ Church experimented with offering a form of prasad to members of the landscape who were tourists and not in communion with the Church as is offered to those attending Hindu temples but this was said to fail because it caused great confusion as well as upset to some older more regular members of the cathedral congregation. Of course, the more evangelically minded did not see things this way at all. For them the church as a tourist church had a ministry for tourists. They reasoned that through embracing the tourists they could reach far more people than they ever could otherwise. However, in a further twist when I spoke to tourists after they had visited Christ Church Cathedral, they all told me that they loved the remarkable peace of the place and its sense of history, which is of course precisely what their presence was threatening to disrupt. Christ Church's visitor's book is full of comments by tourists that echo these sentiments showing this to be a dominant perception.

Christ Church distinguishes itself from St Michael's Cathedral in that it has far fewer recent converts to Christianity. Therefore it may be presumed that within it, Christ Church Cathedral holds the capacity for a greater level of skilled engagement and yet its position at the top of the Mall draws and attracts far greater numbers of tourists and Hindus throughout the year than St Michael's does and this creates tensions in the landscape as different styles of engagement push up against each other. I can remember on several occasions tourists having to be ejected from the cathedral because of their wish to take photographs at inappropriate times and while the visitor's book demonstrates the great warmth that tourists felt upon entering Christ Church and joining with its landscape, that very joining with that landscape did indeed threaten to disrupt it by changing the nature of the worship that was and is being undertaken there both in the present and through the depositing of the trace of action presumably into the future. In addition to tourists and local Christians there is a third group to consider, for whom the church is very important and who are very important to the life of the church, these are the majority of Hindu residents of Shimla. Most Christians in Shimla live embedded within a wider Hindu community and during my fieldwork I was no exception. Therefore, I had plenty of opportunity to talk with local Hindus about their thoughts on Christ Church. As I have elsewhere argued (especially Chapter Five) many have long and complex history of involvement with the church which is both literally and metaphorically central to their conception of life in Shimla.

iii) Hindu and Christian or Jesu Bhakti

When in December 2009 I stood in the courtyard of Christ Church Cathedral during the Christian Satsang. I noticed several local Hindus and Sikh's stood on the edges of the courtyard with a look of intense interest on their faces. I moved over to talk to a coolie from Kashmir who was taking a break to ask him his opinions. His response, like others from recent migrants, that I later solicited, was generally positive, if a little confused. However, those long-term Hindu residents of Shimla that I spoke to about this were far less positive about the event. Some said that they were not sure why the Christians were not happy to do their own thing and questioned why they wanted to copy other religions. A small minority raised concerns that this might be a conversion tactic and behind the comments of the majority lay a sense that if the Christians abandoned traditional forms of worship then they were also abandoning the creation of something that was seen as traditional and important to the wider Shimla community.

The evangelical elements of Shimla's mainstream churches therefore find themselves in a tricky position. They naturally want to make the message of the healing and uplifting power of the Holy Spirit more accessible to other non-Christians. At the same time, they are confronted by those who believe that the main purpose of the church is to continue to sensitively recreate (all be it in a nuanced form) the contemplative ways and practices handed down to them by their Christian forefathers. Moreover, they have to cope with the suggestion that the challenge they present to the status quo also represents a challenge to organically evolved systems that allow the church to act as a witness to a distinct way of life that has become central to the identity of all of Shimla's residents. Strangely, it is precisely the blend of colonial traditions and postcolonial innovations that generate powerful landscapes of worship, which are capable of holding together a diverse congregation and the identity of a city with such a complicated past. For, the church landscape is not only central to the lives of Shimla's Christian minority, but also of extreme importance in the lives of its many Hindus and Sikhs, who at varying times also help to constitute these special landscapes.

The landscapes of worship that surround Christ Church Cathedral shift with the seasons and with the people who worship there. Yet despite these transformations they are landscapes that bond the Christians and act as bridges to the wider society. They are, however, not simply arenas of communitas, but also powerful sites of contestation. They are sites that reflect the traumas of the past and the diverse backgrounds of the people who constitute the Christian landscape. They are then modern landscapes of the migrant city, which blur the traditional anthropological categories of region, caste and historical founding that have traditionally been used to sort Christian groups in India. In Shimla today all these elements draw together, sometimes harmoniously, sometimes painfully. Often the pipe organ leads a worship that speaks to the past, while at others Satsang can be heard exploding out of the church in a way that speaks to those gathered together of their hopes and fears for the future.

9

The Salt in the Stew: Conclusion

This book is a significant waymarker in a fifteen-year journey into, along with, and out of, the landscape of Shimla's Christian communities. It is a journey that appears to have begun quite by chance, as I rather blundered into a series of encounters in the landscape that were to have a profound effect on both my life and that of others. However, I hope that by this point in the book it is now clear that the book's origin is bound up with my own history and the fact that I found myself in a particular environment, at a particular time, with certain predispositions that drew from that history. What is more, I was also presented with a relationship, a connection with elements in that environment that would not have been available to others. I therefore used what skill I had to follow the trail that was opening before me through a sort of wayfinding (Ingold 2000: 219–242). Rather than first mapping out my research before me and then engaging in a strict navigation of the field along pre-planned tracks, I have instead taken a more craft cantered approach (Grimes 2011), or rather, an approach focused on crafting and wider practices of enskilment. If I had taken the more conventional view of the landscape as an object to be classified, through well mapped research that then flowed along established paths, then I would undoubtedly have entirely missed the significance of the Cathedralscape.

In my more grandiose fantasies, I might suggest that I had sufficient skill to engage sensitively with my environment, but this somewhat ego-centric statement would miss that actors in the community had the will and the skill to engage with me. I was led to a community that, as my earliest field notes record, I felt embraced by. I was taken into what felt like a privileged place, where I felt the generation of spiritual capital and the power of religious bonding capital. That said, it is important to note that this personal engagement was seen by me as initially just that. It took a radical event for me to begin to understand that it was also the start of a more academic venture. Of course, in common parlance, being academic can mean turning away from the world, but through a focus on material religion, I have been able to position this project as a turning of the discourse of the academy to the world. Yet, I never would have achieved this if I had not been first bidden to do so by an emotional connection, drawn out by Sita's tears, which led me to an intellectual realisation – a realisation that there was an imbalance that amounted to an injustice.

i) Prophetic anthropology and the wisdom of the hills

My first engagement with Shimla, dramatically revealed a series of connected prejudices. This revelation was not purely intellectual, but was rather primarily emotionally driven. Sparked by a strongly felt conviction that the people who surrounded me in Shimla, who I had not known long, but already felt a connection to, perhaps owed a debt to, were prejudicially, unjustly, marginalised and dismissed. What is more, these prejudices I also held, I to could have quite easily dismissed the value of the community had circumstances played out differently. Shimla's Christians are not a hidden community. Anyone who enters the landscape must instantly acknowledge that they are highly visible; the trace of their actions being the most striking thing in the state capital of Himachal Pradesh. And yet, in all my reading I had never encountered them and because of that they were (both in the ethnographic record and in the first contact of the visitor) completely hidden in plain sight. They were hidden therefore but not hiding. This was not a positive cloak of concealment it was a deliberate denial of existence that drew from prejudice: prejudices around notions of enculturation and inculturation, worship and identity, faith and belonging.

By revealing both the extent of academic prejudice and the value of looking beyond it in Shimla, we may see this approach ripple into other regions and areas. For, if these prejudices operated to repress the wisdom of Shimla then it seems only logical that they may well also exist elsewhere. To some extent we have seen a similar thing happen with both the anthropology of Christianity movement, which was in its infancy in 2006, and the material religion development, which only found a strong voice with the coming of the new millennium (Meyer, Morgan, Paine, Plate 2010). This book would not have been possible if were not for the academic support offered by development in both of these areas. I understand this book however as more than a simple development within these wider movements, although it of course speaks to them. Rather this book is in itself the foundation of what I trust will be a wider movement of in what I am terming 'prophetic anthropology', after the wisdom literature of the prophets of ancient Israel. For, this was indeed an exercise of going up a mountain before returning with a message for those in power.

This book is offered as an important comment to those in power within the academy, in power within the church, as well as, to a lesser extent, within politics. It has been, from the beginning, a corrective to dominant narratives – a voice that does not so much join with the chorus as strike a discordant note. By prophetic I of course do not intend to suggest any special status for myself, or claim that I can in some way look into the future. Prophetic anthropology is not really about forecasting the future, it is more concerned with shaping it. This is undoubtedly a dangerous proposition, given the history of religious studies and anthropology in areas of colonial oppression (Pels 2008). However, I have something radically different in mind. For, I do not see 'prophetic anthropology' as being concerned with drawing information from oppressed minorities in order to provide those in power with more power. Rather 'prophetic anthropology' draws wisdom from entering sympathetically into the sacred landscapes of others before using the researchers own, subsequent, enskilment to reform those in power, which in this case includes the established practices of the academy.

Ultimately prophetic anthropology is but a formulation (and formalisation) of already long-standing practices. We have already mentioned the way that material religion shifted the focus away from elite texts and towards what we might call vernacular religious practices (Bowman and Valk 2014,) and we could also point to the long-standing desire to give a voice to the voiceless (see for example Ranger 1978). However, it is clear that these people have a voice and that my voice is not theirs. What I bring to this book, I hope, is the unfolding of my entanglements with this community, through which I open my own experiences of enskilment for the benefit of others. In the book therefore I have endeavoured to show myself not as the master but as the apprentice, as a way of demonstrating both the mastery of others and the importance of paying attention to their teachings.

ii) Christians and the Cathedralscape

This book began as an act of prophetic anthropology that was focused particularly on exploring Christian communities in an area where their existence was largely denied by contemporary anthropology and religious studies. The project and consequently the book however quickly transformed as an engagement with material religion moved the focus to first Christian landscapes and then the Cathedralscape. As I constantly reformed my understanding of what exactly the process was that I was bound within I began to realise that my study of the Cathedralscape meant incorporating the importance of Hindu actors, many of whom have also been kind and wise teachers. As we have seen, the Cathedralscape draws into it flows of Hindu residents and tourists who then knot and wind around nodes of significance within the Cathedralscape, transforming it as they themselves are transformed by it.

To join with the Cathedralscape is to move from the position of an individual, with a limited existence, to a dividual, or rather multividual, personhood (Halbmyer 2012). For, within the Cathedralscape our being stretches back before us, it joins us with the ghosts of ourselves, the ancestors of the land and the truths of existence. The Cathedralscape draws from and gives to resident and tourist, Hindu and Christian, colonial and postcolonial. The Cathedralscape stretches out to the future and draws together the traces and memories of the past. And this of course explains the mystery of Shimla's landscape. A mystery that drew me into the landscape even before it struck me, for even before I had encountered Shimla's Christians I was drawn onward by the trace of Christian action in Shimla. The mystery arises from the fact that despite the city now being home to largely Hindu postcolonial population the Cathedral as its living essence. What is more, it soon became apparent that in this I was far from alone: Shimla's central mall, with its old colonial Cathedral at the heart is in the heart of so many of its contemporary residents.

From the perspective of this end of the book, the Cathedral's continuing centrality no longer seems so mysterious. Christ Church Cathedral is the preeminent symbol of Shimla precisely because of its positioning at the centre of a Cathedralscape that is both alive and active as an arena of enskilment and significance. The implicit mythology that is gathered up and drawn into the Cathedralscape in turn draws its members on deeper into an entanglement of meaning, through performative mimesis and other significant performative acts. This process of constant renewal ensures that the Cathedralscape acts as a constantly adapting, yet anchoring, mythological base for the city. It forms a template, or to put it another way, offers a key to unlocking the processes of engagement with the wider environment that promotes wellbeing. The Cathedralscape draws together actors from different times and places to develop a sense of dùthchas in a land of migration (Murphy 2011). Just as MacLean's Ghosts connected him to the land through a traumatic history, so too the ghosts of Shimla point to a way for the present to meaningfully meet with the past.

The Cathedralscape connects residents with each other and with the ancestors of the place. As Simon said, 'this is ours, our people built this, we should be proud of it' (discussed in Chapter Six). But it is not only today's Christians who feel connected with the actions of the past. As we saw in Chapter Five, the sign at the entrance to the Mall so conveniently reminds us (in its message of shared heritage and identity) it is also the majority population who can benefit from a connection through time. So, we have seen that Hindu residents speak of Christ Church Cathedral as a site homecoming (Chapter Five). They write poems about the Cathedral and paint pictures of it. Diaspora communities spend time meditating on it, to remember home, and the tourists fought to be photographed within the Cathedral as a way of claiming at least a transient connection with this rich vibrant landscape. The Cathedralscape is claimed by a diverse and dispersed range of people as 'our heritage, our identity and yet, of course, these bonds and bridges, forged within the Cathedralscape, are not without tensions (as discussed in Chapter Eight). These tensions that have been there since the Cathedral's foundation and will, I am certain, continue as long as buildings stand and humans walk these lands.

The Cathedralscape is for some an arena of enskilment, while for others it is a fragile ecosystem, which requires skill, in the form of skilful engagement. There is a pulling in opposite directions here, in these contradictory visions. The first vision suggest stumbling into the environment to engage in a process of enskilment that will most certainly alter the environment as surely as it alters the people who constitute it. The second vision demands a careful, maybe even habitual, action to preserve and protect the Cathedralscape for future generations. Finally, there are the disruptors, a small but significant group who believe that the Cathedralscape is not working for everyone (this to some extent is true) and needs some sort of transformation. This minority element has been in the landscape from the beginning, we see this in the description of Simla as a pantomime stage set designed by a child (Pubby 1885: 15). We also see it in the Christian Sadhus who turned away from the landscape of Simla (Chapter Two) and more recently, have sought to radically reshape it (Chapter Eight). Yet these tensions do not tear the Cathedralscape apart, rather they bind it ever more closely together.

In 2007 the Catholic authorities started a campaign to get everyone pulling the rope in the same direction. Of course, in Shimla, this does not happen, but nor I imagine does it happen anywhere and if the rope pulls in two distinct directions then, unless there is perfect balance of force, eventually it will move one way. Many people who fear for the future of Shimla see it in these terms and want to make sure that they are on the winning side of the tug of war. I however have tried to present a rather different vision in this book. Following Ingold, (2013) I have suggested that it is better if we do not think of Shimla's Cathedralscape so much as a singular artefact, but rather a mass of threads tangling together as they are pulled further apart. This is not to deny that the Cathedralscape is changing and always has been, it is merely to suggest that it is able to give the impression of stability, while incorporating change much as Lévi-Strauss suggests cold culture mythology operates (discussed in Chapter Four).

We have seen, in Chapter Three, the significant transformation that occurred when materials from near and far were brought together by human action, endeavour and imagination into what we now call Christ Church Cathedral. There were those then who were dismayed by the changes that they saw in the landscape and this fact, importantly, points our discussion back to the wider idea of religion as a form of an enskilment. In Chapter Six, we saw how we, as humans, seek to reckon with our environments at the same time as a transforming them and ultimately us. So far, I have viewed this enskilment primarily as a way to engage with the postcolonial landscapes and the potential traumas of colonialism. I believe, however, that we need to see the process of religious enskilment as extending beyond this. It must take us beyond a false division between Shimla and the wider Himachali environment. The lessons of the Cathedralscape must have some degree of transferability to engagement with the environment of the surrounding Himalayas.

The final question I would like to ask of this remarkable landscape then is this: does the element of replication in the Cathedralscape of Shimla, as we have conceived it, only connect us to local history and Christian prehistory, or does it have the potential to engage with the wider prehistory of the Himalayan range? I believe that we have seen in this book that indeed it does, albeit in an indirect way. For we have seen, especially in chapters Three and Five, how first Simla and then Shimla has been viewed as more than just paradise, but also a dham, or house of the God. It is for many Mount Meru (see Chapter Two), the sacred axis around which the world can spin and from which it is possible to know the centre of existence. Even in its dissident mythologies the Cathedralscape shows a relation to the high Himalayas. It points outs from the centre, to the periphery, out to its connections with Kailash and the Maharishi, and out to the plains that stand in balance with the mountains. Finally, the Cathedralscape points outward in its general enskilment. This is what we saw the clergy term the development of a spiritual mindset, which has the capacity to transform human relations with their environment. Through enskilment in the Cathedralscape I have come to know the value of living attentively in relation to the environment, of caring for all people, humans, animals, buildings and trees. As well as the joy of slow and purposeful movement within a landscape of meaning. It is no wonder then that Shimla's Mall Road is known as one of the finest pedestrianised roads in the country. For it stands in stark contrast to the general pattern of roads rapidly filling with combustion engines that choke the air and acts as a reminder that progress and development need not take us away from, as Tagore (1933) would have it, education about the earth through the feet.

iii) Salt, sugar and dilithium crystals

We have talked at length about the wider Cathedralscape and the centrality of Hindus within it. This was important as a way of establishing that we are not simply discussing something that is only of concern for a small minority, however it is important in this that we have not lost sight of the Christian community, whose tears opened the possibility for this book. In all our journeys across and through the Cathedralscape they have remained with us guiding our journey in the same way that they sit at the centre of the Cathedralscape guiding the interactions that take place there. This is not a simple process of vicarious religion (Davie 2007), where they perform rituals for the benefit of those who cannot or will not engage directly with the landscape. Rather, we see Shimla's Christian community operating as an important facilitator of enskilment for those, from all religious backgrounds, who do wish to meaningfully engage with the landscape. Although of course not all of the Christian community are agreed on either the extent of openness or the degree of prerequisite aptitude.

Usha Chug, who is both a local member of the Christian community and an accomplished academic, has suggested that the presence of Christians within Shimla's landscape is like the pinch of salt placed in the stew, a tiny ingredient, but nonetheless essential for its overall flavouring (Chug 2000: 253). In an interesting parallel, Stuart Hall, when discussing migrants in Europe, famously describes them as the sugar in the tea, a small dose that makes everything sweeter (1991: 48). I find commendable, in both of these analogies, the sense that there is some added value to be gained from the presence of the other within, which changes (for the better) the overall composition, as a result of new elements being added to it. I do, however, struggle also with the way that these metaphors seem to relate to the multicultural melting pot theory (Reisch 2008) in which everything is boiled down together. What is more, neither salt, nor sugar are entirely necessary additives for food and beverages and too much of either is generally agreed to be bad for overall wellbeing. This metaphor therefore seems to lay the ground for arguing for a strict limiting the influence of minority cultures, although I am sure that is not what either author intended. In the case of Shimla, presumably trying to restrict the nature of change, within a landscape or Cathedralscape, possibly through immigration policies of one sort or another.

I have argued that instead of seeing Shimla as pot, or a cup we should view it as a landscape. A landscape draws people together and does not see them as fillings for bounded entities, or containers. Sacred landscapes naturally and seditiously work against the religions that would claim them by resisting the unnatural divisions of world religion, denomination and sect. A sacred site, from the perspective of landscape studies, is an ongoing process, it is always trailing things before and behind it. This process of trailing leaves open the capacity for movement in, out and around. For the formation of connections with some at certain points and with others at others. It allows for the maintenance of the agency of the individual, which is never entirely lost in the Cathedralscape, being only rather drawn into it. This is not to say that it is not necessary to relinquish some agency to those you encounter there. To engage in a process of enskilment is, in my understanding to be partly guided by others, however it is not just this, but also to engage, sensitively and directly with the environment. This is a radically different prospect to a sort of living resomation. Even if the feeling of loss of the self in the other is a key aspect of spiritual capital uplift (as discussed in Chapter Five), it is not the same as a minority group, such as Shimla's Christians, being asked to imagine themselves dissolved to a wider Hindu culture.

It is interesting to note that Usha Chug was herself a member of Shimla's Christian communities and her comment, while sounding like an upbeat ending, may have a hint of melancholy about it. The idea of being dissolved into the larger culture certainly resonates with the fears of several key actors that I encountered at both Christ Church Cathedral (as discussed in Chapter Eight) and St Michael's Cathedral (as discussed in Chapter Six). In chapters One, Six and Eight we considered these fears further as we explored the comments and actions of people genuinely concerned about a coming process of enculturation/inculturation. These fears were also there at the start of this book, they were behind Sita's tears and the dawning of this project. Over a decade later I feel that I have a note of optimism to sound here, for I have learnt from my time in Shimla that we are not dissolved into our environment so much as bound up with it and I believe that this vision can beneficially protect those in need, if it is shared.

In contrast to seeing Shimla's Christians as ingredients in stew I would like to see them as elements that when brought together with other elements in the society can be a powerful force for a prosperous future. For sure, if this bringing together is hostile then it may be explosive, but if it is done sensitively, carefully and with an eye to respect for other elements of the environment then it should be a source of power. I am inspired to think in this direction by the poet Mohja Kahf's Hijab Scenes. In '"Hijab" Scene #3' Khaf relates to her struggles as a minority Muslim woman in America, but in doing so puts forward a remarkable vision and plea for how different elements might work together when she writes:

"Can we save the ship we're both on,
can we save
the dilithium crystals?"

Kahf 2003: 25

This poignant line is one that I can imagine poets of Shimla, such Professor Madden, truly enjoying. For, in this poem, Kahf, evokes the idea of different communities in the same landscape being, if not on the same journey, then at least travelling together for a while. To move forward they need to work together to save the dilithium crystals, a dual (di) power source (famous from Star Trek) that needs both its elements to work. Therefore, the generation of the vitality and power that will move everyone forward, towards the stars, a bright, shared future, is precisely the existence of multiple elements that come together to create something far greater than either could be on its own. I would like to suggest that rather than being like salt in a stew, or sugar in tea, the Christian community are an important activator of the vitality of the Cathedralscape (the Cathedralscape Capital, or Implicit mythology). Not because they stand on their own, but rather because, when they are drawn together, for whatever period of time with other elements they spark with vitality. Sometimes the sparks are dangerous, but most of the time Shimla is extremely peaceful and the secret of this is careful (and caring) engagement between a wide range of actors in the environment. These ongoing relationships can occur synchronously across living actors, or diachronically through engagement with shared ancestors, ghosts and memories.

iv) Developments and future areas for exploration

Throughout this book I have been very careful to place myself in it at a particular time and a particular place because I realise that I could not capture the entirety of experience in Shimla: life in Shimla moves ever on. One of the advantages of publishing a book after such a long and ongoing engagement with an area is that I have been able to see transformations in the landscape slowly emerging. Even as I write, new avenues are opening for future explorations that I may take myself, but also invite others, who have been inspired by this text, to either undertake alone or alongside me. For, it is clear that all I have written is contingent on my own engagement with the landscape and a different person's engagement would yield an even richer range of insight.

The most obvious way that life in Shimla has altered since 2006 is evidenced by the way that as I write this section I am still bound up with Shimla, constantly receiving communications from there in a way that simply would not have been possible in 2006. This is of course a result of the growth of the profile of Shimla in cyberspace. When I first went to Shimla, I neither took a smartphone with me, nor do I remember ever seeing one. We were fortunate enough to be able to arrange internet at our home in the hills, but it has to be said that this internet was remarkably slow to the extent that if we wished to view a short video then we would set it buffering and go and make some food in the hope it might have completed by the time we had finished cooking. Of course, there were internet cafés, but these too were largely slow, dependant on slow connection and uncomfortable places to spend a long time in. To make a call back to Europe involved going to a special phone box, a good distance from the house and with limited guarantee of success. To be in Shimla was then to be present there and to have only limited avenues for connection with others elsewhere.

Shimla today is highly connected. It is one of thirty official 'smart cities', which are the poster children of the national government's data development drive. This combined with the smartphone revolution and the cheap rates of affordable data in India have meant that there is a boom of websites, forums and Facebook groups, all talking about Shimla, with an almost universal tendency to focus on its heritage. As might be expected many of these, which I am a long-term member of, focus especially on landscape this is particularly the case with Christ Church Cathedral. We have of course already explored a little (in Chapter Four) some of the Facebook groups in existence that focus on the Cathedralscape (such as *We love Shimla* and *Shimla Queen of the Hills*), but these could form the subject of a book-length study in themselves and this would have interesting implications for our focus on landscapes and the vision of enskilment as practice of practical engagement.

It would be easy to dismiss online forums as lesser replications of the 'real', lived-in world and it does seem that most of the online use of images in these groups is in the mould of the idea of landscape as a fixed backdrop, or pantomime stage set. Viewing Christ Church Cathedral as a material object, rather than a series of materials that are constantly recrafted through the processes of material religion. Yet, even my nascent exploration of these sites suggests that these forums reveal them as sites of interaction, even though the bodily movements (of type and vision) are mediated through technology. The photographs that are placed there are never entirely innocent, nor are the videos. They always draw the eye to one thing at the expense of another. In some complex filters and postproduction leave little to doubt , directly filtering out elements of the environment and enhancing others. What is more, some of these videos and online forums are run by tourists as a way of marking the periphery of their journey to Shimla. These groups contain material that is posted following visits to Shimla that is interacted with by people before they visit Shimla. This process creates an increasing narrowing of the gaze, what we might call a specialisation, an adaptation, or even the development of a habit (as discussed in Chapter Seven). This practice leads to an enhanced ability to engage with certain aspects of the environment in certain ways, but is distinct to the flexibility of skill that we have previously discussed.

Finally, it would be wrong to overlook the vital role that these online forums, groups and repositories, play for those (like myself) who want to maintain a sense of connection to the landscape while apart from it. This way of sharing in the landscape does not require the complex processes of replication and can provide a crucial link to something that is so central to your own identity at a distance. It offers the ability for engagement with others who remain in the landscape and offers a way to at least virtually interact with the landscape. We have already seen how this can operate in relation to guiding the actions of others, who will enter the landscape as a kind of proxy. However, a perhaps more profound role that these forums play is in connecting people across the globe, through shared engagement, in an online platform. This platform is inevitably focused on a somewhat nostalgic representation of a landscape that has already moved forward; it is in many ways a walk not so much with ghosts of present as into the land of the dead.

Throughout my time in Shimla I have benefited from the wisdom of those residents who have an active memory of the traumas of partition and the movement to the postcolonial period. These are increasingly becoming traces on the landscape rather than actors within it, albeit ones with the power to exert influence over the landscape, as long as they live in the memories of those who walk the Mall today. As the influence of these figures fades, the landscape will again become increasingly more susceptible to the politics of possession. Towards the end of a long period of time in Shimla I was walking down the Mall with the ever-uplifting Professor Madan. We usually had conversations that were filled with hope and happiness, but today I was angling to get some more 'useful' research information and I pushed the conversation into unusually uncomfortable territory. In what was one of my deepest regrets of my time in Shimla, I attempted to change position from friend and apprentice to that of inquisitor and authority:

"Do you ever feel that it is strange to be walking through this landscape" I inquired
Not realising my tone, he replied light heartedly
"No, this my home"
Unfortunately, I was far from at my best and I pushed on
"But look at these buildings, they don't look very Indian and well the Church is a Christian building after all"
I had only ever seen his serious gaze once before, when I suggested playing football near his house, but he turned that gaze full to me now as he said
"Do not push things apart in this way, saying this is this religion and this is that, following that path can only lead to trouble".

On that day I was foolish and ashamed of myself, but it will not be the only time that someone will pursue a more divisive agenda and I worry that as people with the skill, sensitivity and understanding of Professor Madan move further away from the centre of influence in the city it will become more troubled. This shift in the landscape could open Shimla to the shifting politics of the increasing nationalistic rise of a certain kind of understanding of religion, which runs counterwise to Professor Madan's vision and that which I have tried to develop in this book. As Carrithers (2000) has demonstrated, this vision of religion has a rich history in India and yet, there is a growing sense of religion as a bounded commodity, which directs identity and limits the range of action. For those who are held tightly within this religion's container, there is no place for the rich vision of the dilithium crystals, polytropy, or Professor Madan's worldview. How this will affect Shimla, where we have seen so little conflict to date remains largely to be seen.

There is already one obvious way that shifting politics have begun to affect the landscape of Shimla. This is the way that the landscape has shifted after the construction of the world's largest high-altitude Hanuman. There is a well-established pattern of post-independence constructions of giant Hanumans all over India and many of these follow a set template, regardless of the environment that they find themselves within (Lutgendorf 1994). Shimla's Hanuman comes relatively late to this scene but follows the template of being funded by money from outside of Shimla and designed by an artist from Rajasthan. The giant, saffron coloured, Hanuman stands next to the ancient Hanuman temple that lies in the forest behind Christ Church Cathedral. Its head peers above the trees as though peeking out at the scene bellow. My initial research into this emerging area suggests that Hanuman has generated a mixed response, but I sense that one of the great strengths of Shimla is that the landscape has been able to adapt and change to new politics and ideas that sit within its overarching theme. Hanuman always was on top of that hill in the minds of those bellow, it is just now he has become both more corporeal and human, but as the years go by Hanuman may be incorporated peacefully into the landscape of those that move around the hill and the city below. As time passes by the people of Shimla may well shift the landscape again, so that Hanuman will come to more sensitively relate to his surrounding environment and the ecology of relations built throughout the Cathedralscape, just as his older more occult and less human presence did.

A final area for consideration of change within Shimla that needs to be addressed is the ability of the landscape to respond to a different kind of trauma to that which we have been exploring in this book. For in the future I feel that along with coping with traumas of historical population movement it will need to be increasingly responsive to the traumas wrought on the environment by historical and ongoing global human action. Shimla is not at present well equipped to face these coming challenges. The city is located in a potential earthquake zone, while being perched on top of a mountain, with many buildings that are less stable than is normally desirable. St Michael's Cathedral is already in danger of falling off the mountainside and St Andrew's Kirk is said to be crumbling due to neglect. There are no substantial rivers near the city and it suffers increasingly from water shortages, although it is thankfully safe from the imminent perils of sea level rise. How the Cathedralscape can adapt (if indeed it can) to meet these environmental challenges remains to be seen and will undoubtedly form a part of any future study in the region. Yet, for now I want to end with a note of hope. There is reason to be hopeful about the future of Shimla, for the way that care for the environment within the Cathedralscape may yet translate to care for the environment more generally, as the clergy at St Michael's Cathedral imagined it would. Moreover, care for each other, built through rich religious bonding capital may help with the need to be compassionate in the distribution of increasingly scarce resources.

If we look, lastly, beyond Shimla, then I believe that this book has much to offer in the way of opening avenues for further explorations around the world.

The concepts developed within these pages, especially that of Cathedralscape capital, seem to resonate well with the findings emerging from the recent flourish in Cathedral scholarship. The emphasis on a crafted form of material religion, and the extension of that to the notion of enskilment, will have utility for those who are intent on pushing forward with the agenda of doing justice to the lived reality of religion. To further explore how religion in other parts of the world also operate through processes of skill and the consequences of this for our reckoning with the world. It is my deepest hope that through this model of religion as enskilment we can engage in a form of prophetic anthropology that stops the academy and schools from artificially and harmfully dividing people into containers of religious belief. Shifting instead to a focus on the way that seemingly distinct faiths are in reality bonded and drawn together around sites of significant action. As well as the naturalness of this way of being, becoming and growing, into the world. So that rather than a skilful approach to religion being seen as something, unusual, problematic, or less desirable, it is understood as a rich and meaningful way to engage with the sacred.

This challenge I put forward through my call for prophetic anthropology, which is a form of exploring religion that is actively engaged in speaking to power from experience. This is a challenge that I will take forward myself over the coming year and I hope that others will join me. For, while it may seem strange, to some of our more quantitatively, or philosophically minded, colleagues to build a fifteen-year research project around an unexpected emotional response, it has proved a highly profitable way to do research. For the gift of this emotional connection given by a comparative stranger, in a distant land, led me into Shimla's landscapes. Here I came to know its human and non-human people, its past, its present and its dreams for the future. It is out of this process that this book was forged, which aims to create a ripple effect that will transform understanding of the value of Christian communities in the Western Himalayas. Beyond this, I offer the wisdom that I derived from a guided engagement with this landscape to those who live in other places and at other times, in the belief that it will prove helpful for all who seek to understand the way that religion as a process of enskilment opens possibilities for living sensitively in the world. Finally, I offer this book both to those who dwell in Shimla now and those who will remake its landscape in the future; including those, who like me, would seek to develop a way of working with material religion that explores the rich possibilities of a other people's engagement with the environment, while acknowledging that the analyst is also, undeniably, entangled in the processes that they seek to explore.

Notes

Chapter 1

1 *Material Religion: Embodiment, Materiality, Technology*, held at Duke University, September 2015.

Chapter 2

1 The way that engagement with both nature and sport can trigger an emotional state of uplift that is reminiscent of Durkheim's (2001 [1912]: 163) concept of religious effervescence has been wonderfully discussed by Eric Dunning (2013) and need not be repeated here.
2 The concept of a body of material that might be termed myth is central to this book's exploration of material religion and we will explore both the value of the term and exactly why I apply it to a wide-range of material in a later section (Chapter Four), where the idea becomes crucial to the argument. For now, however it is simply important to note that by terming the recitals of Stokes' life a form of mythology I am not intending to imply that they are contrived, made-up, or untrue. To the contrary, I intend to suggest that they reveal important truths about contemporary life in the Shimla Hills.
3 Stokes' conversion is often couched as being in response to British political aggression, however his granddaughter relates a more personal combination of push and pull factors. The first of these is the desire to belong, which it is suggested Stokes came to believe could only happen with full adoption of Hinduism, spurred by events such as being stuck in a blizzard with his young family and abandoned by local Hindus. The second of these is the pull of Hindu mythology, which apparently was initiated by his own mother's instance that before converting Hindus you have to understand them. Hindustan Times *Granddaughter introduces American who brought apple to Himachal*, 22 October 2013.

Chapter 3

1. A good example of this is when, on her return to Britain, Fanny notes how 'wretchedly mean [it looks], especially the houses ... it was cold and gloomy ... no wonder ... I felt a little disgusted.' (Parks 1850: 330–331).
2. Solomon (2013) has thoroughly documented and discussed the range and significance of Human/Monkey interaction in Shimla.

Chapter 4

1. This is not an unusual reaction and several accounts record a similar feeling of Christ Church as a happily displaced sacred space (cf Jutla 2000, Pandey 2014, Khan 2014).
2. For all its problems, 'Pulleyar and the Lord Buddha' (1962) remains an excellent example of the way these seemingly distinct categories are profitably rolled together in Leach's analysis.
3. For more information see 'Caroline Homans and Neville Priestley Wedding', *The Boston Post*, 2 September 1896.

Chapter 5

1. Chapters Five and Six draw some of their ideas from part of an earlier article (Miles-Watson 2012), published in *Suomen Antropologi*. These chapters however are not a simple replication of that article, for they contain a substantial amount of important information/analysis that cannot be found there and there is some material in that article that is not covered in either of these chapters.
2. The term 'soundscape' has been technically deployed to suggest a sonic way of knowing that is opposed to a visual way of knowing (Helmrich 2007: 623), this debate is valuable for drawing our attention beyond the purely visual aspects of landscape, but also has issues arising from both its situatedness (cf Ingold 2007c). In using the term, I do not wish to imply that I am taking a stand on one side or the other of this debate. I simply employ it as a convenient shorthand for the auditory elements of the general landscape.

Chapter 6

1. I first introduced the concept of Cathedralscapes in an earlier book chapter (Miles-Watson 2015). The information contained in this subsection however is not a

simple replication of that article, for it both contains information that cannot be found there and does not discuss some of the material that is covered in that piece.

Chapter 7

1   I am in no way here wanting to suggest that Bergmann's development of this concept is dependent upon my own. Rather I outline the chronology of the publications listed above as a way of demonstrating that both strains of thought develop independently in similar, if not identical, directions, from a common source (Ingold), across an overlapping period of time, one in the sphere of anthropology the other in the realm of theology. Indeed, I can see the seeds of the development of Bergmann's thought in publications that predate his outlining of a clear treatise on religion as skill (2015, 2017). Several earlier works (2009, 2010, 2012), for example, mention the idea of the spiritual and aesthetic skills needed to live well in the modern world while discussing the challenge of climate change.

Chapter 8

1   This chapter draws some of its ideas from part of an earlier article (Miles-Watson 2013), published in the *Journal of Culture and Religion*. It is not however a simple replication of that article, for it both contains information that cannot be found there and does not discuss some of the material that is covered in that piece.

References

Ames, E. S. (1928), 'Religion and Art', *The Journal of Religion*, 8 (3): 371–383.
Aravecchia, N. (2001), 'Hermitages and Spatial Analysis: Use of Space at the Kellia', in S. McNally (ed.), *Shaping Community: The Art and Archaeology of Monasticism*, 29–38, Oxford: Archaeopress.
Asimos, V. (2019). *The Slender Man Mythos: a structuralist analysis of an online mythology* (Doctoral dissertation, Durham University).
Baker C, Miles-Watson J (2010), 'Faith and traditional capitals: defining the public scope of spiritual and religious capital', *Implicit Religion* 13(1):17–69.
Baker C, Skinner H (2006) 'Faith in action—the dynamic connection between spiritual and religious capital', William Temple Foundation, Manchester
Bascom, W. (1965), 'The forms of folklore: Prose narratives', *The Journal of American Folklore*, 78(307), 3–20.
Basso, K. H. (1996), *Wisdom Sits in Places: Landscape and Language among the Western Apache*, Albuquerque: University of New Mexico Press.
Bateson, G. (1965), *Naven: a survey of the problems suggested by a composite picture of the culture of a New Guinea tribe drawn from three points of view*, Stanford University Press.
Bateson, G. (2000), *Steps to an Ecology of Mind: Collected Essays in Anthropology, Psychiatry, Evolution, and Epistemology*, Chicago: University of Chicago Press.
Bauman, C. M. (2008), *Christian Identity and Dalit Religion in Hindu India, 1868–1947*, Grand Rapids, Mich: William B. Eerdmans Pub. Co.
Bayly, S. (1989), *Saints, Goddesses and Kings: Muslims and Christians in South Indian Society, 1700–1900*, Cambridge: Cambridge University Press.
Bayly, S. (2001) *Caste, Society and Politics in India From the Eighteenth Century to the Modern Age*, Cambridge: Cambridge University Press.
Berger, P. (1967), *The sacred canopy;: elements of a sociological theory of religion*, New York: Doubleday,.
Berger, P. & Heidemann, F. (2013), *The Modern Anthropology of India: Ethnography, Themes and Theory*, London: Routledge.
Bergmann, S. (2009) 'Climate Change Changes Religion', *Studia Theologica - Nordic Journal of Theology*, 63(2): 98–118
Bergmann, S. (2012). 'Religion in the built environment: Aesth/ethics, ritual and memory in lived urban space'. Gómez, L. & Van Herck, W. (eds.). (2012). *The sacred in the city*. 73–95, London: Bloomsbury.
Bergmann, S. (2015), 'Making oneself at home in climate change: Religion as a skill of creative adaptation', in Brunn, S, D. (ed.), *The Changing World Religion Map* (pp. 187–201). Springer, Dordrecht.

Bergmann, S. (2017), *Religion, Space, and the Environment,* London: Routledge.
Bergmann, S. & Gerten, D. (2010). *Religion and dangerous environmental change: Transdisciplinary perspectives on the ethics of climate and sustainability.* Berlin: LIT.
Berreman, G. D. (1972), *Hindus of the Himalayas: Ethnography and Change,* Berkeley: University of California Press.
Bhardwaj, D. S. Chaudhary, M. & Kandari, O. P. (1998), *Domestic Tourism in India,* New Delhi: Indus Publ. Co.
Bhasin, R. (2009) 'Quite the adopted child: the legacy of Shimla's architecture', in M. Chaudhry (ed.), *Whispering Deodars: Writings from Shimla Hills,* New Delhi: Rupa.
Bhasin, V. (1998), *Himalayan Ecology, Transhumance and Social Organisation; Gaddis of Himachal Pradesh,* Delhi: Kamla-Raj Enterprises.
Bhasin, R. (1992). *Simla, the summer capital of British India.* New Delhi: Viking.
Bialecki, J. Haynes, N. and Robbins, J. (2008), 'The Anthropology of Christianity', *Religion Compass,* 2 (6): 1139–1158.
Bialecki, J. Coleman, S. Csordas, T. Gooren, H. Howell, B. Lurhmann, T. Robbins, J. Shoaps, R. (2010), 'Belief, Participation, Circulation: Challenges in Participant-observer Fieldwork with Evangelical, Pentecostal, and Charismatic Christianities'. Discussion at the *Annual Meeting of the American Anthropological Association,* New Orleans, November 2010.
Bielo, J. S. (2017), 'Replication as Religious Practice, Temporality as Religious Problem', *History and Anthropology,* 28 (2): 131–148.
Bishop, P. (2000), 'The Death of Shangri-La: The Utopian Imagination and the Dialectics of Hope'. *A Journal of Social Ecology,* 2, 7–26.
Bisht, G (2018), 'After Allahabad, Shimla could be renamed: Himachal govt wants to call it Shyamala', *Hindustan Times,* 21 October.
Blaikie, P. and Brookfield, H, (1987), *Land degradation and society,* Methuen, New York
Boas, F. (1927), *Primitive Art,* Oslo: H. Aschehoug & Co.
Boddy and M. Lambek (eds.), *A Companion to the Anthropology of Religion,* 257–273, Hoboken, NJ: John Wiley and Sons.
Bourdieu, P. (1983), 'Forms of Capital', in Richardson (ed.), *Handbook of Theory and Research for the Sociology of Education,*, 241–258. New York: Greenwood Press.
Bowman, M. & Valk, U. (2014), 'Introduction: Vernacular Religion, Generic Expressions and the Dynamics of Belief', in M. Bowman and U. Valk (eds.), *Vernacular Religion in Everyday Life,* 13–32, London: Routledge.
Boyd, J. (1928), 'Travelling with Troops in India', *BMJ Military Health* 51:300–306.
Boylston, T. (2013), 'Food, Life, and Material Religion in Ethiopian Orthodox Christianity', in Boddy, J. & Lambek, M. (eds.), *A Companion to the Anthropology of Religion,* Hoboken, NJ: John Wiley & Sons.
Brookfield, H. (1984), 'Intensification revisited', *Pacific Viewpoint* 25(1):15–44
Brookfield, H. (1986), 'Intensification intensified' *Archaeology Ocean* 31(3):177–180.
Brookfield, H. (2001a), *Exploring Agrodiversity.* New York: Columbia University Press.

Brookfield, H. (2001b), 'Intensification, and alternative approaches to agricultural change', *Asia Pacific Viewpoint* 42(2–3):181–192.

Braun, H. (1972), *Cathedral Architecture*, New York: Crane, Russak.

Buck, Edward, (1925), *Simla Past and Present*. Bombay: The Times Press.

Buckley, M. (2008). Shangri-La: A travel guide to the Himalayan dream. Chalfont St. Peter: Bradt Travel Guides.

Campbell, H. A. & Lövheim, M. (2011), 'Introduction: Rethinking the Online–Offline Connection in the Study of Religion Online', *Information, Communication & Society*, 14 (8): 1083–1096.

Cannell, F. (2006), *The Anthropology of Christianity*, Durham: Duke University Press.

'Caroline Homans and Neville Priestley Wedding', The Boston Post, 2 September 1896.

Carsten, J. (2008). *Ghosts of memory: essays on remembrance and relatedness*, Oxford: John Wiley & Sons.

Caplan, Lionel. (1987), *Class and Culture in Urban India: Fundamentalism in a Christian Community*, Oxford: Clarendon Press.

Carey, W. H. & Wyman & Co. (1870), *A Guide to Simla: With a Descriptive Account of the Neighbouring Sanitaria, Subathoo, Dugshaie, Sunawar, Kussowlie, Kotegurh, Chini, &c.* Calcutta: Wyman & Co.

'Caroline Homans and Neville Priestley Wedding', The Boston Post, 2 September 1896.

Carrithers, M. (2000), 'On polytropy: Or the Natural Condition of Spiritual Cosmopolitanism in India: The Digambar Jain Case'. *Modern Asian Studies*, 34 (4): 831–861.

Carsten, J. (2008). *Ghosts of memory: essays on remembrance and relatedness*, Oxford: John Wiley & Sons.

Castañeda, Q. (2006), 'Ethnography in the Forest: An Analysis of Ethics in the Morals of Anthropology', *Cultural Anthropology*, 21 (1): 121–145.

Cavendish, A. (1995), 'Major General J. T. Boileau, F. R. S., R. E.' *Journal of the Society for Army Historical Research*, 73 (296): 225–233.

Certeau, M. D. (1984), *The practice of everyday life*, Berkeley: University of California Press.

Chandramouli, C. (2011), *Census of India 2011: Provisional Population Totals*, New Delhi: Office of Registrar General and Census Commissioner, India.

Chatterton, E. (1924), *A History of the Church of England in India since the Early Days of the East India Company*, Toronto: Society for Promoting Christian Knowledge.

Chaudhry, M. (2005), *Ghost stories of Shimla hills*. New Delhi: Rupa & Co.

Chug, U. (2000), *Politics of a Dispersed Minority Community: A Study of the Christians of Himachal Pradesh*, PhD thesis, Himachal Pradesh, India: Himachal Pradesh University.

Clymer, K. J. (1990), 'Samuel Evans Stokes, Mahatma Gandhi, and Indian Nationalism', *Pacific Historical Review*, 59(1): 51–76.

Colebrooke, H. T. (1827), 'On the Valley of the Setlej River, in the Himalaya Mountains, from the Journal of Captain A. Gerard', *Transactions of the Royal Asiatic Society of Great Britain and Ireland, 1* (2): 343–380.

Coleman J (1988) 'Social capital in the creation of human capital', *American Journal of Sociology*, 94:95–120.

Coleman, S. (2019), 'On praying in an old country: ritual, replication, heritage, and powers of adjacency in English cathedrals', *Religion, 49*(1), 120–141.

Coleman, S. (2015), 'Accidental Pilgrims: Passions and Ambiguities of Travel to Christian Shrines in Europe', *Brown Journal of World Affairs*, 22 (1): 71–82.

Coleman, S. & Bowman, M. (2019), 'Religion in cathedrals: pilgrimage, heritage, adjacency, and the politics of replication in Northern Europe', *Religion, 49*(1), 1–23.

Coleman, S. & Crang, M. (2002), *Tourism: Between Place and Performance*, New York: Berghahn Books.

Collins, Paul M. (2007), *Christian Inculturation in India*, Aldershot: Ashgate.

Conkey, M. (2013), 'Style, Design and Function', in Tilley, Keane, Küchler, Rowlands & P. Spyer (eds.), *Handbook of Material Culture*, 355–360, London: Sage.

Cox, J. (2002), *Imperial Fault Lines: Christianity and Colonial Power in India, 1818–1940*, Stanford: Stanford University Press.

Cox, R. (2011), 'Thinking Through Movement: Practising Martial Arts and Writing Ethnography', in T. Ingold, *Redrawing Anthropology: Materials, Movements, Lines*, 65–76, Farnham, Surrey: Ashgate.

Davie, G. (2007), 'Vicarious Religion: A Methodological Challenge', in N.T. Ammerman, *Everyday religion: Observing Modern Religious Lives*, 21–36. S.l: OUP USA.

Davies, D. J. (2011), *Emotion, Identity, and Religion: Hope, Reciprocity, and Otherness*, Oxford: Oxford University Press.

Davies, E. (1804), *Celtic researches: On the origin, traditions & language, of the ancient Britons: with some introductory sketches, on primitive society*, London: J. Booth

Della Dora, V. & Sooväli, H. (2009), 'Sacred Space and Uncomfortable Memories: The Alexander Nevski Russian Orthodox Cathedral in Tallinn, Estonia', Leveque, Arbol and Pop (eds.), *Heritage, Images, Memory of European Landscapes*, 215–39, Paris: L'Harmattan.

Dempsey, C. G. (2001), *Kerala Christian Sainthood: Collisions of Culture and Worldview in South India*, Oxford: Oxford University Press.

Dobe, T. (2015), *Hindu Christian Faqir: Modern Monks, Global Christianity, and Indian Sainthood*, Oxford: Oxford University Press.

Dumont, L. (1970), *Homo Hierarchicus*, Chicago, IL: University of Chicago Press

Dunning, E. (2013). *Sport matters: Sociological studies of sport, violence and civilisation*. London: Routledge.

Durkheim, E. (2001), *The Elementary Forms of Religious Life*, Oxford: Oxford University Press.

Dutt, M. N. (1896), *Markandeya Puranam*, Calcutta: Elysium Press.

Eden, E. (2010), *'Up the country': Letters written to her sister from the upper provinces of India*. Cambridge: Cambridge University Press.

Eck, D. L. (1987), 'Mountains' in Eliade, M. (ed.), *The Encyclopedia of Religion*, (Vol. 10) New York: Macmillan, 130–134.

Eck, D. L. (2012), *India: A Sacred Geography*, New York, N.Y: Three Rivers Press.

Eigler, F. U. (2014), *Heimat, Space, Narrative: Toward a Transnational Approach to Flight and Expulsion*, Woodbridge, Suffolk: Boydell & Brewer.

Eliade, M. (1959) *The Sacred and the Profane: The Nature of Religion*, New York, NY: Harvest.

Eliade, M. (1963) *Myth and Reality*, New York: Harper & Row.

Elmore, M. (2016), *Becoming Religious in a Secular Age*, Oakland, California: University of California Press.

Emery, E. (2001), *Romancing the Cathedral: Gothic Architecture in Fin-de-Siècle French Culture*, Albany: State University of New York Press.

Emilsen, W. (1998), 'The Great Gulf Fixed: Samuel Stokes and the Brotherhood of the Imitation of Jesus', in Oddie, G. (ed.), *Religious Traditions in South Asia: Interaction and Change*, 91–106, Richmond: Curzon.

Engelke, M. (2002), 'The Problem of Belief: Evans-Pritchard and Victor Turner on The Inner Life', *Anthropology Today*, 18 (6): 3–8.

Engelke, M. Tomlinson, M. (2006), *The Limits of Meaning: Case Studies in the Anthropology of Christianity*, New York: Berghahn Books.

Ewing, K. (1994), 'Dreams from a Saint: Anthropological Atheism and the Temptation to Believe', *American Anthropologist, New Series*, 96 (3): 571–583.

Field, J. (2003), *Social Capital*, Routledge: London.

Fraser, F. J. (1896), 'Little Number Three.' *Belgravia: a London magazine*, London: Chatto and Windus, 356–437.

Freud, S. (1918), *Totem and taboo: Resemblances between the psychic lives of savages and neurotics*, London: Kegan Paul.

Frykenberg, R E. (2010), *Christianity in India: from Beginnings to the Present*, Oxford: Oxford University Press.

Fuller, C. (1976), 'Kerala Christians and the Caste System', *Man NS*, 11 (1): 53–70.

Galinier, J. (2004), 'A Lévi-Straussian Controversy Revisited: The Implicit Mythology of Rituals in a Mesoamerican Context', *Journal of the Southwest*, 46 (4): 661–677.

Gazetteer (1889), *Gazetteer of the Simla district, 1888–89*, Lahore: Sang-e-Meel Publications.

Gazetteer (1904) *Gazetteer of the Simla district, 1904*. New Delhi: Indus Pub. Co

Geddes, J. (1872), 'Art. VIII.-Independent Section', *Calcutta Review*, 55 (110): 340–381.

Geertz, C. (1966), 'Religion as a Cultural System', in Banton, M. (ed.), *Anthropological approaches to the study of religion*, 87–125, London: Tavistock.

Gillespie, M. (1995), *A Case-Study in the Interpretation of Two TV Versions of The Mahabharata in a Hindu Family in West London*, 354–80, New York and London: Routledge.

Goldsworthy, A. (2009), *Andy Goldsworthy*, Eastbourne: Gardeners Books.

Gooch, P. (1998), *At the Tail of the Buffalo: Van Gujjar Pastoralists Between the Forest and the World Arena*, Lund: Lunds Universitets Publication.
Gow, P. (2001), *An Amazonian Myth and its History*, Oxford: Oxford University Press
Greenagel, F. L. (2001). *The New Jersey churchscape: encountering eighteenth and nineteenth century churches*. Rutgers University Press.
Griffiths, B. (1982), *The Marriage of East and West: A Sequel to The Golden String*, Springfield, IL: Templegate.
Grimes, R. L. (2011), 'Ritual', *Material Religion*, 7(1): 76–83.
Guest, M. (2007), *Evangelical Identity and Contemporary Culture: A Congregational Study in Innovation*, Milton Keynes: Paternoster.
Halbmayer, E. (2012), 'Amerindian Mereology: Animism, Analogy, and the Multiverse', *Indiana*, (29): 103–125.
Hall, S. (1991), 'Old and New Identities, Old and New Ethnicities', in A. King (ed.), *Culture, Globalization and the World System*, London: Macmillan.
Hall, S. (1999), 'Un-settling "the Heritage", Re-imagining the Post-nation Whose heritage?' *Third Text*, 13 (49): 3–13.
Harkin, M. (2000), 'Sacred Places, Scarred Spaces.' *Wicazo Sa Review* 15 (1): 49–70
Harvey, G. (2014), *Food, Sex and Strangers: Understanding Religion as Everyday Life*, New York: Routledge.
Hausner, S. L. (2008), *Wandering with Sadhus: Ascetics in the Hindu Himalayas*, Bloomington, Ind: Indiana University Press.
Hedlund, R. (2000), *Quest for Identity: India's Churches of Indigenous Origin*, Delhi: Indian Society for the Propagation of Christian Knowledge
Hendry, J. (1992), 'The Paradox of Friendship in the Field: Analysis of Long Term AngloJapanese Relationship', in J. Okley and H. Callaway (eds.), *Anthropology and Autobiography*, London: Routledge.
Helmreich, S. (2007). 'An anthropologist underwater: Immersive soundscapes, submarine cyborgs, and transductive ethnography'. *American Ethnologist*, 34(4), 621–641.
Hicks, D. & Beaudry, M. C. (2010), *The Oxford Handbook of Material Culture Studies*, Oxford: Oxford University Press.
Hilton, J. (1933), *Lost Horizon*, London: Macmillan.
Hinnells, J. R. & King, R. (2007), *Religion and Violence in South Asia: Theory and Practice*, London: Routledge.
Howell, B. (2007), 'The Repugnant Cultural Other Speaks Back: Christian Identity as Ethnographic 'Standpoint'', *Anthropological Theory*, 7 (4): 371–391.
Houseman, M. (1988), *Naven Or The Other Self: A Relational Approach to Ritual Action*, Leiden: Brill.
Hugh-Jones, C. (1988), *From the milk river: spatial and temporal processes in Northwest Amazonia*, Cambridge: Cambridge University Press.
Hugh-Jones, S. (1979), *The Palm and the Pleiades: Initiation and Cosmology in Northwest Amazonia*, Cambridge: Cambridge University Press.
Hugh-Jones, S. (1988), 'The Gun and the Bow: Myths of White Men and Indians', *L'Homme*, Vol. 106–107.

Hugh-Jones, S. (2007), Interview by Alan Macfarlane, Anthropological Ancestors Visual Archive, 14 February 2007.
Hulme, L. (2013), *The Religious Life of Dress: Global Fashion and Faith*, London: Bloomsbury.
Ingold, T. (2000), *The Perception of the Environment: Essays in Livelihood, Dwelling and Skill*, London: Routledge.
Ingold, T. (June 01, 2007a), 'Materials against Materiality', *Archaeological Dialogues*, 14 (1): 1–16.
Ingold, T. (2007b), *Lines: A Brief History*, London: Routledge.
Ingold, T. (2007c). 'Against soundscape', in Carlyle Angus (ed.), *Autumn leaves: Sound and the environment in artistic practice*, Paris: Double Entendre, 10–13.
Ingold, T. (2007d), 'Earth, Sky, Wind, and Weather', *Journal of the Royal Anthropological Institute* 13: S19–S38.
Ingold, T. (2010), 'Footprints through the Weather-World: Walking, Breathing, Knowing', *Journal of the Royal Anthropological Institute*, 16: S121–S139.
Ingold, T. (2011), *Being Alive: Essays on Movement, Knowledge and Description*, London: Routledge.
Ingold, T. (2013), *Making: Anthropology, Archaeology, Art and Architecture*, London: Routledge.
Ingold, T. (2015), *The Life of Lines*, London: Routledge.
Ingold, T. (2018), 'Five Questions of Skill', *Cultural Geographies*, 25 (1): 159–163.
Irvine, R. D. G. (January 01, 2011), 'The Architecture of Stability: Monasteries and the Importance of Place in a World of Non-places', *Etnofoor*, 23 (1): 29–49.
Jain, P. (2009), 'From Kil-Arni to Anthony: Portrayal of Christians in Indian Films', *Visual Anthropology*, 23(1): 13–19.
Jeremiah, A. H. M. (2013), *Community and Worldview Among Paraiyars of South India: 'Lived' Religion*, London: Bloomsbury.
Joshi, V. (2012), *A Matter of Belief: Christian Conversion and Healing in North-East India*, New York: Berghahn.
Jutla, R. S. (2000), 'Visual Image of the City: Tourists' Versus Residents' Perception of Simla, a Hill Station in Northern India', *Tourism Geographies*, 2 (4): 404–420.
Kahf, M. (2003), *E-mails from Scheherazad*, Gainesville: University Press of Florida.
Kanwar, P. (2003), *Imperial Simla: The Political Culture of the Raj*, Delhi: Oxford University Press.
Kanwar, Y. (1996). 'St Michael's Cathedral, Shimla', *The Hindu*, 30 December
Kapadia, N. (2001), Triumphs and Disasters: The Story of Indian Football, 1889–2000, *Soccer & Society*, 2(2), 17–40.
Kashyap, C. M. and Post, E. (1961) '"Yankee in Khadi: The Story of Samuel Evans Stokes," *Span* 1(3): 23–28
Kaufmann, S. (1981), 'A Christian Caste in Hindu Society: Religious Leadership and Social Conflict among the Paravas of Southern Tamilnadu', *Modern Asian Studies*, 15(2), 203–234.

Keith, A. B. (1915), 'The Date of the Ramayana', *The Journal of the Royal Asiatic Society of Great Britain and Ireland*, 1(1–2): 318–328.
Kennedy, D. K. (1996), *The Magic Mountains: Hill Stations and the British Raj*, Berkeley: University of California Press.
Kent, Eliza F. (2004), *Converting Women: Gender and Protestant Christianity in Colonial South India*, Oxford: Oxford University Press.
Khan, S. (2014), 'Walking the Walk: an Evaluation of Pedestrian Tourism on the 'Mall Road'', Shimla. *International Journal of Hospitality and Tourism Systems*, 7(1): 39–48.
Kilde, J. H. (2005), 'Material Expression and Maternalism in Mary Baker Eddy's Boston Churches: How Architecture and Gender Compromised Mind.' *Material Religion*, 1 (2): 164–197.
Kinsley, D. R. (1998), *Tantric Visions of the Divine Feminine: The Ten Mahāvidyās*, Delhi: Motilal Banarsidass.
Knott, K. (2010), 'Cutting through the Postsecular City: A Spatial Interrogation', in *Exploring the Postsecular, International Studies in Religion and Society*, 13: 19–38.
Kunin, S. D. (2012), Structuralism and Implicit Myth', *Suomen Antropologi: Journal of the Finnish Anthropological Society*, 37(4).
Laycock, J. (2010), 'Myth Sells: Mattel's Commission of The Masters of the Universe Bible', *The Journal of Religion and Popular Culture*, 22 (2): 4–4.
Leach, E. R. (1962), 'Pulleyar and the Lord Buddha: an aspect of religious syncretism in Ceylon', *Psychoanalytic Review*, 49(2): 81–102.
Leppman, E. J. (2005), 'Appalachian churchscapes: the case of Menifee County, Kentucky', *Southeastern Geographer*, *45*(1), 83–103.
Lefebvre, H. (1991), *The production of space*, Blackwell: Oxford.
Lévi-Strauss, C. (1955). 'The Structural Study of Myth'. *The Journal of American Folklore*, 68 (270): 428–444
Lévi-Strauss, C. (1967),'The Story of Asdiwal' in Leach, E. (ed.), *The structural study of myth and totemism: material presented at a conference on recent anthropological studies of myth and totemism*. London: Tavistock, 1–49.
Lévi-Strauss, C. (1977), *Structural Anthropology: Volume I*, London: Allen Lane.
Lévi-Strauss, C. (1981), *The Naked Man*, New York: Harper & Row.
Lévi-Strauss, C. (1983), *The Way of the Masks*, London: Cape.
Lévi-Strauss, C. (1988). *Jealous Potter*. University of Chicago Press.
Lévi-Strauss, C. (1990). *The raw and the cooked*. Chicago: University of Chicago Press.
Lévi-Strauss, C. (1995). *The story of Lynx*. University of Chicago Press.
Lorenzen, D. N. (1999), 'Who Invented Hinduism?', *Comparative Studies in Society and History*, *41* (4): 630–659.
Lucas, E, D, and Thakur Das, F. (1938), *The Rural Church in the Punjab: a Study of Social, Economic, Educational and Religious Conditions Prevailing amongst Certain Village Christian Communities in the Sialkot District*, Lahore: Northern India Print. and Pub. Co.

Lutgendorf, P. (1994), 'My Hanuman is Bigger than Yours', *History of Religions*, 33 (3): 211–245.
Macaulay, D. (1973), *Cathedral: The Story of its Construction*. New York: Houghton Mifflin Harcourt.
MacLean, S. (1992), 'Hallaig' [with English translation, 'Hallaig'], *Lines Review*, 120 (3): 14–17.
Madan, T. N. (1965), *Family and Kinship: A study of the Pandits of Rural Kashmir*, Bombay: Asia Publishing House.
Mäkelä, K. (2008), 'Ethical Codes and Ethical Control in the Social Sciences', *Suomen Antropologi: Journal of the Finnish Anthropological Society*. 33 (3): 57–66.
Malinowski, B. (1922), *Argonauts of the Western Pacific: An Account of Native Enterprise and Adventure in the Archipelagos of Melanesian New Guinea*, London: G. Routledge & Sons.
Malinowski, B. (1926). *Myth in primitive psychology*. New York: Norton.
Marcus, L. (2007), 'Spatial capital and how to measure it: an outline of an analytical theory of the social performativity of urban form'. In: *Proceedings of the 6th international space syntax symposium*, İstanbul
Marriott, M. (1966), 'The Feast of Love', in M. Singer (ed.), *Krishna: Myths, Rites, and Attitudes*, Honolulu : East-West Center Press.
Mather, J. (2017). Captivating Readers: Middlebrow Aesthetics and James Hilton's Lost Horizon. *CEA Critic*, 79(2), 231–243.
Mathur, N. (2015), 'A "Remote" Town in the Indian Himalaya', *Modern Asian Studies*, 49 (2): 365–392.
McDannell, C. (1995), *Material Christianity: Religion and Popular Culture in America*, New Haven: Yale University Press.
McKay, A. (2015), *Kailas Histories: renunciate traditions and the construction of Himalayan sacred geography*, Leiden: Brill.
McLean, A. (2007), 'When the Borders of Research and Personal Life become Blurred: Thorny Issues In Conducting Dementia Research', in A. McLean and A. Leibing (eds.), *The Shadow Side of Field Work: Theorizing the Blurred Borders between Ethnography and Life*, 262–287, Malden, MA: Blackwell.
Merleau-Ponty, M. (1962), *Phenomenology of Perception*, London: Routledge.
Meyer, B. (2015a), 'Picturing the Invisible: Visual Culture and the Study of Religion', *Method & Theory in the Study of Religion*, 27 (4–5): 333–360.
Meyer, B. (2015b), 'How Pictures Matter. Religious Objects and the Imagination in Ghana', in Ø. Fuglerud & L. Wainwright (eds.), *Material Mediations: People and Things in a World of Movement*, Oxford: Berghahn.
Meyer, B. Morgan, D. Paine, C. & Plate, S. B. (2010), 'The Origin and Mission of Material Religion', *Religion*, 40 (3): 207–211.
Miles-Watson, J. (2006), *A neo-structuralist analysis of the Mabinogion* (Doctoral dissertation, University of Aberdeen (United Kingdom)).

Miles-Watson, J. (2008), 'Incorporating and obviating history: the importance of Lévi-Strauss cold culture theory for contemporary landscape studies'. Paper presented *at Estonian Institute of Humanities Symposium in Social and Cultural Theory: Taking the Spatial Turn*, Käsmu, Estonia, July 24–25.

Miles-Watson, J. (2010), 'Ethnographic insights into happiness', in Steedman, I. Atherton, J. R. & Graham, E. (eds.), *The practices of happiness: Political economy, religion and wellbeing*, 125–33, London: Routledge.

Miles-Watson, J. (2012) 'The cathedral on the ridge and the implicit mythology of the Shimla hills', *Suomen antropologi journal of the Finnish anthropological society*. 37 (4):. 30–46.

Miles-Watson, J. (2013), 'Pipe Organs and Satsang: Contemporary Worship in Shimla's Colonial Churches', *Culture and Religion*, 14(2): 204–222.

Miles-Watson, J. (2015a) 'Indian summers: A Tale of Theft and Betrayal', https://durhamabbeyhouse.wordpress.com/2015/02/27/.

Miles-Watson J. (2015b), 'Ruptured Landscapes, Sacred Spaces and the Stretching of Landscape Capital', in H. Sooväli-Sepping, H. Reinert and J. Miles-Watson (eds.), *Ruptured Landscapes. Landscape Series, Vol 19*: Springer, Dordrech.

Miles-Watson, J. (2016), 'Teachings of Tara: Sacred Place and Human Wellbeing in the Shimla Hills', *Anthropology in Action*, 23(3): 30–42.

Miles-Watson, J. (2019), 'From Page to Place', in J. Miles-Watson & V. Asimos (eds.), *The Bloomsbury Reader in the Study of Myth*, 204–207, London: Bloomsbury.

Miles-Watson, J. & Asimos, V. (2019), *The Bloomsbury Reader in the Study of Myth*, London: Bloomsbury.

Miles-Watson, J. Korpela, M. (2010), 'Indiascapes: Reflecting on India at the 11th EASA Conference', *Suomen Antropologi: Journal of the Finnish Anthropological Society*, 35 (3): 71–79.

Miles-Watson, J. & Miles-Watson, S. (2011). 'Conflicts and Connections in the Landscape of the Manimahesh Pilgrimage', *Tourism: An International Interdisciplinary Journal*, 59 (3): 319–333.

Miller, D. (2005), *Materiality*, Durham N.C: Duke University Press.

Miller, D. (2011), *Tales from Facebook*, Cambridge: Polity.

Millington, P. (1898), 'Someone had Blundered', *Temple Bar*, 1860–1906, 115 (456): 362–383.

Mir, S. (2014). *Muslim American women on campus: Undergraduate social life and identity*. UNC Press Books.

Monchamp, A. (2008), 'Ethics, Advocacy and the Truth: A Response to Klaus Mäkelä's "Ethical Codes and Ethical Control in the Social Sciences"', *Suomen Antropologi: Journal of the Finnish Anthropological Society*, 33 (3): 57–66.

Morgan, D. (2010), *Religion and Material Culture: The Matter of Belief*, London: Routledge.

Morrow, V. (1999), *Conceptualising social capital in relation to the well-being of children and young people: a critical review*. Sociological Review 47(4): 744–765

Mosse, D. (1996), 'South Indian Christians, Purity/Impurity, and the Caste System: Death Ritual in a Tamil Roman Catholic Community'. *Journal of the Royal Anthropological Institute*, 2 (3): 461–483.

Mosse, D. (2012), *The Saint in the Banyan Tree: Christianity and Caste Society in India*, Berkeley: University of California Press.

Mullen, E. (2016), 'Orientalist commercializations: Tibetan Buddhism in American popular film', *Journal of Religion & Film*, 2(2) 5: 1–16.

Murphy, J. (2011), 'From Place to exile', *Transactions of the Institute of British Geographers*, 36 (4): 473–478.

Nagar, D. (2006), 'Hindu Myths', *Journal of American Folklore*, 119 (474): 496–497.

Nagy, J. F. (1986), 'Orality in Medieval Irish Narrative: An Overview', *Oral Tradition*, 272, 301.

Nanda, M. (2003). *Prophets facing backward: postmodern critiques of science and Hindu nationalism in India*. Rutgers University Press.

Narayan, K. (1993), 'How Native Is a "Native" Anthropologist?', *American Anthropologist*, 95 (3): 671–686.

Negi, G. R. (2002), 'Christian Missionary Activities and their Impact on Himachal Pradesh AD 1840–1947', PhD thesis, Himachal Pradesh University, Himachal, India.

Nelson, R. K. (1983), *Make Prayers to the Raven: A Koyukon View of the Northern Forest*, Chicago: University of Chicago Press.

Nelson, R. K. (1989), *The Island Within*, San Francisco: North Point Press.

Olney, F. & Burton, L. (2011), 'Parish Church and Village Community: The Interchange of Social Capital in a Rural Setting', *Rural Theology*, 9 (1): 27–38.

Olwig, K. (1996), 'Recovering the Substantive Nature of Landscape', *Annals of the Association of American Geographers*, 86 (4): 630–653.

Palang, H. Printsmann, A. Sooväli, H. (2007). 'Seasonality and Landscapes', in Palang, H. Sooväli, H. Printsmann, A. (eds.), *Seasonal Landscapes*, 1–11, Dordrech: Springer.

Pálsson, G. (1994), 'Enskilment at sea', *Man*, 29(4): 901–927.

Pandey, S. (2014), 'Simla or Shimla: the Indian Political Re-appropriation of Little England', in D. Maudlin and M. Vellinga (eds.), *Consuming Architecture ; On the Occupation, Appropriation and Interpretation of Buildings*, 149–169, London: Routledge.

Parks, F. (1850), *Wanderings of a Pilgrim, in Search of the Picturesque, During Four-and-twenty Years in the East: With Revelations of Life in the Zenāna* (Vol. 2), London: Pellham Richardson.

Parry, J. P. (1979), *Caste and Kinship in Kangra*, London: Routledge & Paul.

Pass, A. (2011), 'British Women Missionaries in India, c. 1917–1950', PhD Thesis, University of Oxford, England.

Patulny, R. (2009), 'The Sociability of Nations: International Comparisons in Bonding, Bridging and Linking Social Capital', in G. T. Svendsen & G. L. H. Svendsen (eds.), *Handbook of Social Capital: The Troika of Sociology, Political Science and Economics*, 402–428, Cheltenham: Edward Elgar.

Peirano, M. G. S. (2000), *The Anthropological Analysis of Rituals*, Brasília: Departamento de Antropologia, Universidade de Brasília.

Pels, P. (2008), 'What has Anthropology Learned from the Anthropology of Colonialism?', *Social Anthropology*, 16 (3): 280–299.

Phan, P. C. (2011), *Christianities in Asia*, Oxford: Wiley-Blackwell.

Pinault, D. (2001), *Horse of Karbala: Muslim Devotional Life in India*, New York: Palgrave.

Plate, S. B. (2015), *Key Terms in Material Religion*, London: Bloomsbury.

Pubby, V. (1988), *Simla, Then & Now: Summer Capital of the Raj*, New Delhi: Indus Pub. Co.

Putnam, R. (2000), *Bowling alone: the collapse and revival of American community*, Simon and Schuster, New York

Pye, M. (1978), *Skilful Means: A Concept in Mahayana Buddhism*. London: Duckworth.

Raj, S. (2002), 'Transgressing Boundaries, Transcending Turner: The Pilgrimage Tradition at the Shrine of St John de Brito', in S. Raj and C. Dempsey (eds.), *Popular Christianity in India: Riting Between the Lines*, 39–60, Albany, NY: State University of New York Press.

Raj, S. J. & Dempsey, C. G. (2002), *Popular Christianity in India: Riting between the Lines*, Albany: State University of New York Press.

Raj, S. J. & Dempsey, C. (2015), 'Letting Holy Water and Coconuts Speak for Themselves', in T. Pintchman and C. Dempsey (eds.), *Sacred Matters: Material Religion in South Asian Traditions*, 195–217, State University of New York Press.

Rangachar, S. (1964), *Early Indian Thought: The Philosophy of the Vedas, Upanishads and Post-Vedic Literature*, Mysore: Rao and Raghavan.

Ranger, T. (1978), 'Personal Reminiscence and the Experience of the People in East Central Africa', *Oral History*, 6 (1): 45–78.

Reisch, M. (2008), 'From Melting Pot to Multiculturalism: The Impact of Racial and Ethnic Diversity on Social Work and Social Justice in the USA', *British Journal of Social Work*, 38 (4): 788–804.

Robinson, R. (1998), *Conversion, Continuity and Change: Lived Christianity in Southern Goa*, New Delhi: Sage.

Robinson, R. (2003a), *Christians of India*, New Delhi: Sage.

Robinson, R. (2003b), 'Christianity in the Context of Indian Society and Culture', in V. Das (ed.), *The Oxford India Companion to Sociology and Social Anthropology*, New Delhi: Oxford University Press.

Roose, E. (2012), 'Constructing Authentic Houses of God: Religious Politics and Creative Iconographies in Dutch Mosque Design', *Material Religion*, 8 (3): 280–307.

Sahu, D. K. (2013), 'The Church of North India (United)', in Markham, I. S. Hawkins, J. B. Terry, J. & Steffensen, L. N. (eds.), *The Wiley-Blackwell Companion to the Anglican Communion*, 319–328, Chichester: Wiley-Blackwell.

Said, E. W. (1979), *Orientalism*, New York: Vintage Books.

Saikia, Y. (2004), *Fragmented Memories: Struggling to be Tai-Ahom in India*, Durham: Duke University Press.

Sankhyan, A. R. (1996), 'Badhai' in K. S. Singh, B. R. Sharma, and A. R. Sankhyan (eds.), *People of India: Himachal Pradesh*, (Volume XXIV), New Delhi: Anthropological Survey of India.

Sax, W. S. (1991), *Mountain Goddess: Gender and Politics in a Himalayan Pilgrimage*, New York: Oxford University Press.

Sax, W. S. (2013), 'Uttararkhand and Himachal Pradesh', in P. Berger and F. Heidemann (eds.), *The Modern Anthropology of India: Ethnography, Themes and Theory*, 276–285, London: Routledge.

Schmalz, M.N. (2011), 'Christianity: Culture, Identity, and Agency', in I. Clark-Decès (ed.), *A Companion to the Anthropology of India*, 277–294. Oxford: Blackwell.

Segal, R. A. (1999), *Theorizing about myth*, University of Massachusetts Press.

Shackley, M. (2002).'Space, sanctity and service: the English Cathedral as heterotopia', *International Journal of Tourism Research*, 4(5), 345–352.

Sharma, A. (2008), *An American in Gandhi's India: The Biography of Satyanand Stokes*, Indiana University Press.

Sharma, T. R. (1997), 'Horticultural Development in Himachal Pradesh: A Case Study of Apple Cultivation', *Indian Journal of Agricultural Economics*, 52(3): 656.

Sharma, U. (1986), *Women's Work, Class, and the Urban Household: A Study of Shimla, North India*, London: Tavistock.

Sharpe, E. J. (1976), 'Sadhu Sundar Singh and his critics: An episode in the meeting of East and West', *Religion*, 6(1): 48–66.

Sheldrake, P. (2001), *Spaces for the Sacred: Place, Memory, and Identity*, Baltimore: Johns Hopkins University Press.

Shneiderman, S. (2010), 'Are the Central Himalayas in Zomia? Some Scholarly and Political Considerations across Time and Space', *Journal of Global History*, 5 (02): 289–312.

Singh, K. S. (1996), *People of India: Himachal Pradesh'*, New Delhi: Anthropological Survey of India.

Singh, N. (2013) 'Granddaughter introduces American who brought apple to Himachal', *Hindustan Times*, 22 October.

Sneath, D. Holbraad, M. & Pedersen, A. (2009), 'Technologies of the Imagination', *Ethnos*, 74(1): 5–30.

Snellgrove, D. L. (1961), *Himalayan Pilgrimage: A study of Tibetan Religion*, Oxford: B. Cassirer.

Soja, E.W. (1996), *Thirdspace: journeys to Los Angeles and other real-and-imagined places*. Cambridge, MA: Basil Blackwell.

Solomon, D. A. (2013), *Menace and Management: Power in the Human-Monkey Social Worlds of Delhi and Shimla*, UC Santa Cruz: Anthropology.

Srinivas, M. (1962), *Caste in Modern India and Other Essays*, Bombay: Media Promoters and Publishers.

Streeter, B. and Appasamy, A. (1921), *The Sadhu: A Study in Mysticism and Practical Religion*. London: Macmillan.

Sud, O. C. (1992). *The Simla story, the glow & afterglow of the Raj: a sketch book*. Shimla: OC Sud.

Tagore, R. (1933), '"My School"' (a lecture delivered in America)', *Personality* London: MacMillan.

Thapar, R. (1989), 'Imagined Religious Communities? Ancient History and the Modern Search for a Hindu Identity', *Modern Asian Studies*, 23 (2): 209–231.

Thompson, P. (2005). *Sadhu Sundar Singh: A Biography of the Remarkable Indian Disciple of Jesus Christ*. Singapore: Armour Publishing.

Tucker, R. (1982), The Forests of the Western Himalayas: The Legacy of British Colonial Administration, *Journal of Forest History*, 26(3): 112–123.

Turner, E. (1993), 'The Reality of Spirits: A Tabooed or Permitted Field of Study?', *Journal for the Anthropology of Consciousness*, 4 (1): 9–12.

Turner, E. (2012), *Communitas: The Anthropology of Collective Joy*, New York: Palgrave Macmillan.

Turner, V. (1973), 'The Center out There: Pilgrim's Goal'. *History of Religions*, 12 (3): 191–230.

Tylor, E. B. (1871), *Primitive culture: researches into the development of mythology, philosophy, religion, art, and custom*, London: Murray.

Vásquez, M. A. (2011), *More than Belief: A Materialist Theory of Religion*, Oxford: Oxford University Press.

Von Fürer-Haimendorf, C. (1939), *The Naked Nagas*, London: Methuen & co. ltd.

Wagner, A. (2013), *The Gaddi Beyond Pastoralism: Making Place in the Indian Himalayas*, New York: Berghahn.

West, J. (1992), *The Quaker reader*, Wallingford, Pa: Pendle Hill Publications.

Wheeler, V. (1986), 'Travelers' Tales: Observations on the Travel Book and Ethnography', *Anthropological Quarterly*, 59 (2): 52–63.

Whitehead, A. (2013), *Religious Statues and Personhood: Testing the Role of Materiality*, London: Bloomsbury.

Whitehead, A. (2018), 'Devotional Bodies, Working Shrines: The Ritual Dynamics of Devotion in an Andalusian Marian Shrine', *Magic, Ritual, and Witchcraft*, 13 (2): 212–230.

Whiting, R. (2010), *The Reformation of the English Parish Church*, Cambridge: Cambridge University Press.

Whitmore, L. (2018), *Mountain, Water, Rock, God*, University of California Press.

Wilkinson, J. E. (1903), *The Parochial History of Simla, 1836–1900*, Simla: Thacker, Spink & Co.

Woodward, I. (2007), *Understanding Material Culture*, London: Sage.

Wylie, J. (2007), *Landscape*, London: Routledge.

Index

agriculture, 31, 69
    apple crops, 32 (*see also* Stokes)
    drought, effect of on, 157
    forestry and 114, 157 (*see also* trees)
    labourers of 107, 139
    landowners of, 32, 73
    reform of (*see also* beggar and beth), 32
alterity, 76, 83–6
Anglo-Indians, 107, 121, 132
    family life of, 139
    gender roles within, 73
    religion of, 82
apprenticeships, 147, 156
archetypes, 30, 36
architecture, 48, 64–5, 74, 92–3
    Gothic, 1, 11, 47, 51–2, 55, 65, 78, 99
    Sveitserstil, 47
    Tudor, 1–2, 55–6, 130, 134
atheism, 19, 80
Auckland House, 72–3
autoethnography, 2, 19, 106 (*see also* reflexivity)

Bagua, 116
Bascom, W., 62 (*see also* folklore)
Basso, K., 6 (*see also* place)
Bateson, G., 5, 41, 114, 116
    Grace in, 99, 105, 116
Bayly, S., 15, 133
belief, 10, 24, 66, 74, 92, 138, 158
    shared, 35, 132
    systems of, 24, 111, 113 (*see also* Geertz)
Bergmann, S., 21, 112, 161
    skill in the thought of, 21, 112, 161
Bhasin, R., 11, 44, 47, 80
Bielo, J., 42
Bishop Cotton, 55
Bishop Cotton's School, 72–3
Bishop Milman, 67, 75
Blaikie, P., 107 (*see also* landscape capital)
Boileau, Major General J.T., 48–9
Boileauganj, 49, 56

boundaries, 64, 72, 79, 115–16, 124
Bourdieu, P., 103–4, 117 (*see also* Habitus)
Bowman, M., 4, 42, 92, 94, 101, 147
British India, 8, 137
Brookfield, H., 107–8 (*see also* Landscape Capital)
Buck, E., 35, 43, 48, 50–1, 67, 131–2
Buddhists, 15, 173

capital, 21, 32, 91–2, 103–8, 121–2, 145, 152
    (*see also* Putnam)
    cultural, 32, 103–4, 117, 121
    landscape, 21, 91, 107–8
    religious, 21, 91, 103–5, 121–2
    social, 92, 103–4, 107, 117
    spiritual, 104–5, 145, 152.
Carrithers, M., 156 (*see also* polytropy)
caste, 15, 16, 34, 63, 90, 120, 133, 138, 143
    (*see also* class)
Cathedralscape, 22, 52, 91–6, 99–104, 107, 109–10, 112–14, 117, 119–23, 125–7, 129, 137, 145, 147–54, 157–8, 160 (*see also* churchscape)
    capital and, 21, 91, 117, 153, 158
    centrality of, 52, 109
    definition of, 107
    paintings of 60–1, 67, 87, 93.
Cathedral Village, 93–4
Catholicism, 17, 51, 91, 120, 123, 138, 149
    (*see also* St Michael's Cathedral)
    authority within, 149
    choir music, 132–3
    community of, 17, 51, 91, 120
    Hindi within, 119–20, 138
    local manifestations of, 137, 146, 152
    music within, 118
    Shimla's population of, 123, 138
Christ Church Cathedral, 1, 3, 5–6, 13, 17, 20–2, 48, 50–2, 58–61, 65–7, 69–78, 80–1, 86–9, 93, 95–7, 99, 101–2, 110, 118, 120, 123, 125, 129–34, 137–43, 148–50, 152, 154–5, 157

colonial period of, 77
congregation of, 73
construction of, 17, 142
ghosts of, 81–7
music within, 132–3, 143
paintings of, 60–1, 66, 93
Christianity, 14–15, 34, 51, 67, 69, 72–3, 77, 91, 103, 107, 120, 123–4, 138, 146, 149, 152,165
anthropology of, 14–15, 77, 124, 165
Catholic, 17, 51, 91, 120, 123, 138, 149
enculturated, 36, 51, 71, 106, 118, 129, 137, 146, 152.
evangelical, 34, 135–6, 139, 142
missions, 48, 67, 69, 72–3, 103.
Protestant, 16, 72, 107.
Christmas, 17, 67, 72, 134
celebration of, 88, 130 133
Chug, U., 17, 35, 48, 72–3, 132–3, 138, 151–2
churchscape, 20–1, 59–69, 78, 91–3, 96, 102 107–8, 117–18 (*see also* cathedralscape)
class, 14, 18, 73, 87, 118–19, 133, 137–9 (*see also* caste)
labourer, 133
lower, 133
upper, 133, 139
clergy, 121–2, 126, 128
Coleman, S., 8, 42, 47, 92, 94, 101, 124–5
Coleman, J., 103–4, 107, 117
colonialism, 9. 12. 15, 53, 77, 79, 89, 129, 132–4 150
craftsmen and, 77
officers of, 9, 12
period of, 9, 15–16, 35, 49, 54, 57, 71–2, 78, 80, 129, 132–4
politics of , 15
population, 53, 79
rupturing and, 71
trace of, 19–20, 77, 96, 119
communion, 27, 29, 86, 88, 141
communitas, 29. 92. 105–6, 143
Cosmic Mountain, 24–7, 39, 44, 47, 61, 150 (*see also* Mount Meru)
cosmology, 25, 27–8, 61 (*see also* Hinduism)
crafting, 5, 55, 145
Csordas, T., 125
cyberspace, 154

dance, 129, 135–7, 140
Davie, G., 122, 151
Davies, D., 24, 46
Dempsey, C., 15–16, 129
dilithium crystals, 151, 153, 156
Dobe, T., 34–5
dogs, 44–6, 97
Douglas, M., 136
dreams, 35–6, 132, 135, 158
dress, 75, 118, 132
adopted local, 33
colours of, 17
customary, 131
riding, 48
drought 157 (*see also* water)
Dumont, L.,133 (*see also* caste)
Durkheim, 105, 159 (*see also* effervescence)
dùthchas, 40–2, 148
dwelling, 43, 54, 111

ecology, 5, 65, 157
fragility of, 121
systems of, 114, 122
ecosystem, 123, 126, 149
Eden, E., 24, 46, 53–4
effervescence, 29, 99, 105, 159
Eliade, M., 2, 25, 88
Engelke, M., 14–15, 77, 124
enskilment, 21, 111–17, 121, 126–7, 129, 137, 145, 147, 150–1, 154
arena of, 148–9
general, 150
notion of, 116, 158
process of, 21–2, 110–11, 113–16, 126–7, 149, 152, 158
profitable, 122
subsequent, 147
entanglement, 51, 147–8
environment 5, 17, 24, 29, 40–1, 52, 55, 60, 67, 69–70, 79, 85, 91, 94, 110, 112–16, 121–2, 126–7, 131, 145, 148–50, 152–3, 155–8 (*see also* ecology)
architectural, 41
challenges of, 157
church, 75
impact upon, 40
natural, 99, 123

rural, 67, 108, 119, 131–2
secular, 63
temple, 54
urban, 45
Episcopalians, 51

Facebook 154
faith, 2, 16, 36, 65, 67, 72–3, 87–8, 101, 115–16, 118, 124–6, 129, 146
mixed, 116
fakirs
Father Christmas, 126, 134 (*see also* Christmas)
fear, 33, 36, 39, 84, 116, 118, 122, 129, 138, 143, 149, 152.
fields, 32
fieldwork, 2, 4, 6–7, 10, 17, 29, 65, 97, 101,106, 120, 124–6, 142
focus groups, 74, 106–7, 121, 1, 37, 139–40, 157
food, 45, 64, 151, 154
football, 28–9, 32, 53, 156.
forest, 29, 43–5, 114
density of, 29
Hanuman and, 54
Jakhoo, 61
northern, 114
forest monkeys, 54
Fürer-Haimendorf, 10

Gandhi, 33
Geertz, C., 111, 113
geography, 25–6, 41–2, 51
Himachal's, 23
ghosts, 20, 42, 55–9, 61–2, 71–89, 96, 114, 126, 148, 153, 155
Christ Church's, 65
colonial, 80
fertility, 80
haunting, 54
violent, 86
ghost stories, 55–6, 61, 84
globalization, 89
goddesses, 43
Kali, 43, 45, 96
Shymla Devi
Tara

gods, 2, 7–8, 18, 26–7, 29, 37, 43–4, 47, 54, 64, 256–7
Shiva, 27
Hanuman 2, 43, 54, 64, 156–7
Grace, 99, 105, 116, 122
Gothic, 47, 51, 78, 99 (*see also* architecture)
Gow, P., 89
graveyards, 56, 68, 80, 82
Griffiths, B., 33, 63, 88
Guest, M., 93

Hallaig, 41–2
Hanuman, 2, 43, 54, 64, 156–7
sacred hill of, 2
temple of, 61
harmony, 14, 18, 25, 94, 101, 129
haunted sites, 59
hauntings 68
Hausner, S., 11, 18, 27, 131
healing, 25–7, 140, 142
heritage, 16, 79–80, 92, 117–18, 149, 154
buildings, 139
claims to, 118
identity and, 79 149
symbols, 79
Heterodoxy, 21, 91–101
Hilton, J., 8, 24 (*see also* Lost Horizon)
Hinduism, 8, 30–1, 33, 36, 131, 140, 159
cosmology, 22, 28, 61
epics, 26
mythology, 26, 47, 159
population, 30, 79–80
residents, 83, 87, 142, 148–9
Holy Spirit, 120, 139–40, 142
Homans, C., 69, 75, 160
homelands, 19, 40, 53, 78
hope, 143, 156–7
houses, 45, 47, 49, 52–3, 61, 98, 130, 150, 154, 156, 160
Hugh-Jones, S., 62, 64, 88, 124
hymns, 75, 118–19, 126, 133, 135, 139
hypermodernity, 8

identities, 21, 66, 122, 127
group, 21
mixed-faith, 22
rural/tribal, 11

identity, 2, 13, 16, 19, 22, 24, 55, 58, 59, 62–3, 66, 79, 80–1, 83–4, 86, 97, 104–5, 117, 122–3, 125–6, 129–30, 137–9, 141, 143, 146, 149, 155–6
  faith and, 22, 30, 72, 78, 80, 87, 93, 112, 118, 129, 132.
  fluidity of, 126, 138
  formation of , 110, 130
  nationalism and, 26
Illud Tempus, 2 (*see also* time)
implicit mythology, 21, 60–6, 70–5, 78–9, 81–9, 92, 100, 109–10, 114, 117, 148, 153
  concept of, 20, 64–5, 75, 81, 87–8, 104
  standardized, 75, 83–4
  reflexive, 75, 77–8, 81–4
  vernacular, 75, 78, 83–4
inculturation, 36, 51, 71, 106, 118, 129, 137, 146, 152
Ingold, T., 5–7, 40, 46, 63–4, 67–8, 109, 111–12, 114–15, 122, 124, 127, 145, 150, 160–1
  landscapes and, 5–7, 40, 46, 63–4, 67–8, 109, 111–12, 114–15, 145, 150
  skill within, 112–15

Jakhoo temple, 43, 45, 54
Jesu Bhakti, 71, 142
Joshi, V., 11
journeys, 13–14, 25, 27, 29, 31, 34–5, 39, 75–6, 87, 99, 128–9, 145, 151, 153, 155
journal, field, 61, 76, 125.
jungle, 29, 43–5, 114 (*see also* forest)

Kailash, 19, 129, 150
Kali, 43, 45, 96
  Temple of, 96
Kanwar, P., 43–4, 47, 51, 57
key myth, 65, 81 (*see also* mythology)
kinship 139, 159
Kipling, Lockwood, 50, 83–4
Kipling, Rudyard, 54, 83
knots, 65
Kotgargh, 30–1

landmarks, 65, 102
landowners, 32, 73

landscapes, 1, 2, 6–10, 15, 19–23, 25, 30–4, 40–2, 46, 48, 49–51, 53–5, 58–9, 61–3, 65–9, 71–3, 76–80, 90–9, 101, 103–5, 107–14, 126, 129–31, 133–9, 141–6, 148–58, 160.
  capital of, 21, 91, 117, 153, 158
  colonial, 59, 62
  contemporary, 65, 129
  cosmological, 26
  definition of, 6
  material, 5, 36
  mythological, 2, 82
  native, 12
  painted, 60–1, 67, 93
  performative, 101
  postcolonial, 81, 150
  sacred, 2–3, 5, 52, 65, 80, 89, 104, 122, 147, 152
  Simla and, 9, 20, 48, 54, 61, 94, 148, 151, 158
langurs. 44–5
Leach, Edmund, 64
Lévi-Strauss, C., 4, 10, 21, 62–3, 65, 75, 77, 85–6, 88–9, 150
  canonical formula of, 20
  history and, 89, 109
  implicit mythology in, 88
locomotion, 117
Lost Horizon, 8, 24 (*see also* Hilton)
love, 31
lower bazaar, 35, 52, 54, 71, 81, 84, 85, 134

McLean, S., 124 (*see also* Hallaig)
Mahabharata, 26
Maharajas, 57, 80
  dissenting, 80
  Patiala, 57
Maharishi, 19, 34, 39, 129, 150
Malinowski, B., 4, 88
Mall Road, 29, 52, 54, 59, 74, 78, 92, 95, 148
Mar Thomist, 16
martial arts, 116
mastery, 14, 118, 147
materiality, 4, 20–1, 39, 49, 55, 60–1, 66, 91, 103, 159
  Christianity and 24
  culture and, 3, 4, 10, 18, 21–2, 33–4, 39, 64, 131
  skill and, 21, 103

memorials, 20, 56, 69
memories, 30, 58, 61, 66, 78, 107, 130, 148, 153, 155
   collective, 76
   discordant past, 70
   first, 81
   folk, 74
   personal, 82
Merleau-Ponty, M., 5
Meyer, B., 5, 66, 146
migration, 77, 148, 152
Morgan, D., 4, 50, 66, 146
Mosse, D., 15–16, 63, 133
mountainscapes, 2, 19, 39
Mount Meru, 24–7, 39, 44, 47, 61, 150
Mount Olympus, 19, 39, 44, 47
multiculturalism, 12, 16, 151
music, 97, 118, 129, 136, 138
myths, 2, 24–5, 27, 30, 44, 57, 61–6, 78, 81, 86–9, 159
   Eden in, 24
   European, 24, 47
   explicit, 62, 64, 89
   heroes in, 7
   Hindu, 26, 47
   implicit, , 21, 60–6, 70–5, 78–9, 81–9, 92, 100, 109–10, 114, 117, 148, 153
   key, 65
   landscape in, 2, 82
   origin, 43
   toponymical, 19, 62
mythemes, 85–6
mythology, 20, 23, 27, 30, 39, 42–3, 52, 61–3, 82, 86, 88, 111, 150, 159
   definition of, 20
   history and. 89, 109

nationalism, 22, 26
Nelson, R.K., 111, 113–14, 126–7
neocolonial, 9
neostructuralism, 62
numinous, 2, 11, 28, 94, 112, 116

Owlig, K., 6, 108
Olympus, 39, 41, 43–5, 47, 49, 51, 53, 55
omnipotence, 127
Orientalism, 11
Orientalists, 9, 24

Pahari, 12, 32, 46, 55
peace, 18, 59, 61, 76, 83, 85–6
phenomenology, 94, 97
pilgrimage, 11, 28, 41 (*see also* walking)
   activities, 27
   trails, 27
pipe organ, 22, 129, 133, 143
Plate, S., 4, 66, 146
polytropy, 156
postcolonial, 2, 9, 13, 16, 19, 20–1, 55–6, 58–9, 66, 77, 79, 81, 82, 85–7, 89, 118–19, 129, 143, 148, 150
   cities, 4, 10, 96
   developments, 9
   Hinduism, 140, 159
   livelihood, 6
   period of, 12, 29, 44, 59, 62, 79, 123, 155
   population of, 5, 66, 72, 77, 80–1, 148
   Shimla as, 59, 61, 125
   theory of, 3, 22
practice, 111, 113, 115 (*see also* skill)
prayer, 64, 74–5, 113–14, 126, 132–3, 137, 140
preachers, 50, 69
prestige, 53, 86, 97, 122
prophetic anthropology, 22, 92, 126. 146–7, 158
prophets, 147
Protestantism, 107 (*see also* Christianity)
Puranas, 26
Purity 116
Putnam, R., 103–5, 117, 132 (*see also* Social Capital)

Quakers, 31, 33
Queen of the Hills, 54, 66

Raj, S., 15, 129
Rajas, 57–9, 80–1
reflexivity 75, 88, 92
religion, vernacular, 4
religious capital, 21, 91, 103–5, 107, 121–2
religious capital theory, 103
remembrance, 42, 48
replication, 20, 27, 40, 42, 47, 150, 154–5
revelation, 1, 17, 21, 27–8, 30–1, 83, 92, 117, 146
   central, 20–1

Ridge, the, 1, 3, 20, 47, 51–2, 60, 84–5, 96–9, 105, 129–30, 134
ritual, 21, 27, 63–5, 67, 71, 75, 82, 103, 109–10
  calendrical, 22
  extraordinary, 18
  historical, 75
  mimesis and, 63
  practice of, 97
Robbins, J., 14–15, 124
Robinson, R., 15–16, 63
rock, 1, 51, 99, 138
rupture, 22, 66, 70–1, 77, 80, 89–90, 130, 133

sacred sites, 18, 27
sacred spaces, 74
sadhus, 19, 28, 33, 132, 149
saffron robes, 34, 131–2, 134
St Andrew's Kirk, 52, 97, 99, 101–2, 157
Saivite renouncers, 27, 28
Satsang, 22, 129, 142–3
Sax, W., 10–12
scandal point, 51, 57–8, 92
schismogenesis, 41
Scottish churches, 52, 86 (*see also* St Andrews)
seasonality, 55, 60, 64, 140, 143
secularism, 29–31, 53, 63, 67, 79
sentimentality, 107, 141
Serafin, John, 93–5
Shamballa, 24
Shangri-La, 8, 10–11, 18, 24–5, 29, 39 (*see also* Hilton)
  Orientalism and, 24
  conception of, 25
  placing, 25
Sheldrake, P., 5, 88, 94
Shiva, 27 (*see also* gods)
Shymla Devi, 39, 43, 54
Sikh religion, 35
Singh, S. 11, 19, 28, 33–7, 39, 50–2, 129, 131–2, 139
Skill 74, 77, 91–2, 107, 110–16, 118, 120, 122, 127, 137, 141, 145, 149, 156, 158, 161.
  martial arts and, 116
  practice of, 113
  religion as, 116
  worship as, 110

social capital, 104, 107 (*see also* capitals)
soundscapes, 77, 118, 160
spatial capital, 21, 108–9 (*see also* capitals)
Star Trek, 153
St Michael's Cathedral, 21–2, 51, 91, 97–100, 102–3, 105–6, 109–10, 118, 121–2, 125, 129, 133, 138, 141, 152, 157 (*see also* Catholics)
St Michael's Cathedralscape, 104
  architecture of, 100
  Catholicism and, 51, 133
  congregation of, 22
Stokes, S., 19, 28–38, 50–2, 54, 129, 131–2, 159
St Thomas, 52, 72, 131
St Thomas's church, 52, 71
St Thomas's School, 72
Sundar Singh, 19, 28, 34–5, 39, 51–2, 131–2, 139 (*see also* Singh)

Tagore, R., 151
time, 67, 89, 140
  abolished, 89, 140
  cyclical, 67
  linear, 67
tourist board, 72
tourism, 1, 8, 55, 59, 66, 72, 79–80, 99, 101–2, 123, 125, 133, 137, 140–2, 148–9, 155
  landscape of, 101–2
  worship and, 102
town planning, 47, 49
trauma, 5, 20, 42, 70–1, 77, 88–9, 123, 129, 143, 150, 155, 157
trees, 2, 29, 32, 42, 44, 61, 95, 98, 151, 157 (*see also* forest)
  birch, 41–2
  deodar, 1–2, 29, 44
truth, 20, 30, 62–3, 88, 127, 148, 159
Tudor, mock, 2, 47, 55–6, 134 (*see also* architecture)
Turner, E., 106, 124
Turner, V., 25, 29, 63, 105–6, 124–5

Union Church, 52
universities, 73, 96, 102, 105
urban, 8, 12–14, 19, 45, 73, 92, 109
urdu, 35, 52
utopia, 24 (*see also* Shangri-La)
Uttarakhand, 12

Valk, U., 4, 147
Vedas, 26-7
Viceroy, 50-1, 57, 67, 132, 139
Victoria, Queen, 45
villages, 11, 29-30, 32, 48, 51, 67, 78, 119, 140
Vishwa Hindu Parishad, 54
visions, 35

Wagner, A., 11
wandering, 19, 27, 35, 39, 52, 76, 131-2
water, 45, 157
weatherworlds, 19-20, 40, 55
wellbeing, 31, 94, 111, 148, 152
worldviews, 111, 156
worship 74-8

Zomia, 18

www.ingramcontent.com/pod-product-compliance
Lightning Source LLC
Chambersburg PA
CBHW070640300426
44111CB00013B/2184